Stories of the Eight-Year Study

Stories of the Eight-Year Study

Reexamining Secondary Education in America

CRAIG KRIDEL
AND
ROBERT V. BULLOUGH JR.

Foreword by

John I. Goodlad

State University of New York Press

Published by
State University of New York Press, Albany

For information, address State University of New York Press,
194 Washington Avenue, Suite 305, Albany, NY 12210-2384

Production by Diane Ganeles
Marketing by Michael Campochiaro

Library of Congress Cataloging-in-Publication Data

Kridel, Craig Alan.
  Stories of the eight-year study : reexamining secondary education in
America / Craig Kridel, Robert V. Bullough Jr.; foreword by John I. Goodlad.
      p. cm.
  Includes bibliographical references and index.
  ISBN-13 978-0-7914-7053-4 (hardcover : alk. paper)
  ISBN-13 978-0-7914-7054-1 (pbk. : alk. paper)
      1. Education—United States—History—20th century.   2. Progressive
education—United States—History.   I. Bullough, Robert V., 1949–
II. Title.

LA209.K75 2007
373.973'0904—dc22   2006016867

10 9 8 7 6 5 4 3 2 1

In Recognition of the Work of the Curriculum Associates
of the Commission on the Relation of School and College

Harold B. Alberty, Paul B. Diederich,
H. H. Giles, S. P. McCutchen, and A. N. Zechiel

"And perhaps the greatest stimulus of all was the sense of belonging
to an adventurous company which placed a premium upon the
contributions of each of its individual members."

H. H. Giles, S. P. McCutchen, and A. N. Zechiel,
Exploring the Curriculum
(New York: Harper & Brothers, 1942): 308.

I would like to place on the record the fact that my teaching [at the George School, a participating site in the Eight-Year Study] was one of the finest experiences I've had in my life. I saw the very best of contemporary education conducted in a no-nonsense way. . . . I have always viewed with mild amusement the loose charges that Progressive Education was a failure or that it promoted laxity in either study or morals. My classes, if I say so myself, were among the best being taught in America at that time, all with a far above average model of deportment and learning. And through the years my former students constantly write to tell me that they evaluated those years in the same way. A failure? One of the greatest successes I've known.

As to the effect on me: it made me a liberal, a producer, a student of my world, a man with a point of view and the courage to exemplify it. I wish all students could have the experiences mine did. I wish all teachers could know the joy I found in teaching under such conditions.[1]

James A. Michener, 1986

Contents

Contents

Foreword: A Tale of Lost Horizons

John I. Goodlad

From time to time in recent years, various educators have raised the question of whether an initiative comparable to the Eight-Year Study should be undertaken. Since nearly all those introducing the query either were not yet born or were children during the years of planning and conducting the study (the early 1930s into the 1940s) and its reports received little attention, one wonders what they have in mind.

Our memories even of studies gaining much initial attention tend to be short. World War II was just beginning for the United States as the Eight-Year Study was ending. The war overwhelmed almost all else. For example, the paper shortage forced limited editions of the Commission on the Relation of School and College's 1941, 1942, and 1943 major reports. There was no surge of interest when the war ended in 1945. Those of us studying in the University of Chicago's graduate department of education in the concluding years of the 1940s were looking ahead. We failed to take advantage of the rich educational experiences brought by Ralph Tyler and his clutch of colleagues who had just come from the Study's fountainhead at Ohio State University. The Study was marginalized in the history of secondary schooling in the United States. The good news is that this book, the most intimate and comprehensive history of the Eight-Year Study of which I know, comes to us at what well may be the most opportune time in decades.

It is ironic but not surprising that many of those educators suggesting replication of the Study envision a carefully controlled comparison of the academic achievement of students in two sharply differentiated samples of secondary schools. This is the image most commonly represented in references to the Eight-Year Study. It fits today's dominant ideology of what is worth measuring in judging the quality of our schools. But to advance this orientation as the conceptual core is to both distort

and minimize the intent, conduct, and comprehensiveness of this in-
credibly complex, bold, and innovative enterprise.

To launch something intended to be a near-repetition of the Eight-
Year Study without first reading and reflecting on what Craig Kridel and
Robert Bullough have written about it would verge on irresponsibility.
What were the credentials of those involved? How were they able to
schedule the time they put into the work? How were so many of the most
respected educators of the time able to hammer out some major common agreements, even as they differed, often profoundly, in their educational beliefs and perspectives? Was there a chief worrier for the whole?
How were the major commissions and committees constituted? What did
members talk about, how did they connect with the working parties that
were most practice oriented, and how did they move from dialogue to
decisions, action, and appraisal of their work? How was the whole financed, and at what level of expenditure? What would be required to
bring off a comparable study today? Kridel and Bullough do not answer
all of these questions, but they make clear that such questions ran through
and were addressed in the work—indeed, had to be addressed.

No, we do not need another Eight-Year Study. We would find out
pretty much what was found then. Policy makers would not pay much,
if any, attention to it. And educational researchers and critics would
have a great time arguing over methodology and implications. However, what we should do is examine the whole as a case study, learn
from it, and use our learnings to help guide the long-overdue redesign
of public education. Reading this book is a promising place to begin.

Even though I have read a good deal and written a little about the
Progressive Education Association's project, *Stories of the Eight-Year Study*
served as a primer on the subject, ridding me of myths, misunderstandings, and false premises. I was startled to find out that the study
stretched over a dozen years, not eight. The title came from the fact
that it was directed to the nature and relationships of four years of
high school followed by four years of college. To think of the whole
as largely a quantitative evaluation and comparison of two differing
samples of schools is a gross distortion. I was barely into the introduction when I began to realize that I was in for a provocative, humbling
intellectual journey.

For me, the most significant learning about this near-motheaten
landmark educational enterprise is its contemporary relevance. Usually
when my errant thoughts lead to something appearing to be novel, I
soon find myself talking to colleagues thinking along the same or parallel lines. Perhaps this is because there is a surprisingly small number
of good *new* ideas worth talking about. Some of these gain enthusiastic
attention for a few years, are implemented in some form in a few

educational settings, fade away, and then reappear in new dress a couple of decades later before disappearing once more. Meanwhile, the same old ideas and structures of schooling are burnished in still another era of "school reform," crowding out whatever innovative pea patches have managed to gain a brief footing.

The members of the several commissions and committees constituting the infrastructure of the Eight-Year Study managed to come up with an interconnected array of good ideas regarding nearly all of the key elements of schooling. Although what they proposed was progressive, not regressive, they largely left the rhetoric of progressive education to the Progressive Education Association. Fresh ideas were transformed into organizational, curricular, and instructional specifics and introduced into selected schools such as the laboratory school of Ohio State University. And, of course, many were picked up by the member experimental schools of the Eight-Year Study. There was, of course, the slippage from concept to reality with which all of us who have been engaged in the processes are only too familiar.

What comes through to me from *Stories of the Eight-Year Study* is that most of those involved believed in both the necessity and the *possibility* of profoundly changing our schools along lines derived from intensive inquiry. They were not seeking a litany of "what works" but scenarios of what should and could be. The thirty (more or less) schools of the Eight-Year Study served as the "proofing ground." This was no linear process of progressing from wheat to bread. Leave that to the reformers, who so often take failure as a challenge to try a misguided model one more time. The creative minds of the Eight-Year Study pioneered in the workshop ways of learning for individuals, particularly teachers, while opening up new horizons for institutional renewal.

Why do I view the educational implications of what Kridel and Bullough describe as contemporary? And why do I see what they have written as coming to us at an opportune time? The answer to the first question derives from the degree to which the roots of contemporary "good new ideas" can be so readily discovered in the concepts and principles seen decades ago as sound by leading educators of the time. The answer to the second derives from the fact that the last half century of tinkering is now so clearly exposed as a failure that the need for the dawning of a new day is even more obvious.

There was, of course, opposition to and disagreement with the new dawning envisioned by many of those caught up in the ongoing work of the Eight-Year Study. I did not, however, find in *Stories of the Eight-Year Study* any mention of federal mandates that might have gotten seriously in the way. The concepts of local control and state responsibility for schooling were not threatened as they are today. However, dissatisfaction with federal intervention and its consequences is growing, even among policy makers and opinion leaders.

The time has come to align the course of school renewal with the public purpose of education in our social and political democracy and what we already know about both the change process and the powerful ideas that have surfaced again and again only to be pushed aside by the sheer weight of what exists. The center of attention must be, of course, the one currently most ignored—the school and its students, teachers, and parents. All else is supportive. The driving force must be educators. Who else are to be so charged and held accountable?

The urgency of the necessary alignment must not override the exercise of wisdom. The first steps taken are the most critical. We might well begin with a careful reading of the pages that follow. Surely that reading will dissuade us from delaying action until we have before us the results of an Eight-Year or Flexner-type study, valuable though these most assuredly were and still are. And let us be spared still another education summit or commissioned report.

Acknowledgments

We wish to thank three individuals whose help and assistance guided and defined this work.

To Paul R. Klohr, professor emeritus, Ohio State University and former director of the Ohio State University School, who first introduced us to the Eight-Year Study and who upheld the spirit of the project throughout a long and productive career.

To Laura G. Blomquist, director of the Education and Psychology Library at Ohio State University, who on that fateful day decided not to discard those many boxes of unrelated Ohio State materials which proved to be the original documents and extensive supplementary resource papers for the Aikin Commission's *Thirty Schools Tell Their Story*. We would have written *Stories of the Eight-Year Study* even without these resources; however, those four linear feet of materials became the emotional and intellectual center for our archival research.

To Louise DeSalvo, professor of English at Hunter College, whose biographical research and essays have shown that educational researchers and historians have much to learn from the area of creative nonfiction writing.

We are grateful to the following kind and gracious individuals who read portions of our manuscript and offered thoughtful criticisms, caveats, congratulations, and commiserations: Lorin W. Anderson, Mary Bull, Dawn Ann Bullough, Sharon Black, Joseph Featherstone, Sheri Hardee, Robert Johnson, Harvey Kantor, Herbert L. Kliebard, Michael Knoll, Janet L. Miller, William F. Pinar, Sheldon A. Rosenstock, William H. Schubert, Paul Shaker, Robert Sherman, Theodore R. Sizer, Louis M. Smith, Wayne J. Urban, Alan Wieder, Kenneth Wollitz, and William G. Wraga.

We greatly appreciate those who have provided public statements of support: William C. Ayers, Elliot W. Eisner, John I. Goodlad, Maxine Greene, Jay Martin, and David B. Tyack.

We wish to thank the many diligent and conscientious archivists, curators, and researchers who continued to attend to our persistent queries: Marc Bernstein, New York Society for Ethical Culture; Robert

Butche, Ohio State University School Archives; Peggy Caldwell, Shaker Heights City School District; Nancy Cricco, New York University Archives; Gerald Dorfman, Hoover Institution, Stanford University; Raimund Goerler, Tamar Chute, Michelle Drobik, Bertha Ihnat, and Ruth Jones, Ohio State University Archives; Peter Gow and Linda Harding, Beaver Country Day School; Anne-Lise Halvorsen, University of Michigan; Erwin Levold and Roseann Variano, Rockefeller Archive Center; Cornelia Locher, Ethical Culture Fieldston School; David Ment, Teachers College Daniel Meyer and Richard L. Popp, University of Chicago; Pat Sanders, Montclair State University.

Throughout our research, we enjoyed meeting Eight-Year Study participants and their family members. Some are no longer with us and we hope this volume serves as a testimony to the work of Paul Diederich, Wilfred Eberhart, Mary Frank Perry, Robert Gilchrist, Lou LaBrant, Ross Mooney, Chandos Reid, Louise Rosenblatt, Harold Taylor, V. T. and Florence Thayer, I. Keith Tyler, Ralph W. Tyler, William Van Til, and Margaret Willis. We appreciate the kindness and assistance of Helen van Dongen Durant, Heather Jackson, H. S. Thayer, Beatrice Van Til, Nancy G. Zachry, and Stephen Zachry. Our treatment of the Eight-Year Study is merely a beginning which, we hope, will offer new perspectives for research by others. Much more needs to be examined about the Aikin, Thayer, and Keliher Commissions and the Eight-Year Study progressives, that too-long neglected group of educators whose effort to better understand the place of secondary education in a democracy remains both challenging and inspiring.

Introduction

There is currently afoot a simple story of the rise of progressive education, one that has fed mercilessly on the fears of anxious parents and the hostilities of suspicious conservatives. In it John Dewey . . . awakes one night with a new vision of the American school: the vision is progressive education. Over the years . . . he is able to foist the vision on an unsuspecting American people. The story usually ends with a plea for the exorcising of this devil from our midst and a return to the ways of the fathers. This kind of morality play has always been an influential brand of American political rhetoric, used by reformers and conservatives alike. But it should never be confused with history! (Lawrence Cremin, 1961)[1]

This simple tale of progressive education has not changed much since the publication of Cremin's *The Transformation of the Schools* over forty-five years ago. Dewey remains the constant in the morality play—blessed or damned—and accolades or darts are thrown depending upon one's ideology and understanding of progressivism. Much confusion continues today as educators praise and curse progressive education, embracing certain tenets as justification for their work and ignoring other practices as reasons for supposed failings of the public schools. From this commotion has arisen renewed interest in the Eight-Year Study, a project sponsored by the Commission on the Relation of School and College of the Progressive Education Association (PEA) during the 1930s and early 1940s and staged in twenty-nine secondary school sites throughout the United States. After years of neglect, references both complimentary and critical are appearing in the contemporary literature. No curriculum textbook writer now fails to mention Wilford Aikin, director of the Commission, in a typically brief historical overview of curriculum development, and John Lounsbury and Gordon F. Vars have popularized the Eight-Year Study to generations of members of the

1

National Middle School Association. David Tyack and Larry Cuban present the project as a case study in *Tinkering Toward Utopia* to show schools' resistance to change in what they call the "grammar of schooling." The Commission on the Relation of School and College occupies a prominent place in Ellen Lagemann's *An Elusive Science* as an important moment in the history of educational research, setting the stage for the crucial conceptual move from measurement to evaluation. Looking for examples of successful reform involving teachers, Linda Darling-Hammond finds much to praise in the Eight-Year Study as she notes the importance of staff working together and forging shared goals. The project was featured in *Education Week*'s twentieth century historical overview of schooling in America, *Lessons of a Century*, and criticized by Diane Ravitch in *Left Back: A Century of Failed School Reforms*. Alfie Kohn, writing for the general public in *The Schools Our Children Deserve*, describes the Study as "the best-kept educational secret of the twentieth century," while Patricia Graham, in her recent history of American education, *Schooling America*, dismisses the project as culturally blind.[2]

Why is the Eight-Year Study drawing increased attention now?[3] Does its rediscovery reflect a rekindled appreciation of "democracy as a way of life," a phrase common in the tenets of 1930s progressive education? Or, perhaps, with today's emphasis on high-stakes testing and its stranglehold over experimentation, educators are beginning to question the innate weaknesses of standardization. Regardless of the reasons, we hope that examining the Eight-Year Study might spark a reconsideration of secondary education's purposes and practices. From the outset of our research, we have been struck by the boldness and ambition of its leaders, and we can only begin to wonder what might have happened if educators had drawn upon the insights of this project. Both beguiling and disconcerting, this grand experiment continues to capture our imagination. Not only does the work of the Commission on the Relation of School and College invite a reexamination of taken-for-granted public school practices, the research supports a hopeful and an optimistic view of the ability of teachers to improve schools. After years of examining PEA materials, we now view our scholarship as *an act of reclamation*: an opportunity to recall what can be accomplished when educators, students, and parents come together to explore values and to develop practices that represent and reflect the desire to realize our national democratic commitments.

Cremin notes that "Progressivism implied the radical faith that culture could be democratized without being vulgarized."[4] Confidence in a democratic society; trust in thoughtful, open, and civil discussions about values and ways of living; belief that this trust in troubled times is justifiable—these are more crucial today than ever before. Presently, when Americans have lost faith in public education and when democracy is seen merely as the right to choose, we turn to the Commission on the Relation of School and College to recall how educators sought to build a way of life based upon a rich and generous social vision, quite unlike many views prevalent today. The Eight-Year Study reminds us that holding "an essential faith" in school experimentation and in the ability of teachers is not misplaced but vital for school improvement and renewal. True, the policies and practices championed by PEA leaders often seem inappropriate for current times, yet fundamental questions have a way of enduring from generation to generation. Contexts and people change, but the issues persist.

A Brief Description of the Eight-Year Study

The Eight-Year Study, also known as the Thirty School Study, arose from two rather innocuous goals: "To establish a relationship between school and college that would permit and encourage reconstruction in the secondary school" and "To find, through exploration and experimentation, how the high school in the United States can serve youth more effectively."[5] The popular impression, however, that the project was staged from 1933 to 1941 in thirty high schools across the United States is somewhat misleading. Composed of three closely related PEA commissions, the Study actually evolved over a twelve-year period, from 1930 to 1942, and ended only because additional funding was not forthcoming. In fact, the project had no completion date. The general use of the term "eight-year" refers less to the duration of the program and more to the general impression that eight years of a student's academic experiences—high school through college—would be examined. No students, however, were followed for a full eight-year period. And in terms of "thirty schools," only twenty-nine school sites ultimately participated in varying degrees of commitment. Initially, twenty-seven secondary schools volunteered—three sites were added between 1933 and 1934 and one withdrew in 1936—and 284 colleges and universities agreed to cooperate with the proposed college admissions process. Yet among these twenty-nine sites, approximately forty-two high schools and twenty-six junior high programs were directly involved with the experimentation of the Aikin Commission. When all schools that had participated in the activities of the three commissions are tallied, the number more than doubles and touches the educational lives of thousands and thousands of students.

At a 1930 PEA board meeting, the Committee on the Relation of School and College (the Aikin Commission, named for its chair, Wilford

M. Aikin) was proposed. Formal commission status was conferred in 1932, and a five-volume report, aptly titled *Adventure in American Education*, was released in 1942–1943 as the commission officially disbanded.[6] The Aikin Commission brought together educators from schools and universities to examine the relationship between secondary and postsecondary education and to experiment with new school programs in thirty different settings throughout the United States. As efforts proceeded, PEA leaders realized that new types of curricular materials were needed, and in 1932 the Commission on Secondary School Curriculum (the Thayer Commission, chaired by V. T. Thayer) was formed. The Thayer Commission completed its research in 1940, and eleven commission reports were published addressing particular aspects of adolescent research and articulating guidelines for curriculum and instruction in specific subject areas. The Commission on Human Relations (the Keliher Commission, chaired by Alice Keliher), appointed in 1935 and continuing until 1942, extended the Eight-Year Study's research in adolescent development and the social sciences and released six final reports. (See Annotated Bibliography.)

While few contemporary accounts include the Thayer and Keliher Commissions as part of the Eight-Year Study, our review of committee reports revealed overlapping purposes and memberships to the degree that, at times, we were unable to determine which meetings represented which commissions. Many of the actual participants felt the same confusion. One school director described summer workshops where staff members from all three commissions were present. "When Caroline Zachry and Eugene Smith spoke, we didn't really know or care if they were representing the Aikin or Thayer groups. It didn't matter. We were all together and we were trying to sort out how to better our schools. When our teachers came together to work on materials, Aikin workshop activities turned into reports for the Thayer Commission."[7] Alice Keliher deliberately selected members for her commission who served on the Thayer Commission, and activities of Aikin Commission committees were directly linked to those of the Thayer Commission. Aikin Commission staff were also involved in the evaluation of Keliher Commission programs.[8] Clearly the Thayer and Keliher Commissions grew out of the Commission on the Relation of School and College in response to the needs of the participating faculties of the thirty schools. And in the 1938 PEA publication, *Progressive Education Advances: Report on a Program to Educate American Youth for Present-Day Living*, this single program devoted one chapter to each of the three commissions.[9] To approach the Eight-Year Study without recognizing the intertwined purposes of the Aikin, Thayer, and Keliher Commissions overlooks the breadth and vision of this effort to redesign secondary education.

During the 1930s, *exploration* and *experimentation* were hallmarks of progressive schools as teachers sought ways to continuously improve the educational experience for all youth. Commission leaders realized that to experiment meant breaking the hold of the Carnegie unit on secondary school curricula. If programs of study could be developed embracing the tenets of progressive education without sacrificing the academic preparation of the college-bound student and others, then the PEA would have greatly advanced its case for experimentation. This goal came to represent the underlying mission of the project: to design experimental programs "without compromising any student's chances of a successful college education."[10] Select high schools would experiment with curriculum, and as later decided, hundreds of their graduates would be followed into college; yet the overall effort to better articulate instruction between colleges and high schools was initiated to help *all youth* and not just those moving on to postsecondary education. As curriculum design, teacher development, student assessment, and educational aims were reexamined and reconceived, courses of study were changed without losing their emphasis upon subject matter. Contrary to a common misperception, the Eight-Year Study never excused the participating high schools from standardized testing or from various measures of accountability. Numerous tests were administered to students, and data were gathered on the effects of implemented programs. Increased freedom was granted to experiment with the basic structure of schooling, but teachers and administrators were still held responsible for the quality of their academic programs. A focus on course content was never lost.

Accounts of the Eight-Year Study characteristically describe the college success of a matched set of students, one group having attended the participating progressive high schools and another group attending traditional programs. Known as the College Follow-up Study, this research component is often mistaken for the entire project. As we will discuss, the Thirty School Study involved much more than merely comparing students' college achievements. More importantly, the Aikin, Thayer, and Keliher Commissions encouraged in many of the schools dramatic departures from common curricular practices. The commissions constructed a complex conception of adolescent needs and of core curriculum, explored new roles and responsibilities for teachers, developed creative types of student assessment and innovative teaching materials, and clarified the meaning of democracy for themselves and for others. The lasting testimony of the Eight-Year Study demonstrates that educators can experiment with secondary school practices in ways that lead to greater curricular coherence, stronger democratic communities for teachers and students, and innovative programs that are responsive to the needs of adolescents, regardless of their career and education choices. The Commission's experimental methods opened up numerous fresh possibilities for educating the young, including many avenues for college preparation. In essence, the project proved to be an experiment in support of experimentation rather than the mere comparison of a group of college-bound students.

The Perceived "Failure" of the Eight-Year Study

We must discuss one more dimension of the Study, a myth that has permitted the project to be unfairly dismissed by some critics. At issue is a conception of educational success and impact, a view of what educators should expect from school renewal and systemic reform. The Eight-Year Study is too often judged by the outcomes of the College Follow-up Study, which compared the college grade point averages of 1,475 students who had attended participating schools to the averages of 1,475 students who had attended an assortment of traditional high schools. The project is typically deemed unsuccessful based on these oft-cited results: "*slightly* higher total grade average" and "*somewhat* better job than the comparison group." Since the students' college grades were not notably superior, critics began to cite these results shortly after the publication of the final reports to suggest that progressive schools were no better than traditional high schools. We believe this conclusion is unwarranted.

The Follow-up Study was conceived well after the selection of the participating schools, and we are convinced that the Eight-Year Study was never regarded by its leaders as a scientific experiment to determine progressive or traditional schooling as the best preparation for college-bound students. Fitting together the activities of all three commissions supports our conclusion. In fact, this issue was addressed specifically at a 1939 PEA Board of Directors meeting: "The point was emphasized that the distinguishing factor was not one of 'progressive or non-progressive' but of freedom from a fixed pattern of preparation for college versus the traditional preparation."[11]

Other, more serious problems arise with this limited view of the Study. The participating schools identified themselves as "progressive" in many different ways, and these characterizations of progressivism varied considerably. Even the Aikin Commission staff realized that not all of the participating schools were innovative, and some offered strikingly traditional college preparatory programs. When planning the Study, Commission staff members sought participation from a loosely representative cross section of America's schools, including traditional college preparation to highly experimental programs and from conservative to radical schools.[12] The staff recognized that avoiding a dichotomous sample offered a truer picture of what most secondary schools could initiate if college entrance requirements were lifted. Further, the Carnegie Foundation for the Advancement of Teaching, the first funding agency of the project, insisted that rather conservative academic schools participate, urging the Directing Committee to include more private boys' academies.[13] While many of the participating schools would not necessarily be classified as "innovative," then or now, their graduates were expected to represent the success of progressive education as part of the experimental group in the Follow-up Study. A review of Appendix A, descriptions of the Aikin Commission schools, shows the great diversity among the sites and causes one to wonder how these 1,475 students could have ever been expected to carry the mantle of progressive education.

Further, teachers brought differing degrees of enthusiasm for curricular experimentation too. As late as 1938, schools were assessed by Commission staff as having initiated little real experimentation, and even Frederick Redefer, executive director of the PEA, noted that most of the curriculum revision had not begun until after 1936, when the Follow-up Study students had already been selected and were beginning their college years.[14] In essence, not only did many of the participating teachers fail to embrace the spirit of progressivism or engage in serious innovation, but amazingly the Follow-up Study that now commonly defines the Eight-Year Study included many of the "wrong students"—those who graduated before secondary school experimentation was fully underway. While the worth of the Eight-Year Study may be judged through a variety of criteria, success or failure of innovative curricular practices cannot be determined by the results of its own College Follow-up Study. A sounder basis comes from the typically overlooked "Study within the Study," a comparison of students from what were considered by the Aikin Commission's Evaluation staff as the six most experimental schools. In this sampling, the college success of 323 students was compared to traditional school matchees as well as to students from the other "progressive" schools; college achievements of those graduates from the six least experimental Aikin Commission high schools were also compiled. The graduates from the six most experimental schools substantially outperformed their peers in terms of academic averages and honors, intellectual traits, and personal and social responsibility.[15] While we do not dismiss the Follow-up Study, we consider its value questionable at best when compared to the results of the Study within the Study.

Charges of limited impact for the Eight-Year Study began shortly after the conclusion of World War II and were reaffirmed in an often-cited 1950 *Progressive Education* journal article in which Redefer summarized his dissertation.[16] In "The Eight-Year Study . . . After Eight Years," he reported that of the fifteen schools that responded to his survey only two maintained the "spirit" of the project. Redefer inferred that the Eight-Year Study had no influence on American education and also little enduring impact on its original participating schools. His data, however, are insufficient to support these conclusions. He admits that he was unable to gather information on eleven other schools. Having broken his research codes, we know that Redefer received information from only four of the eight more experimental schools involved in the project (as well as from three of the six least experimental schools). He also notes that nineteen of the twenty-six administrators he contacted were new to the schools since 1941; thus most of those judging the long-term influence of the project were not even present in the schools during the active work of the Study. Ralph Tyler took exception to Redefer's conclusions: "[He] did not realize that the Eight-Year Study was guided by principles of learning and not by a particular curriculum form [pattern]. So he reached the conclusion that the Eight-Year Study had no effect because the forms that were established in various places were not continued thereafter."[17] Nonetheless, many contemporary views of the Eight-Year Study are grounded in Redefer's dissertation research which, clearly, has taken on much more contemporary significance than even he would have expected.[18]

Impact, to Redefer, meant permanence—that programs would persist, relatively unchanged, across time—and proof of the Study's impact would have resulted in a massive transformation of secondary education. Given the vastness of the American school system, this would be overly ambitious for any single project, even one much larger than the Thirty School Study. Herbert Kliebard, when discussing the Eight-Year Study, affirmed, "It appears naïve to assume that the interest of public school people on one hand and academicians in colleges and universities on the other would give way in the face of results from a single experiment, however ambitious and far-reaching."[19]

Rather than speak of success or impact, we have chosen to examine the *significance* of the Eight-Year Study as one of the more important historical examples of educational experimentation. In spite of their organizational sameness, schools are dynamic yet fragile places with shifting faculties and ever-changing student bodies, as Redefer's study showed. School cultures can be destroyed easily and quickly–a principal retires, a teacher-leader is transferred. No specific educational changes endure forever. Knowing this, the Eight-Year Study leaders focused on people rather than on programmatic permanence, recognizing that the most direct and powerful way to improve education is through educating educators and then working to create organizational systems that support and sustain their continued development.

Problems of Representation

We have decided not to write a history of the Eight-Year Study per se but instead to tell some of its many stories. Taken together, these narratives constitute the basis of an argument about the nature of school change and educational reform. We are more interested in exploring the contemporary significance of the project which, of course, required that we work from an historical perspective. We have devoted years to acquisitions: sorting through library remainder tables, uncovering forgotten archival collections, and interviewing Eight-Year Study teachers, students, and Commission members. Yet we always return to the present, even as we have enjoyed exploring the past and delighted in the archival chase. In the process we have come to see the PEA not only as an historical organization, existing from 1919 to 1955, but as a vibrant association encompassing many dynamic and interconnected communities composed of remarkable individuals. The Eight-Year Study produced one such group within the PEA, a community that struggled with certain perennial problems of education. We discuss the Thirty School Study participants knowing full well that they lived within their sensibilities and not ours. At times we wish they had addressed more directly such issues as class, race, and gender. On other occasions we regret the important topics left unattended and those crucial decisions that in hindsight proved unfortunate. We ask readers not to mistake our admiration for uncritical acceptance of their policies and practices. Perhaps we are less prone to judge because we recognize that, with its strengths and limitations, the Eight-Year Study was both a work in progress and an uncompleted project. We know that Commission leaders wished to examine the careers of non-college graduates from the participating schools, and teachers and staff initiated efforts to assist southern African American secondary school leaders to examine their high school programs. Loss of funding prevented these and many other activities from being completed.[20]

Other descriptions severely distort the project. Some accounts refer to Ralph Tyler rather than Aikin as director of the Commission on the Relation of School and College, thereby misrepresenting the orientation of the project from school reorganization to evaluation. In other depictions, the goals of the project have been inaccurately described. Claims were made that the Study sought to prove college admission requirements unnecessary (a point never asserted by the Aikin Commission) or to eliminate college admissions testing (a practice never disputed by the commissions). The Study has been accused of attempting to disseminate progressive education practices to the nation's high schools; however, no specific "progressive" practices were ever endorsed.

Further, the participating schools are at times portrayed as child-centered and ungraded, when in fact one of the most important outcomes of the Study was the development and dissemination of content-oriented secondary school tests.[21] Many questionable assertions emerge as one begins examining how the Eight-Year Study has been characterized in both the professional and popular literature.

We are well aware that our image of progressive education contradicts that of others who have depicted "the movement," in part because we focus on a specific group of Eight-Year Study progressives who worked within as well as outside of the PEA. Further, our interpretations are atypical: recognizing the three PEA Commissions that constituted the Study, for example, or describing the project without including comprehensive accounts of each participating site. Some schools will not be discussed, although Appendix A provides brief descriptions of all. A hallmark of the Eight-Year Study, however, was that there was little "common" practice. All participating school faculties were encouraged to innovate and experiment in different ways. A research program involving hundreds of schools and colleges, hundreds of teachers, and thousands of students cannot be portrayed adequately without such selectivity. Some may feel we have overlooked questionable or misguided methods or ignored unique educational programs from among the participating sites in order to sustain our views. We realize that such criticism inevitably flows from the act of interpretation.

We draw primarily from those public schools selected for the "Study within the Study" as representing the most significant departure from traditional practices and reflecting basic tenets of a very contested and non-uniform progressive education ideology. As others have studied progressive education, we too feature our favorite educators, schools, and universities. Cremin and Patricia Graham refer regularly to John Dewey, Harold Rugg, Teachers College, and progressive schools in New York City. Larry Cuban displays affection for East Denver High School, David Tyack describes Ellwood Cubberley and Stanford University, and Arthur Zilversmit turns primarily to the Winnetka public schools.[22] We focus frequently on the Ohio State University (OSU) School, a public laboratory school particularly representative of the ambitions of the Eight-Year Study, founded at the beginning of the project and starting at its inception to experiment with secondary education. The OSU School represented a literal response to the fundamental question: "What would the secondary school look like if one could start afresh?" There are many other replies, of course, as each school site addressed reorganization in ways that were most appropriate for its specific setting. The first-volume report of the Aikin Commission was titled *The Story of the Eight-Year Study*; in contrast, we offer some of the *many* stories of the project.

Portraying the Thirty School Study has become even more difficult with the resurgence of interest in progressive education and the many definitions and impressions of that term. Often we have found ourselves unraveling good-natured summaries of the PEA and wrestling with definitions of progressivism that are too grand or too narrow. In many respects, this semantic struggle has been ongoing for years. Cremin maintained that "the [progressive education] movement was marked from the very beginning by a pluralistic, frequently contradictory, character."[23] Nonetheless, we feel we must use the descriptor and at times situate the project within the shifting boundaries of this slippery term. For some readers this admission and caveat are meaningless, while for others the use of "progressive education" alone constitutes a red flag.

This brings us to a fundamental question: For whom have we written this book? Most certainly we have not written for the traditional historian who leads a life of facts and footnotes and seeks to document events for the record. Instead, we speak to those educators who may have never come across the Eight-Year Study during their undergraduate and graduate work or who view the project as nothing more than an ill-fated experiment. We are not suggesting that old practices should be restaged but, instead, we are examining experimentation as a process for educational change. We hope our portrayal fosters a curiosity about what could have been, what now could be, and how ideas and practices from the past may help us reexamine secondary education in America today.

Believing in School Experimentation

Efforts to restructure [education] in general like the *Nation at Risk* are absurd. You can't change a whole system that way; you have to begin with problems . . . identify particular problems and actually work with them as was the case with the Eight-Year Study. (Ralph W. Tyler, 1993)[24]

Educational institutions are difficult to change, and as John Goodlad reminds us, "School renewal is context specific." What may "work" in one locale proves disastrous in another.[25] Reforms that merely release schools from bureaucratic strangleholds, without providing clear directions for improvement, do not succeed. And changes in policy do not necessarily touch practice. "For schools to become good, the entire culture of each must be renewed through an intensive process of inquiry. The challenge is how to make this uncommon process common—in other words, how to scale it up without flattening it out to the near level of the conventional."[26] Commission leaders quickly learned that an integral aspect of school reform would include the painstaking process of forging a shared school philosophy through a continuous process of inquiry. This method could not be accomplished merely by sending memos or following district office guidelines. Change requires framing and attacking practical, specific problems. Creating a shared social vision involved exhaustive discussion of solutions as they were conceived, reformulated in the light of data and experience, restated, and restated again and again. Belief in democracy and experimentation represented the most fundamental features of the Eight-Year Study. With faith in the ability of otherwise ordinary persons to live democratically, leaders opened up this process to all. Many teachers deepened their understanding and appreciation of democracy, created and shared a social vision, and pushed well beyond the established schooling practices of the day. Others became frustrated by tedious discussions of educational aims that sometimes led them to unacceptable ideological stands. Yet through intensive study and dialogue, communities formed and strengthened, and common beliefs were articulated and clarified.

Equally important, the participants—teachers, administrators, and Commission staff—viewed their work as having social consequences. Their assorted goals for the project were to transform school practice and thereby to enrich the lives of Americans, young and old. Teachers came to be trusted and their views ultimately respected and valued. Information of various kinds, gathered and analyzed by teachers and Commission staff rather than by distant experts completing their accountability records (as is common practice today), was used for decision making. Definitions of what constituted data were exploratory and expansive; conversations were open-ended, driven by questions that mattered, in search of conclusions hard won but often uncertain. Emerging communities were democratic—and more. These were not mere groups: teachers were given a "*sense of belonging to an adventurous company*," and accordingly they displayed the courage needed to engage in educational change.[27]

By joining such adventurous company, participants gained confidence, believing that results would contribute to the common good. School experimentation and exploration, when pursued with committed others in good faith and with thoughtfulness, ultimately leads to good outcomes. From our research we have come to recognize this as the basic moral framework underpinning the Eight-Year Study: (1) *trust* in the ability of teachers and school administrators to reason through complex issues toward sensible and worthy conclusions; (2) *belief* in democracy as a guiding social ideal, a basis for a community of investigation and endeavor; and (3) *faith* in thoughtful inquiry, including school experimentation, to find ways to make education more life-enhancing for students and teachers. These values resonate throughout each of the subsequent chapters, and from this perspective we write with three aims in mind:

1. We question certain widespread beliefs about progressive education and underscore differences between conceptions of progressivism among elementary educators and the much-overlooked work of secondary progressive educators. We describe a perspective that is markedly different from the so-called child-centered and "free school" definitions common today, one that shifts the focus *from* the child *to* the teacher-pupil relationship. With this change in emphasis, the Eight-Year Study becomes an experimental venture in staff development as much as a curriculum project, revealing rich, dynamic educational venues that were constructed not only for students but also for teachers.

2. We attach faces to the names of those educators who shaped the project, most of whom have been forgotten, obscured by today's progressive education icons. To this end, we include vignettes on specific Thirty School Study participants. Biographic but not comprehensive, the portrayals share what we see as interesting and curious aspects of these individuals' lives and work. While preparing the vignettes, we have come to recognize an overlooked group of educators who do not fall neatly into the past or current categories of progressives. Represented by V. T. Thayer, Margaret Willis, Eugene Smith, Harold Alberty, and Ralph Tyler (who thought of himself as a progressive yet is seldom described as such), these *"Eight-Year Study progressives"* followed Dewey's call to combat "either-or" thinking and thus sought to achieve a balanced position—a middle way—recognizing the complexity of education, the need for continuous experimentation, the value of disciplinary knowledge to solve problems, and the crucial juxtaposition of school, society, and the individual's needs and interests.[28]

3. We portray the Eight-Year Study's educational significance rather than its impact for contemporary school renewal. This will not be done by describing a vast array of contemporary schools whose programs are reminiscent of progressive education practices. We believe the project's importance revolves around the *commitment to and practice of school experimentation,* as demonstrated by developing core curriculum, forming school philosophy, and reconceiving evaluation and assessment. This is what we seek to articulate. Presently much has been written about

the difficulties of school reform and the federal government's expanding role in fostering—some say forcing—school change. The Eight-Year Study brings forth another dimension of change: the need to engage in site-based, context-sensitive, ongoing school experimentation. The PEA supported the view that all school faculties should be actively engaged in such exploration as they conceived their own adventures in teaching and learning. We aim to reemphasize experimentation as a basic and foundational need, not a luxury, for healthy schools and school faculties.

Significance for Education Today

To judge from the ahistorical character of most current policy talk about reform, innovators may consider amnesia a virtue. And in those rare occasions when reformers do discuss the history of schooling, they often portray the past in politicized, stylized ways as a golden age to be restored or a dismal legacy to be repudiated. (David Tyack and Larry Cuban, 1995)[29]

The Eight-Year Study holds valuable insights for those who work with schools, students, and teachers. In the history of American education, such a remarkable collection of talent as found among the three PEA Commissions has not been duplicated. The Study brought together a rising generation of educators and social scientists from secondary schools, colleges, and universities who, nurtured by a distinguished group of elders, would become significant leaders of American education. Several fields of educational study were transformed by the work of the three commissions. Rarely has such an academically diverse group come together not as mere figureheads but as *active* participants in an ambitious educational enterprise without specific predetermined outcomes. In contrast to current practices, these educators and social scientists worked closely together without interference from politicians and well-meaning business executives who would press for quick results. The smaller directing committee of the Aikin Commission included presidents of Bennington College, the University of Cincinnati, Bryn Mawr College, and the University of West Virginia; deans of Columbia University, Lehigh University, and the University of Minnesota; professors from Princeton University and Ohio State University; and school superintendents and directors from the East Coast and West Coast (as well as the editor of the *New Republic*). All academic fields were represented for significant contributions, not for mere appearances or publicity. Commission participants—Ralph Tyler, Erik Erikson, Margaret Mead, Peter Blos, Ruth Benedict, James Michener, Helen Lynd, and Benjamin Spock, among others—represented an emerging new era for the social sciences. They came together with a common interest beyond their own focused work—namely, to discuss matters of secondary education and, with faith in experimentation and democracy, to attempt to synthesize new forms of high school and college education.

The words of PEA President Eugene Smith, in the first volume of *Progressive Education*, the house journal of the organization, resonate across the decades: "Progressive education cannot be static; it must be ever searching, ever experimenting, ever moving on towards higher ideals and more complete realization of them."[30] So it is with education today. The times are different, but the essential issues and concerns are the same. There have never been blueprints—not in 1942, not today. What remains is a desperate need for more searching, more experimenting, and ever more risk-taking in order to realize our society's highest educational ideals.

Vignette

Wilford Merton Aikin (1882–1965): Hope, Success, and Realistic Expectations

Wilford M. Aikin, photograph, 1940, Ohio State University Photo Archives

The Progressive Education Association's 1929 National Conference was a thrilling time for Wilford Aikin, head of the local St. Louis Conference Arrangement Committee. This middle-aged school director, while not then a member of the PEA hierarchy, had corresponded for months with PEA founder and president Stanwood Cobb and executive board members who felt that the conference was handled exceptionally well and that the quality of the sessions and high attendance made the 1929 event one of the best ever.[1] Despite all of his conference responsibilities, Aikin agreed to chair a discussion group arising from one of the formal presentations about secondary education. As director of the John Burroughs School, he was well versed to discuss progressive secondary education since just six years earlier (in 1923) he had founded this private, coeducational, college-preparatory high school and had overseen every aspect of its development, from selecting the site, planning the buildings, and buying equipment to hiring teachers and determining curriculum.

In addition to successfully staging the national conference, the entire year proved rather remarkable for Aikin as well. Described in the *Progressive Education* journal as one of the active leaders in the secondary school field and invited to travel to Denmark later that summer to discuss issues in progressive secondary education at the New Education Fellowship's World Conference, he seemed to have burst upon the national scene. During the next fifteen years he would be involved with important, even legendary, educational reform. He accomplished much, however, today his place in the history of education remains well known yet oddly askew—celebrated but misunderstood. In certain respects, the Eight-Year Study could also be so described. Aikin's educational work as well as the legacy of the Study both reflect recognition with numerous inaccuracies and "success" with unfulfilled promise. We hope such perceptions for both will change.

I

In the late 1920s, a good progressive high school was not easy to find. When the PEA celebrated its tenth anniversary in 1929, *Progressive Education* published essays describing advances in the areas of preschool, elementary, junior high, college, adult, and parent education. Secondary education was noticeably missing. Previously, one author stated, "In the field of secondary education there is as yet no clearly recognizable progressive movement. There are new trends, occasional experiments of importance, and a very few experimental high schools."[2] And in the subsequent *Progressive Education* issue, V. T. Thayer described the reorganization of secondary education as seriously lagging behind advances at the elementary level.[3] Such criticism must have been taken quite seriously by the 1929 PEA Conference Planning Committee. The theme had been changed just months before the event from "child activity," a topic that would have continued the organization's focus on elementary and child-centered schooling, to "Education, an Active Process," a theme that may well have been code for anticipated work in secondary education. Alexander Meiklejohn, then-director of the University of Wisconsin Experimental College, was selected for the keynote session, and many conference regulars conducted sessions on teacher training and secondary education. When PEA members arrived in St. Louis for the 1929 national meeting, they seemed ready to launch a recognizable progressive secondary education movement.

Aikin's own 1929 conference session was informal, and no printed document exists. But the conversation no doubt lingered since, on New Year's Day 1930, he specifically set aside time to compose his hopes for secondary school reform. He asserted, "No problem is more in need of *thoughtful study and vigorous experiment.*"[4] Perhaps this was even an audition for his forthcoming role as chair of the Commission on the Relation of School and College; the essay was later published in *Progressive Education* just two months before he proposed the formation of a committee to address issues of high school-college relations. Since the Eight-Year Study is often criticized for focusing only on the elite, college-bound student, it is worth noting that Aikin's New Year's Day composition was concerned with how to provide secondary school education for all youth, regardless of their educational futures.

"Thoughtful study and vigorous experiment"—in many respects this phrase seemed to be as much of a PEA mantra as child-centered curricula and "learning by doing." Aikin called for curriculum development without decreeing specific content, encouraged secondary school experimentation while also supporting intelligence testing, and embraced an education that was both liberal and responsive to the physical and emotional health of adolescents. The New Year's Day comments represented many of the most basic hopes of the Progressive Education Association. Aikin, while not next in line to assume the PEA presidency, had situated himself to accept a position of leadership.

II

As a headmaster of a private secondary school named for one of the most popular American nature writers of the time (John Burroughs, 1837–1921), Aikin was both a leader in the field of progressive secondary education and a statesperson among private, independent school headmasters. Yet unlike many colleagues—Stanwood Cobb, Perry Smith, who had founded North Shore Country Day School, and Herbert Smith of the Fieldston School—who were all Harvard men, Aikin had not been groomed at a prestigious private college himself. Born in New Concord, Ohio, he was teaching in a one-room country school well before his college studies began in 1903, which was not until age twenty-one. After graduating from Muskingum College (located in his hometown) at twenty-five, he taught English and history in Michigan and Ohio public schools while completing a master's degree from the University of Michigan in 1913. Aikin held brief teaching posts at University of California-Berkeley and Ohio State University in the area of school administration and supervision, and he served as head of a private school in New York during which time he coauthored a textbook on American literature with one of his professors at the University of Michigan.[5]

Accepting the directorship of the John Burroughs School in 1923 at age forty-one, Aikin was recognized as a fine orator and spokesperson with a velvety voice, appealing sense of humor, and twinkly eye. Bill Aikin, as he was called by colleagues, was six feet tall with a face that appears formal yet kind in the four photographs we have located of him. Harold Rugg, in 1933 PEA board minutes, complimented his diplomatic efforts, praising his unique ability to bring people together.[6] He had the demeanor of a "thoughtful and fine gentleman" according to

Paul Diederich and Ralph Tyler of the Commission on the Relation of School and College Evaluation Staff. Such abilities served Aikin well, and many believed these talents permitted him to steer the Eight-Year Study through various potentially volatile situations.[7]

III

Aikin was asked to lead the secondary school discussion at the 1930 PEA conference in Washington, D.C. The topic for the conference did not arise from another presentation as occurred previously but was preplanned and focused on a specific high school issue: "College Entrance and the Secondary School." With 150–200 participants, discussion centered on practical approaches to secondary school improvement; however, frequent mention was made of the constraints imposed by college unit requirements. Unknown at the time, the 1930 Conference proved to be a turning point for the organization. A few weeks after the national meeting, officers met to discuss whether the PEA should engage in research and if so what type and how would it be financed? A decision was made to proceed with an established research agenda and to seek external funds. From this board meeting, the Committee for the Relation of School and College was designated "to enter into a thorough study of college entrance requirements, examinations, and of the whole relationship between schools and colleges. Such a study will require several years and may well be helpful and continuous for an indefinite period."[8] Aikin was appointed chair.

Aikin was well aware of the difficulties before him and before the committee: to develop a number of innovative secondary programs in an effort to encourage reconstruction of the secondary school. Such a challenge may have appeared daunting to others but not impossible to him. He had undertaken such a task before—as had others: Cobb had started the Chevy Chase School, Eugene Smith had formed the Beaver Country Day School, Perry Dunlap Smith had "begotten" the North Shore Country Day School, and, of course, Aikin had founded the John Burroughs School. These educators had already accomplished what the PEA had hoped for—creating secondary schools free from the heavy burden of tradition where curricular and instructional methods would be selected by thoughtful choice and not by convention.

Viewed as a most hopeful beginning for the "right kind of reciprocity" between schools and colleges, the committee demanded much of Aikin's time but at first represented merely an addition to his many responsibilities at the John Burroughs School. Within a few years he found his PEA duties overwhelming, and in 1932 he was given leave from his post to work full time with the Commission on the Relation of School and College. In July 1935 he resigned from the John Burroughs School and moved to Ohio State University to assume a research professorship at the Bureau of Educational Research, where he supervised directly the Commission staff of twenty-four people.

Aikin approached the Eight-Year Study with a then-current conception of school experimentation—less scientific and more exploratory. He set out to improve educational practice but not necessarily to launch a research agenda for secondary education. His expectations, while not modest, reflected more a normative approach to change rather than the demands of applied research. The project in 1932 was not preparing for controlled testing but instead for addressing the implications of "what changes are likely to come."[9] What actually followed were many anticipated and unanticipated events, and much of his work from 1938 onward consisted of countless reports and memos to the General Education Board requesting support for an extension of the project. Funds were not forthcoming, and the completion of the Eight-Year Study, though not previously designated, would soon occur. In July 1940 he moved to New York City, where for the next sixteen months he worked at the PEA national office and completed the first volume of the Adventure in American Education series, *The Story of the Eight-Year Study*. With the release of the five-volume series during 1942 and early 1943, the Eight-Year Study was officially completed.

Aikin kept his many letters of congratulations from the publication. Also among his notes from this period are cryptic queries and applications for school and academic posts. None was offered. Expressing some frustration with his inability to secure a university professorship, he wrote to Ralph Tyler in 1946 wondering whether he had "lived too long to be in line for a position."[10] Perhaps Aikin, at age sixty-four, had reached such an impasse. One of the school directors wrote at the completion of the project saying, "[When] one reaches the age that you have, it isn't so easy to get positions in competition with younger men."[11] His career in the field of progressive education was at its end; at age sixty, he received national attention as director of the Eight-Year Study and little more.

Aikin was far from retirement, however. He had married a former teacher from one of the participating sites (his second wife), and they considered starting a school in the Palo Alto, California, area. Instead, he became a human relations and personnel training consultant for the Standard Oil Company of California and for other companies, an interest that had arisen from the Aikin, Thayer, and Keliher Commissions' research. He remained active in the San Francisco educational community during the 1950s, staying in contact with Tyler and teaching workshops and seminars at Stanford University. Described by his daughter as a "wise, vigorous elder," happy and quite content with his life while remaining active with the community library and school board, Aikin continued professional writing and presentations into his late seventies. His final manuscript addressed the nature of human relations and dignity.[12]

Aikin expressed few regrets about the Eight-Year Study. Reminiscing in a 1953 essay entitled "If We Were to Do It Again," he suggested there was too much disparity among the schools and believed a follow-up study of non-college-bound students would have "yielded even more striking and convincing results."[13] But he certainly was not going to bicker about what should have been done. Rather, he used this essay as an opportunity to underscore (twice) the Study's original decision not to prescribe a curriculum for all secondary schools and remained convinced that successful school reform could occur only with an involved staff that felt ownership over proposed changes.

IV

Opportunities seemed unlimited for Wilford Aikin in 1938, and the same could be said of the work of the Commission on the Relation of School and College. They both met numerous obstacles through the 1930s and 1940s, yet many positive outcomes were apparent: students from the actively involved high schools were doing well in college, secondary school teachers were very pleased with the summer workshops, and the Study's standardized tests were being used throughout the country. In terms of its original goals, the Commission was a remarkable success as Aikin documented in *The Story of the Eight-Year Study*. This causes us to wonder if he and his associates were surprised when in subsequent years the project was characterized as unsuccessful. What would have constituted success? Evidently, in the view of many educators, markedly higher college grade point averages from the progressive school students would have been more convincing.

Fortunately, newspaper articles during 1942 and 1943 judged the project on its own terms and reported the many strengths of the Thirty School Study students: stronger leadership, better intellectual abilities, better understanding of democracy, a keener interest in good books—each a valued outcome for a nation preparing for war. And while the "slightly above average grades" seemed to take on a negative interpretation in later years, period newspaper accounts throughout the United States saw those results very differently: "Survey finds progressive school graduates have edge in college: Eight-Year Study shows they make better grades"; "Rigid curriculum condemned: Graduate of progressive schools found superior in college grades"; "School of future is taking form: Experimental units . . . find that pupils excel in things that matter."[14] British educators saw the results as successful too. In 1942, the Eight-Year Study was applauded as a "bold and ambitious experiment" that was viewed as assessing intellectual qualities and abilities rather than merely tabulating college grades. For the British, a new conception of core curriculum fostering intellectual traits and embracing a sense of democracy mattered, especially when they were engaged in their fight against fascism.[15] To many American critics, however, college grade point averages remained more important.

Fate, too, has been oddly cruel to the historical legacy of Wilford Aikin, literally as well as figuratively. His name in histories and records has been mysteriously transformed into Aiken—an alteration that now appears with regularity. Considering the self-deprecating humor for which Bill Aikin was known, we might say he is a victim of "the Aikin vowel shift."[16] Perhaps there is a natural tendency to misspell the name. Even his daughter described her schoolgirl's jingle: "I'm Margie Aikin, A I K I N that is."[17]

V

> All through the Study, the commission was convinced that the
> principles of democracy should guide its work, and particularly
> so in its relations with each school. Since the commission would
> not dictate, the schools were forced to state clearly the objec-
> tives of whatever they proposed to do. (Wilford M. Aikin, 1964)[18]

For Wilford M. Aikin, the spirit of the Eight-Year Study ultimately took form in three fundamental beliefs: schools can experiment with their programs in fruitful ways without jeopardizing their students' future educational careers; there are many paths for college success; and genuine educational reform cannot be packaged and disseminated. Throughout the duration of the project, Aikin and the Directing Committee refused to prescribe a secondary school program. Some critics questioned this decision, believing that the Study would have been much more successful and exerted more impact upon American education if "circulated" throughout the country as an official and sponsored progressive education course of study. His refusal to concede is somewhat ironic since so much of what is remembered today about progressive education comes from packaged school plans: the Wirt's Platoon System, Kilpatrick's Project Method, Parkhurst's Dalton Plan, and Washburne's Winnetka Plan.

As guide and diplomat, Wilford Aikin assisted school faculties in charting their own journey through educational reform. Many teachers and administrators were initially frightened of the prospect of experimenting with their programs, and some were never able to accomplish many of the innovations they sought. Ultimately, however, Commission staff and teachers understood that every school in a democracy not only should be but must be an experimental school. He maintained that "No aspect of any school's work should be so firmly fixed in practice or tradition as to be immune from honest inquiry and possible improvement. It is only in this way that life and vigor are maintained and progress achieved."[19] Today, as efforts to initiate school reform so often turn to prepackaged programs and as school consultants base their careers upon transplanting programs—best practices approach—from one school to another, we admire Aikin for his conviction not to prescribe an Eight-Year Study "school model." If he had, perhaps fame would have followed; however, we are convinced that success would not have occurred. He knew this too.

Chapter 1

The Educational Context
of the Eight-Year Study

There is no need to re-present the history of progressive education. Patricia Graham's *Progressive Education,* Lawrence Cremin's *The Transformation of the School,* and William Reese's *Power and the Promise of School Reform* have already done so, and their work proves as insightful today as when first published.[1] Yet countless myths still surround both progressivism and the PEA. We wish to discuss lore that affects our conception of the Eight-Year Study as we attempt to broaden the common definition of progressive education in view of current perceptions of the late 1920s–1930s era. We also will examine the societal tensions of the 1930s, particularly those concerning the future of democracy, since public fears greatly influenced the direction of the project. We conclude this chapter with a discussion of the unique type of research conducted by the Aikin Commission staff.

Conceptions of the Progressive Education Association

Although progressive education has no official creed, it has its distinctive points of view and activities. (John L. Childs, 1939)[2]

The Progressive Education Association was far from being united in the late 1920s during the Eight-Year Study's early stages of conception. Formed in Washington, D.C., in 1919 under the leadership of Stanwood Cobb, the PEA, originally titled the Association for the Advancement of Progressive Education, attracted individuals more critical of established school practice rather than those sharing a common vision for bettering education.[3] Having witnessed unsuccessful efforts to form a Montessori society in the United States, PEA members believed the association would fail at the national level if founders focused on any specific approach to schooling.[4] Throughout its history the PEA would explore many different and sometimes contending orientations to teaching and learning—

the ideas of Pestalozzi, Montessori, Rousseau, the American transcenden-
talists, Freud, Steiner—and not just the ideas of John Dewey. While Dewey
(and the early University of Chicago Laboratory School) defines progressive education for us today, he did not embody the movement for PEA
founder Cobb and other PEA members who instead turned to eighty-
five-year-old Charles W. Eliot to lead the organization. Eliot, emeritus
president of Harvard University, declined the PEA presidency due to failing health but agreed to serve as the honorary first president, proclaiming
his belief in the principles and aims of the organization.[5] Years later, after
Eliot's death in 1926, Dewey would serve as honorary president.

The PEA is also often viewed as a small, obscure organization of
Dewey disciples centered at Teachers College, Columbia University, or
a group of "dauntless women" who started private, elite elementary
schools centered on developing the interests and fostering the creative
spirit of children. Historical narratives continue that the PEA turned to
a more political, social reform agenda, sparked by George Counts's
1932 "Dare Progressive Education Be Progressive?" speech that led to
great turmoil and fragmentation within progressive education circles.[6]
The tale of the PEA concludes with the association imploding in the
late 1940s and disappearing in the 1950s in what follows a general
organizational biography: birth, growth, maturity, and death. These impressions implicitly assume that progressive education was the near-
exclusive domain of PEA members.

This story of the PEA, similar to the morality play of progressive
education described in the introduction, is not necessarily wrong—
merely too simple. As is commonly believed, the PEA was indeed small.
Yet its membership was not quite as modest as some assume and certainly larger than many well-known educational organizations today.
From the first meeting in 1919 with eighty-six in attendance, membership rapidly expanded, increasing fourfold between 1924 and 1930 to
7,600 members. By the late 1930s membership peaked at approximately
10,000, although according to Harold Rugg, the association was more
than twice this size based on conference participation.[7] PEA meetings
were not small gatherings either, and regional conferences were often
as popular as national events. For example, the 1934 PEA Southern
New England Conference attracted over 2,000 attendees.[8] Neither were
these all private school educators, as some may assume. It is true that
the PEA was first composed of an elite, East Coast private school constituency, yet Cobb maintained that this merely reflected opportunities
for educational innovation, since private schools were freer to experiment than were public schools. For Cobb, the PEA encouraged educational reform for all schools, and he maintained, "It is in and through
the public schools that the ultimate success of the progressive move-

ment must be sought."[9] By 1933, approximately 35 percent of PEA members were from the public schools, and the largest subgroup of members consisted of public school administrators.[10] Further, the PEA may not have been quite as obscure as is often assumed. The organization received substantial national attention throughout the 1930s. Newspaper accounts described the Eight-Year Study and its preliminary results in New York City, Boston, Philadelphia, Chicago, and Los Angeles. The cover of the October 1939 *Time* magazine featured PEA Executive Director Frederick Redefer with the subtitle "We are no longer a rebel group," and the then-current U.S. Commissioner of Education, John W. Studebaker (who served in this role from 1934 to 1948), was directly connected to the PEA and the Eight-Year Study as a former superintendent of one of the participating school systems.[11]

One aspect of PEA lore is perplexing, however. Cobb maintained that a Teachers College, Columbia University, group stole the PEA from the founding members. Cremin first described this anecdote in 1959, and Cobb restated the story to Graham in 1962 and again to Bullough in 1974.[12] Since no Teachers College faculty member ever served as president of the PEA, Graham places the comment in a broader historical context and notes that the informal power structure of the PEA did shift from Cobb's private school, Washington-related crowd to the Teachers College faculty, and there clearly were shifts in power and ideology.[13] Counts's 1932 *Dare Progressive Education* conference presentation and the Teachers College-*Social Frontier* group altered progressive education rhetoric in the 1930s and early 1940s, focusing attention on the many Teachers College faculty who were actively involved in progressive education. Even the PEA offices moved from Washington to New York City in 1935.

Yet when asked about Cobb's claim, Donald Cottrell, a faculty member at both Teachers College and Ohio State University during the 1930s–1950s period, expressed doubt and maintained that while Teachers College faculty unquestionably constituted an informal power center in the 1930s, other communities emerged as well, in particular in the Midwest at the University of Illinois and Ohio State University.[14] In addition, PEA activities in California, specifically at the University of California, Berkeley, must not be overlooked as another center of important activity. As we examined Commissions' school accounts, we felt that much of the more interesting work occurred in areas other than New York City, even though recent descriptions of progressive education have tended to feature New York schools. Suffice to say that Teachers College was not the sole center of the Progressive Education Association, although it was certainly one of the more influential.

Cobb was quite correct, however, in saying that "something happened" in the 1930s that dramatically shifted the power structure of the organization. PEA leaders decided to expand their involvement in school research and experimentation, a decision confirmed at a 1930 Board of Directors' retreat when they decided to seek external funding for program development and dissemination (a decision that helped establish the Eight-Year Study). Thus began the Association's rather anxious quest for research funds at a time when the organization was near bankruptcy. When Cobb charges that the PEA was stolen from its membership, we see as culprits not the Teachers College faculty but instead the Carnegie Foundation for the Advancement of Teaching and the General Education Board (GEB) for taking control of the direction of the organization during the 1930s. William Learned and Henry Suzzallo of the Carnegie Foundation and Lawrence K. Frank and Robert Havighurst of the GEB exerted substantive influence in the PEA by determining which projects would be funded and which would not. At times PEA funding seemed to serve Frank's interests as much, if not more, than the PEA's. By the 1940s these foundations moved on to other projects and, having abandoned the PEA, left the organization dependent on outside monies that were no longer available. When in the 1940s the GEB staff decided they were no longer funding general education projects, the decline of the PEA began.[15]

Finally, we wish to address one other general misimpression—namely, that the progressive education movement was synonymous with the Progressive Education Association. Cobb acknowledged that the PEA did not create the movement but gave it "form and body."[16] While this may well be the case, other organizations were heavily involved in developing and promoting progressive practices, most notably the American Council on Education (ACE), founded in 1918 to serve as a national forum for higher education institutions and to provide easier access to college education for larger numbers of students. The Council received financial support from the GEB during the 1930s and through the 1940s that most likely would otherwise have been directed to the PEA. The ACE's American Youth Commission's studies addressed issues of central concern to the PEA membership and to leaders of the Eight-Year Study. In addition, the Council received funding for the Cooperative Study in General Education, a project coordinated by Ralph Tyler from 1939 to 1945 in what was a direct outgrowth of the Eight-Year Study's curriculum development efforts at the college level.[17] There were many other groups working during the 1930s and 1940s to promote progressive education. When Hollis Caswell, president of Teachers College from 1955 to 1964, assessed progressive education during the 1930s, he made a point of highlighting the contributions of the Society for Curriculum Study, the Educational Policies Commission (formed in 1935 by the NEA and the American Association of School Administrators), and the California and Michigan state departments of education.[18]

In addition, other research groups were exploring many of the topics central to the Eight-Year Study. Three years before the Aikin Commission on the Relation of School and College was established, the Educational Records Bureau, described as a Who's Who of progressive educators in the eastern states, formed its own Committee on School and College Relations. This group, also composed of secondary school and college educators, met at the Carnegie Foundation offices to "discuss college entrance problems." The Bureau's committee, chaired by Eugene Smith, former president of the PEA and a key figure in the Eight-Year Study, in essence, functioned in parallel to the Aikin Commission and continued to meet through the 1930s, releasing reports in 1932, 1933, 1935, and 1942. In many respects, the Educational Records Bureau's Committee was more active in its attempt to break the stranglehold of Carnegie units on American secondary education than was the Aikin Commission and was more successful in promulgating the use of the cumulative student record form once this was no longer a focus of the Eight-Year Study.[19]

The PEA's Commission on Secondary School Curriculum and Commission on Human Relations also had counterparts of sorts. The Educational Records Bureau staged a five-year, public school demonstration project in educational guidance (from 1933 to 1938) somewhat similar to the research of the Zachry Committee of the Thayer Commission. With funding from the Carnegie Foundation, the Bureau released its 300-page final report, *Guidance in Public Secondary Schools*, in 1939. Also, the American Council on Education's Committee on the Relation of Emotion to the Educative Process, formed in 1934 and funded by the General Education Board, examined the emotional life and needs of young people in ways quite similar to the "human relations" work of the Keliher Commission and Zachry's Committee, and the ACE's Motion Picture Study, also funded by the GEB, conducted research that was integrated into the work of the PEA's Commission on Human Relations.[20] Our point is merely to note that progressive education of the 1930s must not be reduced to a PEA battle between child-centered educators, clutching their Project Method pamphlets tightly in hand, and *Social Frontier* radicals reading quotations from *Dare the School Build a New Social Order*.[21] While the PEA began its "ultimate demise" and fragmentation in the late 1930s and early 1940s, there was great diversity within progressivism, and many other organizations were involved in similar activities. The PEA was but one group among many that sought to advance the cause of progressive education.

Definitions of Progressive Education

The many myths surrounding the Progressive Education Association are actually less complex than the variety of definitions of *progressive education*, in the 1930s as well as today. In *The Transformation of the School*, Cremin warns against formulating any capsule definition: "None exists, and none ever will; for throughout its history progressive education meant different things to different people.[22] And this was certainly the case when one looks carefully at the PEA, an organization of competing coalitions among its constituency, each holding different views of progressivism. In fact, at the 1938 annual meeting, a committee reported on its efforts to define the term, and while a statement was produced, nearly the entire group objected, explaining that progressive education is not a definition but "a spirit."[23]

Despite the PEA's failure to adopt an official definition, a vague and widely shared description of progressive education has emerged over time, tied to slogans such as "learning by doing," "teaching the whole child," and "fostering creative expression." These catchphrases became the basis of caricatures by critics in the 1950s who popularized images of cheerful children doing as they pleased, greeted with smiling approval from their poorly educated but tolerant teachers, stereotypes that live to this day. William Heard Kilpatrick's version of the "project method," a confusing pedagogical practice from its conception, may have caused more damage to progressive education, particularly to its image, than virtually any other curricular or instructional innovation.[24] Rather than attributing the slogans to Kilpatrick, however, many of today's critics castigate Dewey, often without reading his educational works or appreciating his disciplinary focus.

Whatever the original spirit of progressive education may have been, as we researched the Eight-Year Study we were surprised by various distinctive points of view and many forgotten names. V. T. Thayer, Alice Keliher, Harold Alberty, Caroline Zachry, Burton Fowler, Robert Leigh, and Eugene Smith are just a few of the educators who do not appear in today's descriptions yet who were quite influential in furthering the PEA's mission. While we have tried to make sense of the term *progressive education*, we see little clear pattern in its use. Tyack notes that the loosely applied label represents a diverse group of reformers, philosophies, and practices, and that those identified as "administrative progressives" had little in common with other wings of educational progressivism.[25] At times too focused and at other times too comprehensive, the use of the term is, according to Kliebard, "not only vacuous but mischievous" and was "studiously avoided" in *The Struggle for the American Curriculum*.[26] Aikin must have felt the same. Although the indexer for *The Story of the Eight-Year Study* inserted the term on a variety of pages, Aikin never used "progressive education" except once in reference to a quotation. We have tried to follow Aikin's model and Kliebard's advice and have used the term cautiously and carefully.

At one time, we also thought of preparing a configuration of progressive educators. We concluded, however, that there really is no need for yet another overview, and that the past classifications have been quite helpful as we have tried to make sense of the field. Cremin's designation of progressives as scientists, sentimentalists, and radicals helped sort out many educators working in the early twentieth century. Additional groupings such as Kliebard's social meliorists, Tyack's administrative and pedagogical progressives, and even Rugg's "scientific methodists" and "project methodists" clarified an unwieldy movement.[27] But each arrangement has also raised questions, not just what defines a progressive educator? But does the distinct adherence to a set of beliefs or historical fiat determine one's classification; that is, are progressive educators defined by ideology, or are progressives defined as those educators who lived through the Progressive Era? Cremin, for example, situates the genesis of progressive education in the years immediately following the Civil War. Like him, most educational historians view progressive education as an outgrowth of America's Progressive Era. From this perspective, the movement comes to fruition in the late nineteenth and early twentieth centuries, beginning with Frances Parker's school in Quincy, Massachusetts, continuing through Dewey's laboratory school at the University of Chicago, and followed by developments at the Gary, Lincoln, Winnetka, and Dalton schools. Progressive education seems, then, to have been codified into an ideology before the formation of the PEA. In fact, we found the work from the period 1890–1920, as seen in the diverse practices of Dewey, Ellwood Cubberley, William Wirt, Marietta Johnson, Caroline Pratt, and Margaret Naumburg, differ strikingly from that of the 1930s and the Eight-Year Study. And when progressive education is viewed at the secondary rather than the elementary school level, a new assortment of issues comes to the forefront and a different group of educators as well.

Eight-Year Study Progressives

From all of this, we now come to see a distinctive middle ground where certain progressive educators of the 1930s stood. They were neither administrative nor pedagogical progressives nor would they be grouped as child, society, or subject-centered educators. The descriptors "scientific methodist, social meliorist, and social reconstructionist" also seemed inappropriate. This distinct group, "situated between the extremes," has come to symbolize for us a theoretical practicality and a dynamic, reasoned balance among a constantly evolving set of educational claims. The intensive process of inquiry and continuous school experimentation required "a middle way" if these educators were to respond effectively to the changing demands of schooling. Such a position is not often recognized in accounts of the period. The work of Keliher, Eugene Smith, Thayer, Alberty, Lavone Hanna, Boyd Bode, Margaret Willis, and others has been somewhat overlooked, due, we suspect, to a tendency to bifurcate the "progressive movement" into firm ideological stances and to engage in the sort of "either-or" binary thinking that Dewey so consistently and vigorously challenged.

Ralph Tyler, a self-proclaimed progressive who is often dismissed as not fitting easily into the various configurations, captures aspects of this group. When attempting to describe the way in which educational decision making ought to occur, Tyler found that he needed to differentiate a range of legitimate and competing educational interests. He characterized these as "sources" of aims and included the disciplines (subject matter), the individual "needs" of learners, understood quite broadly, and studies of society. These three areas—subject matter, the individual, and society—were considered as having equal claims on education, even though Tyler most certainly recognized that educators frequently emphasize one source over another as each is "screened" through philosophical and psychological orientations. Tyler's famous curriculum rationale, maturing through his work with the Eight-Year Study, reflected this desire for appropriate balance.[28]

Attempting to transcend those three sources, Eight-Year Study progressives brought these competing claims into intense and intimate conversation so that each deepened the meaning of the others. For example, representing a synthesis of values, "needs" came to be thought of as both personal and social in nature and not merely as expressions of individual desire or of an insistent societal demand. In contrast, other progressives embraced an ideological clarity produced by extending the extremes, that is, Kilpatrick refined a conception of personal interests as fruitful educational experiences, Counts urged the role of social activism for improving schools, and Cubberley nurtured an administrative efficiency to extend the reach of public education. These progressives became better known in part because of their extreme and easily characterized positions. Overlooked were those educators associated with the Eight-Year Study who set out to achieve a reasoned balance of interests while continuing to seek new understandings about the relationships among the subject matter, the individual, and society.

Eight-Year Study progressives embraced an experimental spirit—a process of inquiry—and their bond also became a common set of ideas found in how they positioned themselves in relationship to the three categories identified by Tyler and to other established lines of progressive thought. They held a democratic social vision, albeit evolving, along with a deep appreciation for the power of the academic disciplines and for knowledge as a tool for solving fundamental human problems and enriching human life. Coupled with this, they adopted school experimentation as a way of understanding learning and human development that recognized the unpredictability of outcomes and the centrality of intellectual adventure and exploration. Attending to youth's schooling simultaneously meant thinking carefully about the individual and social implications of student needs and how the disciplines might serve as guides for teachers to design potentially educative environments. Conversely, the means for achieving desired social aims were considered and judged in terms of how they would impact educational communities and shape the quality of students' educational experiences. Aims and means were tightly linked—they could not discuss one without also considering the other—and theory and practice were brought into intimate relationship, what we refer to as theoretical practicality (or middle-range theorizing) leading to intelligent problem solving.

We are not suggesting that these educators held no firm stances. Their beliefs were constantly evolving as they situated their work within specific settings and reexamined the implications of their positions. Their central values were clear as actions adapted to circumstances and demands. Eugene Smith extended the point when he stated that "truly progressive" education must continually be tested by two questions: "Does it keep itself fitted to present day requirements, changing as necessary with changing living conditions and changing needs? Does it keep apace with investigation and discovery in the educational field?"[29] These progressives neither compromised nor conceded their beliefs, nor did they adopt an ecumenical stance as a way to resolve dilemmas, a point of criticism sometimes directed against Tyler. Rather, they sought a reasoned and productive balance, a middle way, evolving and changing with their experimental and implementative research.

By the nature of its design and intent, the Eight-Year Study appealed to educators with this somewhat atypical and now overlooked orientation. They were theorists deeply concerned about practice as a way of enriching theory. Yet they were also administrators and teachers, involved in the daily workings of schools, who viewed theory as a means for thinking more clearly and productively about practice. The first orientation, the *practical theorist*, is well represented by Boyd H. Bode, whose central concern became how democracy through public education could be realized as a way of life. Eugene Smith nicely embodies the second orientation, the *theoretical practitioner*: one who was deeply concerned with scientific and experimental research as a way to better schooling. V. T. Thayer depicts even further both perspectives combined in the career of one individual. As the accompanying vignettes illustrate, Thayer, along with Bode, Smith, and many others, had a deep commitment to school experimentation as an open-ended but also increasingly more sensitive, thoughtful, intelligent, and socially responsive practice. All were progressives, but none saw themselves as sitting comfortably within progressivism nor even within the PEA. Bode and Thayer gladly criticized the better-known leaders—Cubberley, Snedden, Kilpatrick, Parkhurst, Washburne, Thorndike, and Counts—as they later did one another.[30] Thayer may well have seen himself as much a secular humanist as a progressive, and Smith seemed more active in the ACE and Educational Records Bureau than in the PEA (even as its former president). In fact, many of these Eight-Year Study progressives were consistent and outspoken critics of some so-called progressive tendencies, particularly those that underplayed the value of disciplinary knowledge or the "mindless celebration" of individual student needs.

The 1930s: A Lost Generation of Youth

The situation for youth in the early 1930s was desperate. As the Great Depression deepened, young people found themselves unable to obtain employment and increasingly dependent on their parents for ever longer periods of support. In an American Council on Education study, Homer Rainey and his colleagues found that employment opportunities for young people had simply vanished. In 1936, an estimated 4 million youth between the ages of sixteen to twenty-four (the then-defined ages of adolescence) were enrolled in school, a larger than ever proportion, while 5 million were unemployed and seeking jobs. More adolescents remained in school longer, yet these students encountered a curriculum out of touch with their experience. The needs of the 1930s' high school pupil, Rainey concluded, could not be met with the same curriculum determined for "the selected body of students enrolled in secondary school and institutions of higher education in 1900."[31] The high school curriculum was outdated, and his conclusion was widely shared. Following a three-month cross-country trip of the United States, Maxine Davis referred to American youth as a "lost generation" and used harsh words to describe America's secondary schools: "They are, on the whole, concerned with preparing [youth] to enter college, although they know that for all but a few hundred thousand . . . boys and girls in the secondary schools, the last three years of high school are all the education they will ever have."[32] She also lamented the general disconnection of the schools from the wider problems of young people and, perhaps engaging in hyperbole, expressed concern that the schools no longer represented democratic institutions.

School faculties faced their own crises. As teachers were obliged to assume ever greater social responsibilities, expectations were changing. At the same time, education budgets were dramatically cut, building programs delayed, and teaching staffs reduced. Yet as McGill and Matthews observed, "The years of economic crisis have been accompanied by a disposition to examine critically the kind of education that is being offered youth and to adapt it to new and changing needs."[33] To many educators, the traditional high school (college preparation) program seemed not only outdated but also ineffective. Of those few young people who continued to college, not many stayed. Within a group of twenty-five research universities, almost half of the students who entered in 1931 and 1932 withdrew permanently before graduating, and one-third of these withdrew during their first year.[34] As many high schools continued to embrace a traditional college preparatory program, numerous students were ill prepared for either employment or further study.

The situation in Europe was increasingly frightening as well. The growing appeal of fascism, with its glorification of youth, horrified PEA Commission members. The German Youth Movement gave new meaning to the social importance and political potential of adolescents. Eight-Year Study staff—most notably Bruno Bettleheim, Fritz Redl, Peter Blos, Erik Erikson, and Walter Langer—had fled Austria and Germany for refuge in the United States. They arrived with firsthand knowledge of the growing tensions in Europe. Many other PEA members were not hopeful about the future. America was at risk, and democracy was threatened as fewer young people found meaningful connections with the wider society.[35]

The Aikin Commission members recognized the changing role of youth and worried about the future of the secondary school in American society. They were disturbed that so many students were placed in unresponsive college preparatory programs and had such little hope for the future. Secondary education had to change. Yet school administrators were wisely reluctant to jeopardize any student's chance for admission to college, no matter how remote, by altering the traditional curriculum. In the late 1920s, of the 17 percent of high school students who went on to college, 94 percent were accepted solely by their school record and teacher recommendations. Aikin noted, "Under these conditions not many schools were willing to depart very far from the conventional high school curriculum. They could not take chances on having their candidates rejected by the colleges."[36] Thus the educational needs of a very small portion of the adolescent population determined the curriculum for nearly all. While standardized college admissions testing became more popular during the 1930s and lessened somewhat the hold of a rigid college preparatory curriculum on the secondary school, little actually changed, especially in small schools. Burton Fowler stated that in the early 1940s, 60 percent of students were enrolled in high schools with fewer than 200 students that closely followed what college admission standards dictated: "The requirements for admission to Cornell, Michigan, Wellesley, or Yale become the basis of the secondary curriculum in most of the high schools sending one or more pupils to these colleges."[37] Realizing that life was especially precarious and insecure for young people in the early 1930s, educators wondered and worried about the mission of secondary education in a faltering domestic economy and an increasingly uncertain world. This was the context for secondary schooling; these were the problems for American education.

Conclusions

Today's educators come to the Eight-Year Study with varying impressions derived from published accounts of educational progressivism, descriptions of the Progressive Education Association, and interpretations and distortions of the project. One impression must remain, however, since there is no adequate way to convey fully the frustration and fear that many educators felt as the Great Depression deepened. Democracy was in jeopardy, and Americans' most basic beliefs about education were shaken. The secondary school population was changing rapidly, and high school faculties were forced to address issues that would undermine the established political and academic goals of education. New and pressing responsibilities for secondary school education were being identified, and loosely confederated groups of progressive educators—members of the PEA, American Council on Education, Educational Records Bureau, and other organizations—were searching for ways to adequately respond. So emerged the Aikin Commission on the Relation of School and College at the beginning of a twelve-year odyssey in school experimentation.

To understand the Eight-Year Study is to become familiar with a much different conception of school experimentation, one forgotten with the passing decades of "process-product" designs and federal incursion into educational policy making and school practice. Eight-Year Study leaders pioneered a new approach to research: an *implementative study*, the first of its kind in the United States.[38] As such, it differed from the common "status study" (a survey to document current practices), the "deliberative study" (a gathering of data to support normative recommendations for educational change), and the pilot-demonstration project, which so many assume the Eight-Year Study represented.

Implementative studies tested no formal hypotheses, upheld no specific models to be implemented and evaluated, and established no set of predefined outcomes. Rather, the Thirty School Study embraced a robust and determined *faith* in experimentation as an "exploratory process" to include gathering, analyzing, and interpreting data for the sole purpose of improving educational practice. As an example of what William Caspars describes as a process of "open ended . . . ethical deliberation," the Study sought not to "prove" hypotheses with today's conventions of validity and reliability but instead to implement and test the best thinking of seasoned educators.[39] In what was then viewed as the "method of intelligence," this type of study addressed complex and indeterminate problems with an ethical commitment to make schooling better for young people and, we would add, more educative for teachers. Without the burden of reliability, school experimentation focused primarily (if not exclusively) on determining the validity of certain practices as these studies became site specific. John Goodlad has argued that outstanding programs come from working intelligently on local, not national, problems.[40] Arising from these local studies, a faith in school experimentation was formed among teachers and Commission staff. Demonstrating the nature of an implementative study as such, the Eight-Year Study becomes even more important for educators today.

Vignette

V. T. Thayer (1886–1979): A Middle Position of Integrity without Compromise

V. T. Thayer, photograph, ca. 1940, Ohio State University Photo Archives

[Progressive education] prepares for a changing future without dogmatism or rigidity. It conceives of the school as perpetuating in American life the open road and new opportunities for fulfillment which constitute our richest inheritance from the American frontier. (V. T. Thayer, 1944)[1]

Among those who prepared for a changing future without dogmatism or rigidity, V. T. Thayer embodies the work of the Eight-Year Study. Thayer was, in the language of the time, "a schoolman" and much more: a philosopher, humanist, and social critic. He served as director of the Ethical Culture Schools, chair of the PEA's Commission on Secondary School Curriculum, and administrator of various elementary and secondary schools. In these roles he does not fit easily into today's common conceptions of the progressive education movement. He did not follow the well-defined practices of Ellwood Cubberley and the administrative progressives of the early twentieth century but instead developed the idea of "functional democratic administration." While believing in the importance

39

of student needs and life adjustment, he would have bristled at a "child-centered progressive" label, since so much of his professional writing centered on the importance of building a democratic society and the value of a strong general education curriculum. Thayer engaged in school experimentation; however, he would not have considered himself a scientific progressive. In *The Passing of the Recitation*, for example, he criticized Thorndike's psychological research and its underlying assumptions about learning.[2] Neither was he a social reconstructionist, even though he wrote for *The Social Frontier*, contributed to *The Educational Frontier*, and worked with school faculties to lessen common social-economic class distinctions. Although trained as a philosopher, Thayer was first and foremost an educator who observed classrooms, met with parents and students, raised funds, designed curricula, and coordinated the administrative offices of an active school while also living the life of a serious scholar who published essays on Locke, Kant, James, and Dewey and spent his summers teaching at universities across the country. A philosopher who chose to enter the field of education, an academic who accepted a school administrator's post, and a school administrator who gladly taught secondary school students—Thayer was certainly a progressive educator who remains unique among the conventional classifications.

I

If truth is not absolute, if experience is in continuous reconstruction, if the secondary school should reorganize curricula in response to the needs of youth balanced with societal expectations, then how does one direct a school? "With kindness, sincerity, and integrity" is the response of many of those who worked with Thayer as they have described his character and administrative demeanor.[3] The Fieldston School, a participant in the Eight Year Study and one of the educational programs of the Society for Ethical Culture, was his laboratory—a school built on the values of the Ethical Culture Movement while upholding progressive beliefs about preparing students for an uncertain future.

Cultural, religious, and progressive education ideologies combined as Thayer sought to experiment with a program that would integrate vocational, individual, and societal needs in a democratic community. A reserved, affable man possessing an air of great dignity and steeled determination, these same values permeated his career.[4] Thayer's beliefs would never harden into dogma, in accordance with the tenets of the Ethical Culture movement: "sharing a quest for meanings, ever-evolving, ever-changing."[5] At times, however, Thayer's open-ended, self-critical views put him at odds with Felix Adler, the founder of the

Ethical Culture Society and a neo-Kantian idealist who strongly objected to Deweyian pragmatism and humanism. Thayer, commonly linked to Dewey, would often be accused of not adhering faithfully to Adler's beliefs. Yet, despite his differences, he successfully guided the Fieldston School for over twenty years and honored its values without compromise.

II

> I do not wish to give the impression that there were no happy periods in my childhood. There were rainy days when I could retreat with a book and the comfortable insurance that there was no outside work to interfere with the pleasures of reading. Even today, at 89 [in 1971], the sound of an early morning rain brings with it feelings of relief and anticipation! (V. T. Thayer, 1971)[6]

Vivian Trow Thayer was raised in rural Wisconsin by his father and stepmother. Ill health as well as a loss of religious faith caused Thayer's father to leave the ministry where, as a farmer and rural mail carrier, the family always faced poverty, a condition that profoundly influenced Thayer's sensitivity to others' life struggles. While the family lineage was distinguished (being direct descendants from Miles Standish), Thayer was not prepped for admission to Harvard College as were his later Fieldston colleagues. His secondary school experience and start-stop university education were funded by working at various jobs, from sanitarium attendant to restaurant manager. After two years at the University of Wisconsin, he could not afford to continue his studies and during an extended interlude took a position as principal of a rural elementary school in Wisconsin. While Thayer notes, "No one could have been less prepared in the way of training and experience than was I," he still found administration enjoyable while never faltering from his goal of finishing undergraduate and doctoral studies in philosophy.[7]

Upon completing his doctorate in 1922, Thayer faced a difficult choice between an assistant professorship of philosophy at the University of Wisconsin and the principalship of the Ethical Culture High School in New York City: "The decision turned upon a choice between philosophy and education as a career, and between [university] teaching and [school] administration. A choice, as my subsequent career demonstrates, I found difficult to peg down once and for all!"[8] Intrigued by the philosophy of the Society for Ethical Culture, founded in 1876, Thayer became specifically interested in its focus on ethical relationships, social reform, and socialized individualism. A nondenominational, humanistic movement growing out of American Reform Judaism and representing a type of Progressive Era, settlement house organization, the

Society held no theological creed but instead provided venues for individuals to formulate their own metaphysical beliefs "in the worth and dignity of each person and the commitment to help create a better world."[9] Adler called for "deeds not creeds,"[10] and the Society's activities were varied—establishing settlement houses, Workingman's Schools, and free kindergarten for the children of laboring men and women, as well as establishing the forerunner organization of the ACLU and supporting the creation of the NAACP.

Thayer would find the Society's philosophy more appealing than the actual educational program, although the Ethical Culture schools embraced many then-innovative educational practices, including homogeneous grouping, democratic student activities, and an integrated curriculum of common life activities. "Particularly fruitful, did it seem to me, was [Adler's] concept of democracy and of democratic education. . . . Indeed, without its metaphysical assumptions, it gave a concreteness to what was often vague and undefined in John Dewey."[11] After only two years of service, however, Thayer left in 1924 for Ohio State University to work with Boyd Bode, his former University of Wisconsin philosophy teacher, who was building an education faculty that would bring meaning to the phrase "democracy as a way of life." He did not leave on bad terms; during his absence he researched and wrote his first two major works, *The Passing of the Recitation* and *Supervision in the Secondary School*, with many references to practices from the Ethical Culture Schools.[12] During this time, Adler arranged to build a new campus in the Bronx the Fieldston School, as a middle and secondary school program distinct from the Ethical Culture school facility located in midtown Manhattan. Although leaders at Ohio State were planning their own laboratory school and hoped Thayer would remain, Adler had raised sufficient funds by 1927 to begin construction. Thayer accepted the director's position, and the school opened in 1928.

III

The Fieldston Plan, a pioneering venture in both secondary school administration and curricular organization, closely resembled Thayer's own writings. First conceived in 1927 and then with support from the General Education Board from 1933 to 1938 to develop curriculum materials, the program grew out of Adler's belief that vocation would be the most effective means for learning culture. Thayer thought the "implications of this concept of 'living through the radiations' of our unique interests and abilities for education were not only clear, but revolutionary."[13] The intent was not to train students for employment or to use occupations for narrow specialization but to serve as a link to balance interests with what Adler called the "needs of civilization" for cultural studies. Vocation (whether art or business) enabled the thematic organization of culture which, in turn, permitted development of an integrated, "fused" core curriculum for the study of civilizations: "History, science, literature are to be windows through which light will stream in to illumine the vocation, and the vocation will be an opening through which [to] . . . look out intelligently on the world at large."[14] Thayer adopted the term *orientation* as a way of integrating students' interests with a dramatically changing society.

Thayer questioned whether determining adolescent needs could be entrusted entirely to the students, especially since teachers were to guide them toward achieving unity and purpose in their lives. Unlike laissez-faire, child-centered programs, he envisioned the school as an interpretive agency where teachers would assist students "to weave unity and purpose" into their lives "in socially desirable directions."[15] If educators were to take their responsibility seriously, they would require more information not only about individual students but about the nature of adolescence. To this end Thayer organized the Fieldston School's Department of Guidance, led by Caroline Zachry, to initiate new forms of adolescent study and ultimately to become an experimental research center for the Commission on the Secondary School.

Under Thayer's leadership the Fieldston School also explored the role of community service in the education of students. As an expression of functional democratic administration, school governance was restructured to include expanded student, faculty, parent, and alumni participation in decision making and the further education of all members of the learning community. The intellectual development of teachers and administrators and even of parents became an important component of reform; in fact, Thayer and his coauthor, Harold Alberty, concluded their *Supervision in the Secondary School* with a chapter on the growth of teachers.

IV

In 1933, Thayer (along with Dewey) was one of thirty-four signers of the *Humanist Manifesto*, a highly controversial document that helped articulate a (secular) humanism within a context of scientific, philosophical, and ethical thought. Adler, who was extremely ill at the time, was not informed of Thayer's signing for fear that he would become so upset he would die as a result. The *Manifesto*'s fifth proposition, "Religion must formulate its hopes and plans in the light of the scientific spirit and method," represented beliefs held by Thayer, the only professional educator asked to sign the document. These views would, in time, lead him to become extensively involved in discussions over religion, public education, and academic freedom.[16] By the mid-1940s Thayer found himself heavily embroiled in the religion in public education debate, required by his membership on the Academic Freedom Committee of the ACLU. During this period he also published *American Education Under Fire* and *Religion in Public Education*.[17] In 1948 he wrote, "The sap of enthusiasm for my position in the schools [has] been running thin for some time," and he resigned as director of the Ethical Culture Schools.[18] To say that Thayer retired, however, would be misleading. While he severed his institutional ties with the Ethical Culture Schools, he continued to address the role of public schooling in a democracy and published *Religion in Public Education, The Attack upon the American Secular School, Public Education and Its Critics, The Role of the School in American Society*, and *The Challenge of the Present to Public Education*.[19] His faith in public schools and progressive education never faltered.

V

When Thayer considered why the influence of the Eight-Year Study was not greater, he lamented the tendency among many champions of progressivism to oversimplify "complex processes" and to be more "*against* something than *for* something."[20] Thayer's career represented working *for something* and for building educational programs. And this is where understanding his work becomes especially difficult, since many of his ideas were developed in practice and not fully described in print. At the time, "speaking" to the professional community was done in ways other than conference lectures and articles and often involved the then-common practice of school visitation. Thayer would host hundreds of visitors each year to the Fieldston School. Similarly, when Alberty was director at the Ohio State University School, that facility averaged 15,000 visits annually from educators who wished to see rather than to be told how important social and educational issues were addressed.[21] For these Eight-Year Study progressives, there seemed to be little point merely to talk about problems when their laboratory school settings provided venues to demonstrate solutions to the educational and social challenges of the day.

Although perceived differently, race, class, and gender inequalities were among Thayer's challenges. These issues were embedded within the wider concern of extending democratic values and combating totalitarianism, misguided capitalism, and political corruption. Despite charges to the contrary, Thayer and other Eight-Year Study progressives were not blind to issues of race, class, and gender. Student evaluation at both Thayer's and Alberty's schools included a social problems test that consisted of scenarios about race equality (representing considerable classroom discussion), and the Thayer Commission's film and radio projects' curriculum materials both confronted students with issues of race (including lynching) and social inequity.[22] Thayer's 1956 lecture, presented when he was a faculty member at Fisk University, stressed both race and diversity issues, and racial inequality was behind his call for the faculty and students "at Fisk to respond courageously to the call of the new frontier." Yet the title of the speech was "Today's Challenge to Education."[23]

Class issues as well seem missing among those Aikin Commission schools that catered to the economic and intellectual elite. Yet one of the more remarkable efforts to increase student social sensitivity and appreciation of democratic values was undertaken by Thayer and the Commission on Secondary School Curriculum at the 1938 Hudson Guild Farm Camp. Aware of the privileged backgrounds of those many students attending Aikin Commission schools and concerned about their limited experience, students from the Fieldston, Lincoln, and George Schools attended a two month, summer "service learning" camp intended to heighten awareness and sensitivity to social class differences. Advertised as "working together with different groups of people" to "understand more profoundly the meaning of Democracy as a way of life," the adolescents participated in a variety of activities, including farming and construction projects with local residents and numerous visits to textile, mining, and industrial centers where they witnessed the economic struggles of their fellow citizens.[24] The program was described in terms of social adjustment and communal responsibility when in fact students were observing graphic examples in social class inequalities.

Thayer was acutely aware of the destructive tendency to resolve serious issues into either-or stances, into binaries, and for those positions to harden so that whatever truth initially resided within them was lost. Issues of race, class, and gender were understood by him and others as specific instances of a more general problem of how to fully extend the democratic values of social and economic participation. For his part, Thayer continued to adopt a middle position: while recognizing the centrality of schooling as a way to preserve America's democratic traditions, he argued for a curriculum that was responsive to changing social conditions and individual needs while simultaneously valuing academic content as a means to increase human control over an uncertain and unpredictable future.

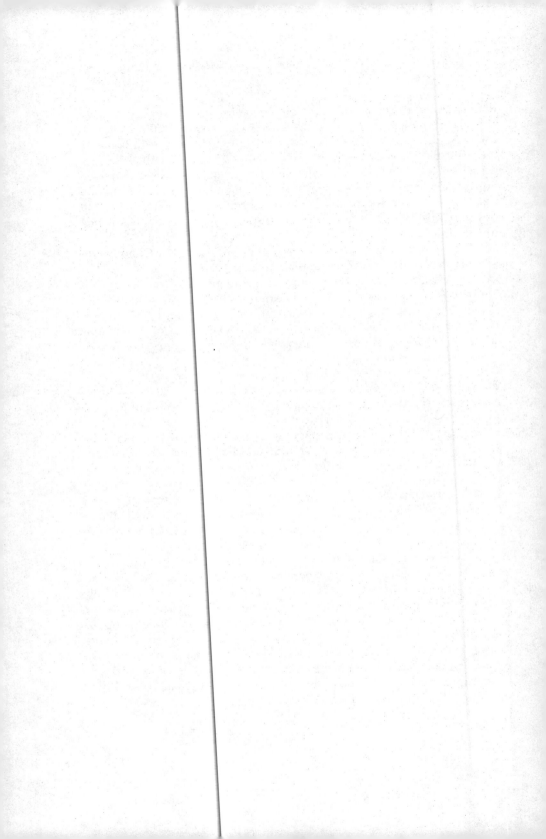

Chapter 2

Tests and Records: The Veneer of College Admissions

Educational reforms are intrinsically political in origin. Groups organize and contest with other groups in the politics of education to express their values and to secure their interests in the public school. (David Tyack and Larry Cuban, 1995)[1]

Introduction

An emphasis on student testing may not have been what one would have expected from the Aikin Commission. The early years of the Eight-Year Study, however, were remarkably different from what is now portrayed. Ralph Tyler, V. T. Thayer, Caroline Zachry, and Alice Keliher, all of whom later accepted leadership roles, had not yet fully involved themselves. Instead, other names—Learned, McConn, Wood, Brigham— appear in the early proceedings. Members of the Aikin Commission's Directing Committee who came together from 1931 to 1933 included those who would later help establish the Educational Testing Service. William Learned, who worked in the Carnegie Foundation for the Advancement of Teaching's Division of Educational Enquiry, was directing the acclaimed Pennsylvania Study, a statewide program of high school and college testing. Max McConn, dean of Lehigh University, served on the American Council on Education's Advisory Committee on College Testing, and Ben Wood assisted with the Pennsylvania Study while directing the American Council on Education's Cooperative Test Service (CTS). Carl Brigham, designer of the College Entrance Examination Board's Scholastic Aptitude Test (and a repentant eugenicist), was also involved in early conversations as a member of the Directing Committee.[2]

Under the influence of these men who sought to establish a national network for secondary school testing, the Directing Committee, with its commitment to open-ended experimentation, found the Eight-Year Study's ends being determined well before the project was even underway. This threatened the spirit of the project and led, ultimately, to a showdown between the leaders of the Carnegie Foundation and an ad hoc group of school principals, a conflict that transformed the direction that the Study would eventually take. The issue proved to be much more than the standard tension between national versus local control of testing or between aptitude versus achievement measures. Underlying the exchanges of the participants rested an issue of professionalism: Can teachers initiate school change, and are they capable of accepting the responsibility of testing and evaluation?

College Admission, the Carnegie Unit, and Testing Bureaus

The college entrance requirements, which effectively determined the major part of the secondary curriculum, preserve the crystallization of that curriculum in sixteen admittedly artificial Carnegie units, . . . so long as those rigid requirements remain in force, the secondary schools . . . are tied hand and foot and simply cannot make any substantial changes in their curricular or teaching procedures. (Max McConn, 1933)[3]

Not all educators viewed the Carnegie unit with such disdain and, although criticized for its stranglehold on the secondary school curriculum, many college administrators maintained a much different view than members of the Aikin Commission. Those "rigid" high school requirements had served a useful purpose—providing structure to a nonstandardized secondary school system. During the 1920s, most college admissions decisions were based on letters of recommendation (often from alumni) in addition to grades and the completion of fourteen to sixteen units of study. The "Carnegie unit," conceived by the NEA Committee on College Entrance Requirements and the North Central Association of Colleges and Secondary Schools rather than by the Carnegie Foundation, represented 120 teacher contact hours and, from the perspective of most college admissions officers, adequately demonstrated students' readiness for college study. Little else mattered. The standardized testing system, so well known today, was not fully developed, but this is not to say that college testing did not occur. Herbert Hawkes, dean of Columbia University, described taking twenty-three different entrance examinations in the 1890s for admission to college.[4] Most often however, such testing merely ascertained placement in class sections rather than determined admittance to college.

By the mid-1920s advances in tests and measurements prompted Learned, McConn, Wood, and others to question the value of the Carnegie unit as the leading indicator of a student's readiness for postsecondary studies. At issue was the fairness and usefulness of content knowledge (achievement) in contrast to intellectual aptitude as a predictor of college success. The field of college admissions was undergoing a transformation as admission officers wondered if capable students, particularly those from less privileged and rural backgrounds, were being overlooked due to their inability to fulfill unit requirements. In addition, secondary programs varied dramatically in quality, and Carnegie units were not commensurate across schools. Hopes ran high for testing; breakthroughs in the new science of measurement could reduce, they thought, the high dropout rate among college students by assuring more accurate placement and by identifying able students regardless of their family background. Eugene Smith, at a 1928 college admissions symposium published in *Progressive Education,* underscored this egalitarian dimension when he noted that testing would enable identification of many deserving students who had needlessly been denied admission to college.[5] William Learned took the same position with the Pennsylvania Study: too many talented students had been prevented from continuing their academic studies. These leaders believed that widespread testing to identify talent would open opportunities for students, and this could be done, from their perspective, not by content-oriented tests, such as the traditional College Board examinations, but by an innovative new type of college-oriented aptitude test.

Members of the Aikin Commission recognized that some form of testing was needed to make college admission decisions. The question became, what type: scholastic aptitude tests, traditional college (subjective essay) tests, or newly conceived objective (multiple-choice) achievement tests? Further, if the Eight-Year Study altered the configuration of high school subjects, there was the question of how school faculties would deal with "the unwillingness of colleges to accept any admissions plan not providing written examinations covering the major fields of knowledge."[6] Was the intent of testing to assist the classroom teacher to improve learning or to aid the college admissions officer in admitting students? Many possibilities would be considered as Aikin committee members explored the various directions for the project.

Another administrative issue arose over the selection and recording of student information. Considering the multidimensionality of student interests, there was some question in terms of how to accurately portray each individual's abilities and potential. Grades communicated little about student learning. If the basic structure of the high school curriculum was to be reinvented, as was the intent of the Eight-Year Study, then what student records should be retained and what sort of new information should be made available to college admissions officers? The challenge was clear: "to devise means by which teachers, without too much expenditure of time, can present pictures of the various pupils with whom they deal."[7] Determining which tests best predict college success and how to maintain student records became the first and most pressing matter for the Aikin Commission.

Given this challenge, the Committee on Tests and Records quickly came to dominate early Aikin Commission proceedings. Representatives of four testing services, each seeking to shape policy and practice in its own image, participated in the deliberations. Of the four, the oldest and most established was the College Entrance Examination Board, described by Nicholas Lemann as "a tweedy, clubby association of a few dozen private schools and colleges [seeking] to perfect the close fit between New England boarding schools and Ivy League colleges."[8] The other three bureaus included the recently formed Cooperative Test Service, the relatively new Educational Records Bureau, and the Carnegie Foundation's Division of Educational Enquiry. All four testing centers and their respective programs were closely interrelated, and each was quite ambitious. In 1932, just as the Eight-Year Study was being conceived, these centers were seeking ways to extend their influence across the nation, and each looked toward the project as a way to disseminate the results of its work. (See Appendix B.)

The testing bureaus, at times allies and at other times competitors, were closely linked by financial support from the Carnegie Corporation's Carnegie Foundation for the Advancement of Teaching and the Rockefeller Foundation's General Education Board. The College Board received Carnegie funds during a difficult period in 1917 and later in the 1940s. The Pennsylvania Study represented a directly sponsored program of the Carnegie Foundation. The Cooperative Test Service was supported by the General Education Board, and the Educational Records Bureau was funded by the Carnegie Foundation. Hawkes, who was involved with both agencies as well as with the Aikin Commission, met regularly with Frederick P. Keppel, president of the Carnegie Corporation, to discuss the merits of various research projects. His recommendations would have been well received by Keppel since the two men were friends and former colleagues, having worked together at Columbia University.[9] As planning began in 1931, the power of the Carnegie Foundation and the General Education Board loomed over Eight-Year Study meetings and framed many of the Aikin Commission's conceptual issues. The maneuverings of the four testing services eventually played out a few decades later in the struggles that resulted in the formation of the Educational Testing Service. At this point, however, the battles among and between various testing groups were just beginning. In some respects, the Eight-Year Study may be viewed as one of the first skirmishes.

The Cummington Meetings

When the Aikin Commission's Directing Committee members first convened in May 1931 at the Cummington Conference, testing and college entrance requirements were far removed from the agenda. Aikin was delighted with the Carnegie Foundation's interest in the project, especially since the Rosenwald Foundation displayed little willingness to allocate funds, and he believed that Keppel and Henry Suzzallo, president of the Carnegie Foundation, would soon approve a $15,000–20,000 grant, a rather large sum given the project's then $800 working budget. Reorganizing the high school curriculum would be the topic for the fourteen members of the Directing Committee, most of whom were university educators and school principals. During this weekend retreat, members described extant examples of school programs, and subcommittees were formed to address three select topics: basic principles, curriculum plans, and college admission. By the end of the meeting, preliminary reports had been prepared, and the group had identified a set of fundamental values that would guide future planning. Much was still unresolved, and the plans would change dramatically through the upcoming year. Initially the Directing Committee considered proposing three or four specific, uniform types of high school programs of study as the basis for school reform. At other times during the weekend, participants discussed whether each (yet to be selected) school should determine its own curriculum. Much attention at this time, however, remained centered on the traditional separate subjects. The enthusiasm of the group is apparent in the minutes of the conference as this educational adventure was beginning to take shape. Ideas were tossed about, and beliefs were confronted in a conceptual free-for-all. The Cummington participants seemed overjoyed by the project's hopefulness and possibilities.

The Directing Committee met again in the spring and autumn of 1931, not at a weekend retreat in Massachusetts, as before, but instead at the offices of the newly supporting foundation, the Carnegie Corporation, in New York City. Conversation turned quickly and rather dramatically away from the original direction of the Cummington Conference—namely, developing innovative curricula in order to free schools from traditional course credits. One principal questioned whether discussing the secondary school curriculum was worthwhile at all and suggested that the time be spent developing tests in the various subject fields. Others asserted that since the colleges were committed to the Carnegie unit and would vigorously oppose any changes at the high school or college level, it seemed pointless to try to redesign secondary school curricula. College faculty were described as having little interest in secondary schools, even preferring that their students arrive at college having taken no high school courses in their chosen fields of college study. During this meeting at the Carnegie Corporation offices, the entire direction of the Eight-Year Study shifted from secondary school curricula to standardized testing as a method to determine students' readiness for college. At the request of Aikin, obviously planned well in advance, Learned proceeded to distribute pamphlets to the group describing the Pennsylvania Study and its newly developed tests. Learned maintained that the Carnegie-sponsored Pennsylvania Study tests were in keeping with the Aikin Commission's values and would greatly help the study.[10] As board members discussed the future of this Carnegie Foundation-funded project, they were informed that the Pennsylvania Study was solving the problems of student assessment and college admissions.[11] The message was certainly clear and unmistakable: follow Learned's recommendations and use the Pennsylvania Study tests.

Selecting the participating schools and determining the process for college admissions topped the agenda at the third and final Directing Committee meeting in 1931. Discussion returned, inevitably, to the relationship of curriculum and testing and to ways the group would proceed in initiating school reform. A new subcommittee was formed that would focus on testing and, as the minutes report, the topic "was considered at some length."[12] In frustration with the direction that the project seemed to be heading, one principal spoke up and said that "it seemed impossible to prepare a group of tests before the nature of the new curriculum is known."[13] In response, the group was reminded that Keppel, president of the parent funding agency, thought that "some new test" should be developed first. Aikin said that he hoped to "tie up" with the Cooperative Test Service, the same bureau that had constructed tests for the Pennsylvania Study. To this comment one participant retorted that "it's all right to tie up if we don't get eaten up!"[14] Much later another participant would ask, "Why should we go to great trouble to set up a so-called experiment if we are merely to exchange our old shackles for new ones which may be equally galling?"[15] Tensions grew as a fundamental issue came to the forefront: all agreed that a rigid high school curriculum, as defined by Carnegie units, needed to be changed. Yet what would replace the unit as a measurement to verify the completion of high school and determine whether students were prepared for and capable of college study? The Directing Committee was being encouraged to view standardized tests as the answer.

More was at stake during the first year of meetings than merely breaking the "crystallization of that curriculum in sixteen admittedly artificial Carnegie units." Access, opportunity, and democracy formed the basis of Learned's justification for testing, since the formal college preparatory curriculum was not accessible to all college-capable students. Standardized tests were thought to be a fair way for all students to display their intellectual capabilities, and ability and knowledge rather than "seat time" should guide the path to college. The Carnegie Foundation staff monitored the direction of the Aikin Commission's discussion with a clear view toward integrating and extending Learned's work. By January 1932, the Directing Committee had prepared the Plan of Cooperation, the first comprehensive description of the project. Through the 1932 calendar year, schools were selected to participate in the "eight-year experiment," and school faculties began discussing their program changes. All seemed to be moving forward as plans were made to meet at Bennington College in early July 1933 for the first formal conference of the participating school teachers and staff.

The Bennington Conference

At the opening session of the Bennington Conference—a full, five-day meeting for Commission staff, school delegates (generally including the school director and a lead teacher), and select college representatives—Aikin reminded the group that the objective of the project was to improve secondary school curriculum and teaching. College testing and examinations were of interest only because they were seen as means for achieving these objectives. The conference focused its attention on the proposed curriculum plans of the participating school sites and the administrative problems arising from implementing such programs. Numerous references were made during the conference to the Pennsylvania Study; however, schools were most concerned with the current difficulties of sorting out new curricular directions and refining their programs. Not until the fourth conference session, scheduled for the evening of July 4th, did the group turn its full attention to testing and a report from the Committee on Records and Reports, now the Subcommittee on Tests and Records. On that day, the participants failed to anticipate the fireworks to follow as school faculty and Commission staff began a sixteen-month struggle to establish their own independence from the Carnegie Foundation and the Pennsylvania Study.[16]

At this evening session, school delegates began questioning the Committee's proposed testing program, annual aptitude tests and English scholastic tests, and additional tests that would be developed from syllabi sent by the schools to Ben Wood. Although some expressed concern that a common testing system "would become as vicious as the College Board Examinations," the group did not object to the idea of testing but instead raised questions about implementation. The meeting ended without a hint of the deep disagreement that would soon develop. The next day, Goodwin Watson of Teachers College described a far-reaching reorganization of secondary education, and the conference dialogue returned to programmatic matters. Presenting the Lincoln School report, Watson encouraged school faculties to adopt a no-preplanned curricular structure, a program with periodic diagnostic tests and an emphasis on students' interests in what would become a "cultural-epoch" core curriculum. Watson may have lost most of his audience when he argued that secondary schools should enable each student to spend "part of his time in the city and part in the country, part in the United States and part in Europe."[17] Rugg, who took issue with his colleague's views, proceeded to lead a discussion that lasted for the next five hours as delegates posed questions about the possibility and viability of such an approach to secondary education.

Stunned and angered by the proceedings, Carnegie staff described the conference in an internal memo as the "craziness up there." From the perspective of the Carnegie Foundation, Watson's comments went beyond radical. Little wonder that Learned, writing to Keppel in the summer of 1933, stated that "the Bennington situation [got] entirely out of hand, with no recognition of the fact that progressive schools will have to submit themselves to some kind of test as a basis of college confidence."[18] Watson's presentation, not particularly well received by the conference participants either, had been intended to challenge the rather conservative curriculum proposals described earlier by the participating schools.

Despite the "craziness," Learned still saw promise in this "Eight Year Experimental Study of Secondary Education." Schools had been selected; colleges had given their approval to the Study; and, with foundation support, Aikin was appointed to serve as executive officer for the project. Yet from the perspective of the Carnegie Foundation, Aikin seems to have been considered more of a figurehead for the work of Learned and Wood. When Aikin had requested funding to work full time on the Study, Keppel advised him not to leave his directorship of the John Burroughs School. Running the time-consuming project in a full-time capacity was not as important to the Foundation's interests as was the development of the testing program.

Clearly the Bennington Conference caused some concern for the Carnegie Foundation. Learned realized that not all participants shared a commitment to the value of adopting standardized tests. Nevertheless, he did not seem to have anticipated serious or organized opposition to these plans. In late 1933, however, the unexpected death of Suzzallo, a staunch supporter of the PEA, seems to have changed everything. Although the death of the president of the Carnegie Foundation did not prevent the approval of an additional $50,000 grant in January

1934, battle lines were forming as leaders of the Eight-Year Study confronted what would one day become a multibillion-dollar testing industry.

The Revolt of 1934

Herbert Smith, principal of the Fieldston School and a member of both the Aikin Commission's Committee on Records and Reports and the Thayer Commission's Committee on Evaluation, became upset with the direction of the Aikin Commission's testing program. In January 1934, he and others objected to requests for the schools to complete large amounts of record keeping, believing that the Committee on Records and Reports was placing itself between "school and college [as] an alien agency for accrediting students" and, thereby, seeking to determine college admissions. The Committee on Records and Reports issued a response to the schools that only sharpened the disagreement. For Smith, "The question can fairly be raised whether many of the objective tests of achievement at present recommended do not distort educational values. Even if it be assumed that these tests are in themselves no worse than those of the College Entrance Examination Board, their application annually makes them more likely to warp instruction."[19] Seemingly, the school directors had struggled and ultimately accepted the merits of a cumulative exit exam. Now they were being confronted with annual standardized student testing for which they had not bargained, certainly ironic for an experiment that aimed at freeing secondary school programs from the curricular expectations of the colleges and universities.

Jesse Newlon of Teachers College assured the Committee that he was not opposed to the use of standardized tests: "We use objective tests in the Lincoln School constantly."[20] Yet riled by Herb Smith, Newlon expressed the frustration and anger that was building: "An elaborate system of testing in the schools is entirely beside the point so far as that objective of our experiment is concerned. . . . I am unable to see what contribution this program of testing can make to the achievement of that purpose. To me it seems much better to leave objective testing entirely to the individual school."[21] Others called attention to the complexity of evaluation and to ways testing would serve different ends. Even the Thayer Commission's Committee on Evaluation recognized what could easily become conflicting factors: "The same test which would be useful to take a quick inventory of a student's knowledge of current affairs or to rouse an interest in them, for example, might be thoroughly mischievous if used to establish unit credit for admission to college in the social sciences."[22]

Many competing interests were at play: Eugene Smith's hopes for cumulative student records; Learned's hopes for national distribution via the PEA of the Pennsylvania Study tests; and Herbert Smith's, Newlon's, and many others' distrust of the new standardized tests. Unhappy with recent events, Herbert Smith called a meeting of school heads for late April 1934 to discuss the implications of the Committee on Reports and Records' response to his objections of the planned testing. In what was considered an insult, Eugene Smith, chair of the Committee on Reports and Records, was not invited to this meeting despite Aikin's and Leigh's pleas for him to be included. A revolt had begun, and the principals were well aware of its implications. Leigh admitted to Herb Smith that the "original plan for the admission to college" (conceived by then-PEA president Willard Beatty, V. T. Thayer, and Leigh himself) "did not contemplate any such ambitious testing program." Leigh added, "It should be recognized that by the Carnegie grant of money the original program was actually changed because the Carnegie people felt that the experiment was not worthwhile except as it included a rather complete testing program."[23] Not all school heads objected to Carnegie's ambitions, however. In fact, Beatty, then-superintendent of the Bronxville Schools, wrote to Herb Smith saying that the testing program seemed quite amenable and "admirably presented" by Learned in a recent address, which he would ask Learned to send to Smith.[24]

Eugene Smith, upon learning of the meeting, wrote to Herb Smith: "I am seriously concerned about you calling a meeting in regard to testing. If the facts are at all as they are being sent to me, I can conceive of no surer way to wreck the whole eight-year experiment."[25] In other correspondence, Eugene Smith believed that the schools simply could not omit testing: "That point is settled by our acceptance of the money from the Carnegie Corporation. It has been thoroughly thrashed out and I do not see that there is any possibility of further discussion in regard to it."[26]

As leaders of the project struggled to find direction, outside corporate forces were converging on what would be a watershed moment in testing and measurement. "Our teachers grow more and more restive under the imposition of another system of testing [by the Aikin Commission's Committee on Records and Reports]. Just when we thought we were getting free, we find we are likely to be shackled even more closely, so that the shades of the prison house will be almost continuous."[27] Further, the Committee on Records and Reports was determining the source of the tests (i.e., the types of tests) as well as how they would be used. Certain laboratory schoolteachers objected to this imposition, implying that they preferred to use their own testing bureau rather than an agency endorsed by the Aikin Commission.[28]

Looking back on this period, Eugene Smith admitted:

The committee's recommendations of tests to be used by the schools was not a success. Although the committee recognized and accepted the variation of aims and methods in the schools, it nevertheless tried to find a group of aptitude and achievement tests general enough to be applicable to every setting, and therefore, *useful for cross-site comparison.* School faculties found, however, that in many cases the tests chosen did not apply to the work they were doing because of differences in content and in purposes, and this program was therefore abandoned.[29]

Originally, the Aikin Commission's Directing Committee was merely seeking to be responsive to its two original goals: to encourage reconstruction in the secondary school and to serve high school youth more effectively. Commission members recognized the role of the secondary school in preparing students both for postsecondary education and for life, and educators were well aware of the important role that evaluation might play in this effort. Eugene Smith pleaded, "Even the most opposed to over-testing, however, do not seem to feel that the small amount of information called upon at this time could be considered at all dangerous."[30] The use of tests was not dismissed, however; in fact, the Commission sought to draw upon the diagnostic potential of testing while not restricting the curriculum. But a warning from the Cummington Conference now proved prophetic: preparing tests before deciding the nature of the new curriculum would seem impossible. Ultimately, a large percentage of the participating school principals and teachers concluded that the Aikin Commission plan would result in over-testing. No doubt they also sensed the Committee's interest in cross-site comparisons, an aspect of the experiment that some might not originally have anticipated. The College Board, at first annoyed over talk of dispensing with all entrance examinations, later discovered that most of the participating schools continued to use two of its tests, the Scholastic Aptitude Test and the Comprehensive Examination in English.[31] To Learned's dismay, however, those instruments developed by the Cooperative Test Service for the Pennsylvania Study were not adopted.

By the 1934 April meeting of participating school heads (not including Eugene Smith), a resolution was approved that "the Directing Committee be asked to assure us that no agency shall be set up to intervene in any way between the school and the college in certifying individual students for admission."[32] In clear opposition to the Carnegie Foundation's expectations for the study, Herb Smith's group sought a sounder basis than testing for improving relations between school and college. These principals demanded a more open, experimental research program. "Many of the schools went into this experiment in such a way

that the proposed uniform testing program becomes both inappropriate and damaging. . . . No one testing scheme from outside can be
applicable to all these experiments."[33] These same principals met two
weeks later (again excluding Eugene Smith) to discuss further the events
of the spring. They agreed that they needed additional time to establish
their curricular programs before they were asked to devote "energy to
any testing program at all beyond what they themselves [found] immediately useful."[34] Their views were heard: the Cooperative Test Service
and Educational Research Bureau would not be using the Eight-Year
Study to distribute tests.

The Carnegie Foundation did not withdraw immediately from the
Eight-Year Study, and its officers remained interested in the experiment
even though the new president, Walter A. Jessup, was, according to
Keppel, not as enamored with progressive education as his predecessor
Suzzallo had been.[35] As the second grant was near completion, a meeting was held in late 1936 with Keppel, Hawkes, Jessup, and Aikin to
discuss the possibility of further Carnegie support. Jessup was satisfied
with the work already completed, and he asked whether "it was time to
put emphasis on the college end."[36] His comment was not merely sug-
gestive but was quite critical. Since 1934 the Aikin Commission had
displayed a strong commitment to secondary education and during the
intervening years had confirmed its intent to help those high schools
struggling with curriculum and instruction. Clearly officers of the
Carnegie Foundation staff had been upset with this turn of events.
Learned reported to Keppel:

> The Committee on Records and Reports, which is the real core
> of the undertaking so far as appraisal of results is concerned,
> had its program for evaluating the work of the different schools
> completely overturned by revolt on the part of the radicals,
> some of whom have not touched solid ground for many years.
> Under the new orientation of the committee, it will be much
> more difficult to ascertain what the undertaking is about or
> what it is accomplishing.[37]

In response to the PEA's request for funding during this 1936
meeting, Jessup stated that he thought the Carnegie Corporation and
the Foundation needed to further examine the project before reaching
a conclusion. Actually, a conclusion seemed to have already been
reached. Carnegie staff member Learned had withdrawn from the
proceedings of the Eight-Year Study, and Carnegie, in fact, was out,
turning its interests in this area more exclusively to the Educational
Records Bureau's Committee on School and College Relations. Sensing

reluctance on the part of the Carnegie Foundation to continue supporting the PEA's Commission on the Relation of School and College, E. E. Day, program officer of the General Education Board, inquired whether there would be an objection to the Rockefeller Foundation taking over funding. Keppel "said he didn't believe so–in fact he was quite sure [the Carnegie Foundation] would not."[38] Soon the General Education Board moved into the major contributor's role for the Commission on the Relation of School and College. When the final reports of the Aikin Commission were published, staff discussed how the Carnegie Foundation would be acknowledged.[39] The Carnegie Corporation was thanked for "generous subventions" in all areas except evaluation, and the PEA issued a statement noting that both Carnegie and the GEB, despite their grants, were not to be considered to be endorsing "any of the statements made or views expressed therein." By the 1950s, when a query arose concerning the Carnegie Foundation's support of the Progressive Education Association, the organization was quick to distance itself from the Eight-Year Study.[40]

Conclusions

> A student's grade record, like the weather, is an excellent subject for light conversation and seldom causes a stir until it reaches extremes. (Dean Chamberlin, Enid Chamberlin, Neal E. Drought, William E. Scott, 1942)[41]

In retrospect, the claim could be made that the program of the Committee on Records and Reports was completely overturned by revolt. Yet during the early years of the Eight-Year Study, few programs were really in place, and all activities of the Aikin Commission were subject to debate. Insistent issues of purpose arose. Should testing be diagnostic in order to assist the secondary school teacher, or should its purpose be to develop a better means to select students for college? Was the role of the Aikin Commission to reconstruct secondary curriculum to provide a more meaningful preparation for college and to ascertain whether this was being accomplished? Many school heads were wondering if not the intent of the experiment should be "to pursue curriculum modifications free from existing restrictions," as had originally been suggested. Ironically, the importance of addressing these issues pertaining to school and college became evident first to the Thayer Commission's Committee on Evaluation, not to the Aikin Commission's Committee on Reports and Records. Thayer, Herbert Smith, and colleagues noted: "The purpose of the experiment was to build up a better kind of secondary education and a better means of passing students on from school to college. Such a program as the Committee on Records is proposing would leave us at the end of the experiment obliged either to accept a cumulative record of tests as a basis of admission to college or else to revert to the College Entrance Examination Board. Cannot some sounder basis of integrating school and college be found?"[42]

The Eight-Year Study began as an experiment in curriculum reform as secondary school educators sought to establish better relations between schools and colleges. What is often overlooked, however, is that participating college and school leaders maintained very different, often contrasting, agendas for reform. For the colleges, *guidance, cooperation,* and *college admissions* were the operative words; yet these terms quickly translated into *tests* and *cumulative records* for the schools. As often happens, institutions of higher education determined the direction. Only by the Revolt of 1934 were the principals able to prevent the colleges from leading the Thirty School Study off course, away from the experimental restructuring of secondary education. Despite the influence of leaders of the Carnegie Foundation, neither were their wishes met. From its beginning, one story of the Eight-Year Study was a saga of foundation power and manipulation, of personal rivalries, and of conflicting assumptions about the proper relations between schools and colleges that eventually led to revolt. In retrospect, the action of the school directors was remarkable—principals proved more determined, even though the Study itself may have been put at risk.

The 1934 revolt occurred not in opposition to student evaluation or even to standardized testing. The Eight-Year Study never attempted to free students from tests but only to release schools from the standard Carnegie units required for college admission. Some colleges still expected students to submit College Board results in order to be considered for admission, and all colleges requested student records that included some form of achievement or aptitude testing. In fact, most of the participating schools administered the American Council on Education's Psychological Examination and continued to encourage their college-bound students to take the College Board's Scholastic Aptitude Test (SAT). The revolt, while centered on the issue of testing, arose from a more fundamental concern: who controlled the project and whether or not the outcomes remained open for discovery or were predetermined.

Previously, we asserted that the Eight-Year Study was much more than the work of one PEA commission and that the Aikin Commission must be understood in relation to the Thayer and Keliher Commissions. Now an additional element must be added: to fully understand the Eight-Year Study, the stories must include the roles of the supporting foundations. These accounts of the project reveal how experimental programs, through the vicissitudes of funding and the ambitions of funding agents, may ultimately contradict themselves and unfold in unanticipated ways. Yet fortunately for "the progressive education legacy," a few members of the Aikin, Thayer, and Keliher Commissions allied themselves with several school principals and, with great courage, spoke out in favor of curricular experimentation. In so doing, they unknowingly may have postponed for a short time the standardized testing juggernaut that rolls forth virtually unchallenged today.

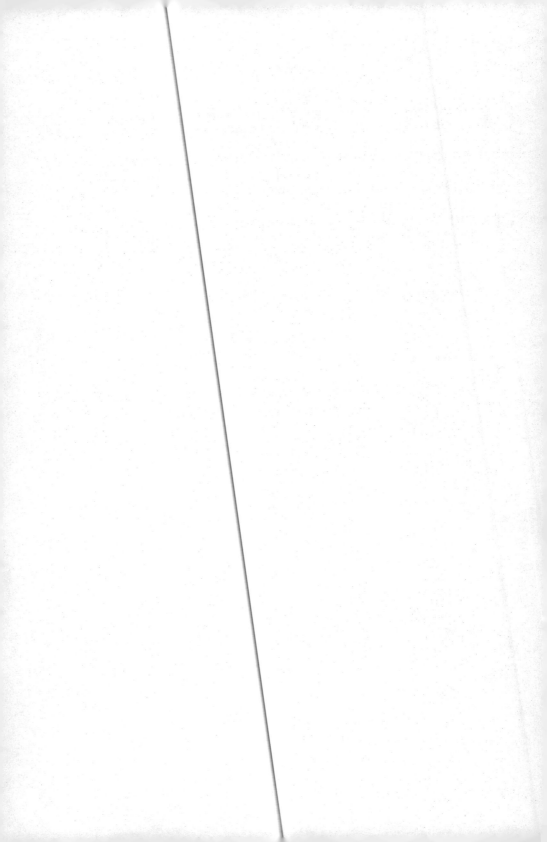

Vignette

Eugene Randolph Smith (1876–1968): Recognizing "the futility of statistics as an end in itself"

Eugene R. Smith, photograph, ca. 1938, Beaver Country Day School

The name Smith seems to permeate Progressive Education Association documents—Eugene Randolph Smith, Herbert Winslow Smith, Perry Dunlap Smith, and Elliott Dunlap Smith. Each takes on different roles in the stories of the Eight-Year Study—leader, provocateur, loyalist, and supporter, respectively. Eugene Randolph Smith, headmaster of Boston's Beaver Country Day School and the president of the PEA from 1923 to 1925, was perhaps second in importance to Aikin on the Commission on the Relation of School and College. Herbert Winslow Smith (ca. 1890–1981), headmaster of two participating Eight-Year Study schools, the Fieldston School and the Francis W. Parker School of Chicago, led the principals' revolt of 1934. Perry Dunlap Smith (1888–1967) served as headmaster of another participating school, North Shore Country Day School of Chicago, and Elliott Dunlap Smith (1891–1976), then-professor at Yale University, was a member of the Commission on Human Relations. While each Smith guided the direction of the Eight-Year Study in significant ways, Eugene Smith, perhaps more than any other member of the PEA, has been most influential in the evolution of progressive education and most unknown and overlooked today.

I

For Lawrence Cremin, Eugene Smith exemplified the progressive educator who used science to improve the traditional curriculum. In fact, Cremin featured Smith in his "scientists, sentimentalists, and radicals" chapter in *The Transformation of the School*, and Harold Rugg would have designated him one of the "scientific methodists" in his configuration of the progressive education field.[1] While we wish not to quibble with Cremin, nor Rugg for that matter, after reading Smith's work we view his interests as being primarily focused on the importance of experimentation rather than on any formal conception of scientific inquiry. "Statistical investigation" or numerical tabulations seems to be a more accurate description of his research. This is not to say that scientific inquiry and psychological measurement were not important to him. In 1920, when in Boston to talk to a group of patrons who would ultimately finance the Beaver Country Day School, he stated that "one of the greatest movement(s) in education today is becoming scientific about education," although Smith's conception of science, as he made very clear to the Boston benefactors, referred to accumulating data in order to better understand students and to describe the learning process.[2] Science—conceived as systematic data collection—should verify one of the most basic beliefs of progressive educators: the importance of educating the whole child. Smith's lifelong conviction remained that "the school must be for the child, not the child for the school or for the convenience and ease of an established system of schooling," and throughout his career his vision remained on the student and on bringing about an "improvement in educational opportunity [for] all the children of all the people" rather than on scientific technique.[3]

While adopting many attributes of "child-centered progressives," Smith's place among the testing experts becomes somewhat difficult to understand, especially in light of these student-oriented views. Smith stood among the founders of the CTS and the SAT and was himself the founder of the Educational Records Bureau (ERB)—entities that combined to form the Educational Testing Service. Further, at this time the early college admissions process was much more discriminatory and racist rather than child-centered. Carl Brigham, SAT designer, championed eugenics before renouncing his position and later becoming a member of Smith's Records and Reports Committee of the Aikin Commission. Columbia University, the leader for the development of college admissions testing and sponsor of the CTS and ERB, openly expressed concern about the moral background and social desirability of its applicants in reaction to an influx of ethnic students. College admission officers embraced meritocracy, democracy, and open access for public school students; however, Herbert Hawkes, dean of Columbia College from 1919 to 1941, also saw entrance exams as a way to distinguish those students with high intelligence from those with high ambitions, that is, separating ability from accomplishment and power from performance.[4] Period vernacular suggests those "most ambitious" were the Jewish students.

How the Eight-Year Study high school principals—Smith specifically—responded to these not-too-covert intentions is unclear. Some of the Aikin Commission participants turned quickly away from the topic of college admissions, perhaps in reaction to the discriminatory intentions of admissions officers. Smith's interests centered less on college admissions testing and more on ways to record student progress. While his work in recording and appraising student progress placed him in the testing community, he devoted himself to solving the administrative logistics of student guidance, "doing each day the right thing for each individual pupil," and to promoting the forgotten topic of transfer, "the passing on of information so that education becomes a continuous process."[5]

II

Similar to many other Eight-Year Study progressives, Eugene R. Smith was an academic who lived with children, teachers, and parents. His life included both the sphere of ideas and the world of youth—of universities and schools. Smith graduated from Syracuse University in 1896 and served as an instructor in mathematics until ca. 1898. He appears in progressive education lore as the first headmaster of the Park School in Baltimore from 1912 to 1922 and as one of the founding members of the PEA. When Stanwood Cobb outlined the plans for initiating the organization, Smith traveled to Washington throughout the winter of 1918–1919 for informal meetings as the association's organizational structure and charter were formed. He is said to have made the most significant contributions in articulating the seven principles that served to define the PEA.[6]

When Smith was offered the director's position at the Park School, a k–12 coeducational day school, he was described as "a charming and very capable young man, open-minded, tolerant, progressive."[7] A 1920 graduate recalls Smith as "a top-notch mathematician and, it turned out, an educational innovator. I remember his twinkly blue eyes, sandy hair, sense of humor as well as discipline, and his musical ability."[8] As headmaster, he allowed students to guide the school's program and sought to soften departmental divisions among the areas of study. Students would work "on any subject so long as enthusiasm carried them," and he "endeavored to make the schedule adapt to learning, rather

than the other way 'round.' "[9] Smith's policies blended a strong Pesta-
lozzian belief in object teaching with a mathematician's love for preci-
sion. After ten years, he was invited to Boston to start the Beaver Country
Day School and served as its director, a position he held for the next
twenty-two years, from 1921 to 1943, during which time he also lectured
at Johns Hopkins University, Wellesley College, Harvard University, and
the University of California, Berkeley.

During this period as a full-time school administrator and teacher,
Smith was also active as a writer. His major work, *Education Moves Ahead*,
was published in 1924 with an introduction by Charles Eliot. Also, Smith
contributed a chapter to the legendary 26th Yearbook of the National
Society for the Study of Education, *Curriculum-making: Past and Present*,
a work whose publication in 1927 is purported to have established
curriculum as a distinct field of study. He published regularly in the
PEA's journal, *Progressive Education*, and the American Council on
Education's journal, *The Educational Record*, and coauthored with Ralph
Tyler *Appraising and Recording Student Progress* in what became the most
popular and widely read volume of the Aikin Commission's final report. His final years were spent in Florida, where he lectured at Rollins
College and published in 1963 a pedagogical memoir, *Some Challenges
to Teachers*, a uniquely conceived collage of comments by Smith and
former teachers and students he had known throughout the years at
the Beaver Country Day School and the Park School.[10] While the term
progressive education does not appear in *Some Challenges*, the "progressive
spirit" is embedded in Smith's work.

III

As a mathematician, Eugene Randolph Smith saw at once the
value of tests and scores as part of the inventory of a child and
as a means of communication among educators. In the same
breath, he saw ahead *the futility of statistics as an end in itself*, and
as a controlling factor in the inventory of a child. [It was] in
this spirit that he became a "founding father" of the Educational Records Bureau and set a standard of sanity for its contribution to education. (Jean T. Sharpless, 1988)[11]

The Cumulative Record Card seemed to combine Smith's interest
in children with his concern for administrative practicalities. All of his
organizational work—with the PEA's Commission on the Relation of
School and College, the American Council on Education's Committee
on Measurement and Guidance, and the Educational Records Bureau's
Committee on School and College Relations—returned to this record

form, a double-sided sheet of tagboard that would fit into a 8.5 × 11-inch student file and would record important information about students beyond the mere listing of course grades, test scores, and cryptic teacher comments. A description of the form, prepared by an American Council on Education committee, actually appears as an appendix in the Aikin Commission report *Appraising and Recording Student Progress.* While the card was oriented for all secondary school students, college and non-college bound, a uniform College Entrance Blank was also devised by the ACE and the National Association of Secondary School Principals (also described in *Appraising and Recording Student Progress*) for those students seeking admission to college. Smith was persistent in his efforts to popularize the form as well as to standardize the type and amount of student data, and he was quick to point out that student records represented a "living document." While "recording student progress" seemed at times merely a convenient form of bookkeeping, student records were no routine matter for Smith.[12] The Cumulative Record Card provided an important service to school administrators and teachers by defining crucial information and offering originality and inventiveness for student record keeping.

As chair of the Aikin Commission's Committee on Records and Reports, Smith oversaw four subcommittees attending to specific aspects of record keeping: student behaviors, teachers' reports, school-to-college transfer forms, and student development. He also worked with individual schools as they experimented with their own student forms. His committee developed a manual to guide and provide commonality for the many different dimensions of what would now be called authentic assessment, including creativeness and imagination, responsibility-dependability, curiosity, social concern, emotional responsiveness, and social adaptability. Descriptors were provided to help teachers make such judgments, and substantial space was left to actually elicit observations rather than to permit the customary numerical ratings.

The Denver public schools were perhaps the most innovative with their cumulative form. Their Cooperative Educational Record preserved for each student information kept cooperatively by teachers, parents, the pupil, and even the pupil's friends.[13] The forty-seven-page form included conventional tables to record examination scores and patterns of behavior, similar to other Eight-Year Study school records, along with many other topics, including formal and informal educational experiences, book tabulations, and additional observations. In essence, the Denver staff reconceived the traditional intent of record keeping; cooperative records became a reciprocal working relationship where parents and students would submit comments along with the school staff's assessments. The forms were much more than a solution to the bureaucratic problems of organizing and maintaining student data and, instead, offered ample opportunity for "everyone who knows about the pupil . . . to contribute whatever will throw light on that person as a living individual, going through an unbroken, continuous development."[14]

Clearly Smith was trying to break the practice of the student record as a "simple book-keeping form on which a few mathematical symbols are entered."[15] The "continuing reports of a pupil's all-round development" became a common and an often-repeated phrase for Smith as he and others viewed student records as portraying the intellectual and psychological development of young people. They assumed that future teachers, as well as students and their parents, would want a log—a portfolio—of this development as a basis for effective guidance and as an educational memoir. Since the field of guidance had not taken on today's more narrow role of career and vocational orientation, any school faculty member may have been asked to offer advice about the student—academic, personal, psychological, career and vocational, and emotional. For this important role, teachers and staff wanted as much information as possible. Yet with guidance came another now generally forgotten topic: *transfer*. This term took on a very specialized meaning, since student records attempted to integrate—to foster "a continuous process"—for student's learning. While the Curriculum Associates helped teachers integrate the secondary school curriculum, the term *transfer* represented Smith's efforts to establish sequence—continuity—for the intellectual and emotional development of the student. A thoughtful high school program would seek not only to integrate the disciplines across the curriculum but also to unify information by the transfer of knowledge for the individual who is developing from adolescence to adulthood.

IV

I am making a prophecy, which is always dangerous, but I am so sure that schools and colleges together are searching for the continuity in education of which I have said so much, and for the flexibility that will best serve each individual. (Eugene R. Smith, 1940)[16]

We have heard the rather common response from teachers, "I won't look at a student's record because I wish not to be influenced or biased by another's view." "Pygmalion in the Classroom" research has convinced us that teachers' unfavorable expectations and labels can negatively affect student performance. This we do not deny. Yet for Smith, cumulative records did not limit the views of a teacher but instead served to inform and expand the image of students. Smith believed that the observations of trained, experienced, thoughtful teachers could be of great value for their own curriculum planning as well as for the planning of future colleagues and administrators. He certainly did not deny the subjective nature of such judgments and even referred to the "halo effect" whereby a teacher projects good qualities onto a student. But his faith always remained with the sound assessments of teachers, individuals whose professional commitment and responsibility placed them in the role of ethnographers and psychologists as they constructed meaning about students' academic and emotional well-being.

Smith offers a sample that captures the flavor of the Cumulative Record Card and the anecdotal reports of the Eight-Year Study schools. This statement is abbreviated but represents the type of information that would fill a student's secondary school file. Such specific details would not necessarily be relayed during the college admission process. (See Appendix C.) A careful reading of the statement reveals its highly interpretive and subjective character; many comments could lead to legal action in today's litigious times. But Smith continued to place his faith in the community of teachers who would come together to discuss the various dimensions of a student—not in a punitive way but in a manner capable of enhancing learning experiences for students and for themselves as the activity took on dimensions of staff development. The recent publication, *Growing Up In University School*, by Robert Butche, offers a much more comprehensive account of the importance of cumulative student records and their beneficial role in helping determine the educational experiences of students.[17]

While student measurement may contradict present impressions of child-centered progressive education, comprehensive record keeping proved to be of even greater importance for those experimental schools, since the principal often was asked to "confirm" the amount of work for college-bound students who completed individual and unconventional study programs. Even though Eight-Year Study colleges accepted students without tallying Carnegie units, admissions officers still requested some assessment of a student's strengths and achievements. Open-ended record keeping permitted such judgments to be made by providing the principal with substantive information to "unscramble" a student's core program into subject units.[18]

Eugene Randolph Smith, considered the father of the cumulative record form and the Educational Records Bureau, stood among the founders of the standardized college admissions test movement. Yet he recognized the futility of statistical representation of student knowledge. Instead, cumulative records became "living, exciting stories," and while no one type of cumulative form was deemed perfect, "every record should move in the direction of becoming such a living document. If we achieve that, education will articulate in a continuous process."[19] Smith's goal was to encourage continuity in education, a transfer of knowledge that was best achieved by thoughtful teachers and parents guiding students based on the accumulation of abundant and well-chosen information.

Chapter 3

An Essential Faith:
From Tests and Measurement
to Appraisal and Evaluation

The first years of the eight-year experiment have been characterized by confident assurance and puzzled questions; clear
thinking and confused fumbling; fresh, vigorous attack upon
our problems; . . . ineffective, tradition-bound attempts to meet
the challenge which our new freedom has brought. (Wilford
M. Aikin, 1936)[1]

Introduction

In the spring of 1934 school headmasters, commission staff, and
teachers were disturbed with the direction the experiment seemed to
be taking. Frustrated with the seemingly ineffective attempts to reframe
their school programs—the confused fumbling—the principals lashed
out at one of the few areas where decisions had been made: the selection of tests for college admissions. As Ralph Tyler recalled, "The thing
was about to go haywire."[2] Perhaps it had. In late April 1934, Herbert
Smith received a letter from Wilford Aikin informing him that he had
"no moral right to upset the machinery for managing the experiment
right at the beginning."[3] At the same time, the *New York Times* wrote to
Smith requesting the results of "the college entrance experiment," inquiring how the schools had met the challenge of admissions.[4] The
Times had announced the project a year before and wanted to know
what teaching methods had been employed in the schools. Ironically,
as reporters pressed for results of the Eight-Year Study after merely one
year, the participants were still attempting to determine the project's
focus and direction. Three years had passed since the initial planning
session, and the most definite statement was that the school faculties
did not want to be part of a Carnegie research program.

Even with the initial tradition-bound efforts, a spirit of independence and open inquiry prevailed among the cooperating school faculties, many of whom firmly embraced school experimentation. Also, the group seemed to be moving toward a yet-to-be-articulated conviction: responsibility for educational reform necessarily rests with school faculties and staff. This faith in experimentation and belief in teachers would soon be expressed in what could be interpreted as outright defiance toward leaders in the field of tests and measurements. The spokesperson was a young educator who, just a few years before, had traveled the back roads of North Carolina offering extension courses to teachers. In the process he had come to appreciate their challenges and needs. The Eight-Year Study would avoid another uprising, and much of the credit belongs to this spokesperson, Ralph Tyler, who joined the Commission staff later that summer.

The 1934 George School Conference: "A Gathering of Craftspersons"

During the spring revolt, Herb Smith's principals' caucus feared that the Aikin Commission's Committee on Tests and Records, headed by Eugene Smith, would emerge as an accrediting agency, standing between their high schools and the colleges. The caucus drafted a document telling the Aikin Commission's Directing Committee that the schools would accept no prescribed testing program and that teachers would be responsible for researching school practice, otherwise "the spark of life will go out unless teachers feel that they are enlisted in research. Such a program as has been proposed will make of them merely clerical assistants."[5]

The warning of Herb Smith and the principals was heeded when for six days in June 1934 cooperating teachers, principals, and Commission staff came together for the George School Conference, the second annual meeting of the Eight-Year Study. Unlike the earlier gathering at Bennington College, where Aikin Commission and Carnegie Foundation staff presented keynote addresses describing the progress of the experiment to a small group of principals, teachers, and college administrators, the George School meeting was open to all participating high school teachers. One can only imagine the excitement at the first keynote session to the ever-present question, "What is all this about?" Obviously trying to respond to concerns of the school faculties, Aikin described the current direction of the "curriculum study," as the Eight-Year Study was called at this time. After the opening session, no formal conference papers were presented; instead, the program was drawn from responses to a questionnaire that had been sent to principals two months earlier requesting information from both teachers and students about their problems and successes to date. Topics were assigned to individual school faculties, and twenty-five of twenty-eight schools reported during the week.[6] Testing was not overlooked at the meeting, although discussion often focused on more immediate issues for the schools: "use of contemporary material," "health education," and staff coordination for developing an integrated curriculum program. Additional issues arose during the conversations and became themes for consideration later in the week. Described as a conference of craftspersons where "teachers in overalls with their boots on" went to work, the George School meeting addressed issues real to the schools and defined itself as being "of, for, and by teachers at work on the reconstruction of secondary education."[7]

The issue of how to initiate educational change would once again become crucial. Prior to the conference, a few principals had recommended that the schools report their activities among themselves seeking, in effect, a "best practices" approach for educational change. Others believed that by discussing specific problems and concerns, teachers could elicit aid from Commission staff to develop solutions. This second approach reflected the belief that genuine experimentation was not a matter of merely transplanting another school's promising practices and that the proper role of the staff was *to assist teachers* rather than to direct them. Securing the services of individuals who could support the school faculties in developing tests and measurements paralleled the decision to establish the Thayer Commission, which was already providing assistance with curriculum and instruction.

After the George School meeting, the Aikin Commission, with GEB funding, decided to appoint Ralph Tyler to oversee the testing and evaluation component of the project. With the Evaluation Staff separate from the influence of the Carnegie Foundation, the Pennsylvania Study, and Eugene Smith's Committee on Tests and Records, the teachers and principals were now firmly in control. Problems were not resolved, however. Many college administrators expressed little trust in the abilities of "school people"—teachers—to meet the challenge of reforming secondary education, and not all believed Tyler capable of guiding the undertaking.

Tyler's 1934 Challenge: No Indubitable Proof

Ralph Tyler was not completely unknown within the testing community. He had published *Constructing Achievement Tests* in 1934, a collection of articles appearing primarily in the *Educational Research Bulletin*.[8] But now he was directing the evaluation of this rather high-profile project, and his debut on the national research stage did not take long. Just five months after accepting the directorship of the evaluation team, Tyler addressed the Third Educational Conference on Testing, talking to the leading tests and measurement researchers and college admissions officers in the country. In this presentation, he described the fundamental tenets of what would become his life's work in evaluation and assessment. Over fifty years later, he recounted this session as "the first one; what's our mission, why we've got to do it, why it is so important."[9] This was, for Tyler, a pivotal moment in his career as well as in the history of assessment.

The New York City conference featured not Tyler but sessions by George Zook, former U.S. Commissioner of Education and then-director of the American Council on Education, and Herbert Hawkes, "the Dean of College Deans," who presented a paper on the "Real and Imaginary Dangers of Testing." Hawkes spoke to the audience not as a test designer but more as a client who benefited from scientific measurement. There were many reasons he would have been chosen to offer a keynote address. The distinguished and beloved sixty-two-year-old Columbia University dean had championed the role of tests and measurement by establishing the Educational Research Bureau and the Cooperative Test Service and by fostering support from IBM and the Carnegie and Rockefeller Foundations.[10] This respected, Ivy League administrator told his audience that the real danger of testing arises from permitting non-experts (namely teachers) to become involved in test construction; testing "should be entrusted only to the expert." For Hawkes, the threat of standardization was merely an imaginary danger, and he assured the audience, "If the testing program does unduly standardize the educational process, it is contrary to the strenuous efforts of those responsible for its existence."[11] To make his point, he argued that those who expected "more than facts" from testing displayed uncritical idealism and dilettantism.[12] These words seemed to be aimed at Tyler and other Eight-Year Study school faculty, including most certainly Herb Smith.

The pro-standardized testing rhetoric did not end with Hawkes's remarks; in fact, it was only the beginning. A Yale admissions officer berated progressive secondary schools for their criticism of the College Board Entrance Examinations and, while commending the experimental work of Learned and the Pennsylvania Study, supported regimentation of entrance examinations. The superintendent of Radnor High School, one of the participating Eight-Year Study schools, spoke in support of Hawkes's views in an address entitled "The Effect of Systematic Testing on Pupil and Teacher." Introduced by Ben Wood, Radnor's school superintendent proudly proclaimed that his school had given "more tests than any other school in the history of the world."[13] Years later, Tyler recalled this educator, remarking that he was so "heavy-handed that the Radnor teachers were fighting him as much as they were working on the [Eight-Year] study."[14]

Battle lines were again drawn. Neither Hawkes nor Wood could have been pleased with Tyler's entry into the project, and Tyler certainly was not with friends among the conference presenters. He had already engaged in a public exchange with Wood that aired their deep differences. At least Tyler could count on the presence of his colleague, Wilford Aikin, to officially introduce the Eight-Year Study in an address immediately preceding his talk. Aikin's remarks, one assumes, would have set a positive tone for his own address. Yet fate seemed to conspire against Tyler, and Aikin cancelled. Eugene Smith, who had just previously introduced Dean Hawkes, was asked to read Aikin's paper. At this time Tyler was wary of Smith, who certainly would not have been viewed as an ally. Finally, there Tyler stood, a youngish-looking thirty-two-year-old before an audience of 460 conference participants, including many of the prominent test and measurement leaders of the day from the other sponsoring organizations: the Educational Records Bureau, the Cooperative Test Service, and the Personnel Methods and Educational Testing committees of the American Council on Education. Following a slate of unsympathetic presenters and introduced by a less than sympathetic colleague whom he had unofficially replaced on the Eight-Year Study, Tyler spoke.

Though introduced to discuss the problems of measurement, Tyler's paper was actually titled "Evaluation: A Challenge and an Opportunity to Progressive Education."[15] While the audience may have wondered if evaluation could offer such opportunities, they did not have to wait long before hearing the challenge. In the second paragraph of his speech, Tyler directly disagreed with Hawkes and asserted an essential faith in school experimentation and in the abilities of motivated school staffs to initiate thoughtful and productive school change. Throughout Tyler's presentation, the central role of the teacher in assessment was clearly articulated. Evaluation was not the sole responsibility of testing experts, as Hawkes had asserted, but a central role of teachers as well. Tyler never disputed the importance or value of testing experts; he just never mentioned them in his talk. Eight years later, when Tyler's staff released their final report on evaluation, one of their most basic convictions rested on the belief that teachers should be intimately involved in the design and construction of all assessment instruments. Testing data were to have value for informing program development and teaching, not merely for making college admissions decisions. During his speech, Tyler called for new methods of collecting student data so that important educational purposes, previously thought to be intangible and incapable of assessment, could be appraised. He went on to argue that no one uniform evaluation program should be implemented among the thirty schools. Then, in what may have been viewed as blasphemy among the testing experts, Tyler suggested that evaluation should *begin* with school staffs formulating their own educational goals, purposes, and objectives. A full one-hour discussion ensued where the audience "seemed convinced [they had heard] a new direction to the testing movement."[16]

The start of a monumental transformation of the Eight-Year Study was embedded in this 1934 challenge when Tyler stated, "[School] evaluations are not likely to represent indubitable proof of the success or failure of current educational endeavors."[17] To this point, the leaders of the Eight-Year Study—Aikin, Eugene Smith, Learned, and others— had viewed the project as a controlled experiment for which success could be proven.[18] This was to change. The schools were not engaged in testing predefined hypotheses nor, as Smith maintained, conducting a scientific, laboratory experiment with controlled variables and clearly articulated propositions. Tyler recognized quickly that each school faculty was implementing its own pilot demonstration, or implementative study, on its own terms and in accord with its situated, idiosyncratic problems and interests. Evaluation of students and of programs had to be, according to Tyler, reasonably objective and accurate, depicting the value of these experimental programs, but it need not provide "indubitable proof" of whether progressive education was superior to traditional education—for example, whether an adolescent needs core program might be better than a topical history course for promoting student learning and development. Tyler did not dismiss scientific inquiry; rather, he highlighted the importance of school experimentation not to prove or predict outcomes but, more importantly, "to suggest" promising directions and possibilities for schooling practice.

The opening paragraph of Tyler's address acknowledges this point along with the expectation that widely differing programs would emerge from the cooperating schools. He reminded the conference attendees that,

> Thousands of schools have not the freedom to embark upon radical educational changes, nor the facilities to conduct pioneering experiments. . . . They have long been looking for suggestions which offer sufficient promise to encourage them to embark upon an improved procedure. They are looking to the experiments in progressive education with the hope that they may find suggestions for the solutions of their own problems.[19]

Having spent the past years conducting "service studies" in schools throughout North Carolina, Tyler was aware that solutions take many different forms in different contexts. This type of applied research, situated "in particular classrooms, in a particular community, with a particular group of pupils, under a particular teacher," had been aimed at initiating changes and improvements in specific situations and settings.[20] These service studies were designed to gather data useful for improving particular teachers' own practices. As Tyler wrote, "The problem will have been satisfactorily solved if the solution is successful in that one classroom."[21] When Tyler told the audience that educators must (literally) enlarge their concept of evaluation, he was in effect moving the field of education from evaluation as tests and measurements to evaluation as program assessment and experimentation.

Further, Tyler, in what even today would be viewed as controversial, was displaying his emphasis upon validity rather than reliability. Given this view, the Evaluation Staff never really stressed test reliability in the conventional sense, arguing instead that constantly changing situations and contexts require school staffs to ascertain and reformulate problems in a continuous quest for renewal. Instead, he encouraged discussions among teachers and staff pertaining to test validity. As Tyler continued his work with the Eight-Year Study, validity, not reliability, remained of utmost importance.

Tyler Builds His Research Team

To what degree Tyler would work with Smith's Committee on Records and Reports was initially unclear. The relationship between Tyler's team and Smith's committee would evolve. Tyler was not necessarily welcomed with open arms, and he felt "hesitation and almost suspicion" from a few principals still loyal to Learned and the Pennsylvania Study. Tension would exist between Smith and Tyler and their staffs well into 1938.[22] Yet Tyler was not beholden to Smith or the Carnegie Foundation grant since his funding from the General Education Board was independent of the Records and Reports Committee. In time, the name and orientation of this committee would merge with Tyler's staff, but out of courtesy Tyler distanced himself from Smith's primary work, that of developing a student records form. The final Aikin Commission's report on evaluation, *Appraising and Recording Student Progress*, "coauthored" by Smith and Tyler, reveals how very independent and separate these two groups were and how priorities shifted over the life of the Study.[23] Of the 497-page report, the final forty-one pages were allocated to student records, Smith's lifelong interest, while the first 456 pages describe the work of Tyler's group.

Tyler aficionados will recall various accounts of the formation of the Eight-Year Study Evaluation Staff, especially his ability to recognize talent. His hiring decisions, however, represented a fundamental belief: Content knowledge was more important than knowledge of tests and measurements, and subject-area specialists could, he believed, learn to become testing experts. The GEB encouraged Tyler to train a group of individuals who would in time become leaders in the field of evaluation and education.[24] And this he did. Eventually members of his team included Louis Raths, a math teacher from the University of Chicago's University School, who later helped define the areas of human relations and values clarification; Hilda Taba, a German teacher from the Dalton School, who furthered the fields of social studies and curriculum; Paul Diederich, a Latin teacher from the Ohio State University School, who proceeded to become a founding figure of the Educational Testing Service; Bruno Bettelheim and Peter Blos, Austrian refugees, who both developed important lines of thought in the areas of psychology and psychiatry; and, for a short time, Oscar Buros of Rugers University, who established the Institute of Mental Measurement and founded the annually published *Mental Measurement Yearbook*. The abridged listing is impressive; each team member would impact greatly his or her field of interest as did Tyler's many assistants, primarily teachers and graduate students in the humanities and sciences. While Tyler selected his staff with great care, there were tensions within the group. Innovative, experimental work seems to necessitate skepticism and critique, and he encouraged such discourse at his staff meetings that proved disconcerting for some.[25]

Tyler looked for thoughtful, independent staff members who could productively assist teachers to identify their instructional aims and to clarify their objectives for student and program evaluation. The staff walked a narrow line between enlightened evaluators and content area specialists. Emphatically, they were not to serve as external testers who would prepare and administer standardized paper-pencil instruments. The staff helped the schools by recommending evaluation instruments when available and by developing new tests. They also advised teachers in forming educational hypotheses (noteworthy since Tyler provided an option to those faculties who wished to conduct what was called "an experiment in the technical sense"), and they offered assistance for collecting evidence of student success. Underlying the orientation was a fundamental belief in open discourse since, for Tyler, evaluation consisted of a process by which the *values* of an enterprise were articulated and ascertained. In essence, e-valuating—or drawing out values— was conceived as first and foremost a philosophical rather than a technical activity. For Tyler, evaluation represented a way *to enrich and to improve* the decision making critical to curriculum and instruction, and thus he insisted that his staff should not appraise a school program but should instead support school facilities in meeting *their* obligations and expectations.[26]

Tyler's group broke ranks with Learned, Wood, and other Aikin Commission members who had been requesting the development of "power tests" (requiring differing levels of intellectual power) as an alternative to "speed tests" (determining "the limits of capacity" of students to complete questions within a set time).[27] The Evaluation Staff did not attempt to create tests with bell-shape curve distributions or new instruments such as Learned's "innovative" true-false and multiple choice questions. In fact, Tyler ridiculed the hypothetical questions then being hotly debated by test constructors: "Should the true-false test or the essay-type test be used?" These individuals, derisively called "test technicians," were unable, Tyler felt, to produce useful tests because they lacked subject matter mastery and "appreciation of the aesthetic values to be derived from work in the humanities."[28]

Through their conversations with the school staffs, Tyler's team was able to bring stability to the Eight-Year Study at a time when the project seemed to lack direction. All but two schools approved of the evaluation program, and all the other sites were actively engaged with Tyler and his staff. In 1937, no other than Herbert Hawkes himself would write, "They [the teachers] think of the [evaluation] program as an important aspect of teaching rather than a special adjunct irrelevant to their main purpose. . . . The evaluation program has really promoted the building of an improved curriculum."[29] Perhaps their most important accomplishment, as noted in this 1937 independent report, was its success in changing the schools' attitudes toward evaluation, especially in light of the deep mistrust arising from the circumstances of the spring of 1934.

The 1935 Conference Epilogue: Defining and Measuring Objectives as Conversation and Dialogue

It is no easy task to formulate objectives. Schools are frequently tempted to accept a glib statement which may have come to their attention rather than to think through their own serious purposes. . . . We ask, "What does your school mean by this objective?" "What are you trying to accomplish?" We want to keep the discussion focused upon the real purposes of each school and not upon the conventional definition of terms. (Ralph W. Tyler, 1936)[30]

Tyler returned to the Fourth Educational Conference on Testing and, with a presentation entitled "Defining and Measuring Objectives of Progressive Education," reconfirmed the point that establishing objectives should be as important, if not more important, to the field of measurement as test design. Also, while correcting any misconceptions about the Eight-Year Study that had arisen, he maintained that teachers could and should develop tests to meet their own instructional and programmatic purposes. Further, Tyler stated in no uncertain terms that the participating experimental schools were teaching facts and information and that students would be tested in a variety of ways to ascertain whether they retained such knowledge. This was mentioned, no doubt, in reaction to the common public perception that "child-centered" progressive schools were not interested in the disciplines and were ignoring serious academic content.

Tyler coined the term *comprehensive appraisal* for his approach to evaluation, where instruments were designed to ascertain student development and not merely to determine the acquisition of knowledge and factual learning. For him, evaluation should begin with teachers discussing "what kinds of changes in its pupils the new educational program was expected to facilitate."[31] Conversations were never confined to what could be measured. Rather, teachers' hopes for their students became the point of departure for discussion. The process of defining objectives was recursive, requiring cycles of thoughtful questioning and reworking by staff and groups of teachers until what was written could fully capture what was intended. For example, one school sought to foster in students a sensitivity to significant problems. This term, *social sensitivity*, as Tyler reported,

> was discussed, worded, reconsidered and re-worded until it was finally clear that the schools were using [it] to mean that they hoped to develop pupils who are aware of significant problems of modern life, who are able to analyze these problems to indicate the more definite crucial difficulties involved, who are really concerned in trying to help in overcoming these difficulties, and who develop a plan of action for themselves with reference to each problem which is appropriate for their abilities and opportunities. These four types of behavior are more clearly understood than the original phrase and the problem of evaluation is clarified.[32]

From a single, vague aim emerged four objectives that were used to strengthen the focus of instruction and to provide structure for assessment. Despite the claims of some critics, Tyler did not consider listing behaviors to be the starting point of evaluation. He ultimately stated educational goals in behavioral terms, but the conversation began with classroom problems and teachers' wishes for their students' development rather than specific behaviors.

By Tyler's 1935 conference session, the Evaluation Staff had organized educational objectives from originally eight into five very broad categories—skills, understandings and appreciations, interests, good thinking, and social maturity. Tyler believed that existing evaluation programs were too narrowly conceived and that student data did not provide a comprehensive picture of the development of students. He maintained that educational areas then considered intangible and incapable of evaluation could, through extensive discourse and reexamination, ultimately lead to some form of appraisal useful to teachers. The categories eventually evolved to become appreciation, interests, aspects of thinking, social sensitivity, and personal and social adjustment. Defining behaviors and setting objectives, a process that grew from the continuous process of inquiry, served as a means for articulating broader goals and for clarifying the larger purposes of schooling.

The Work of the Evaluation Staff

There are numerous examples of what transpired when Tyler's staff visited a school or when teachers traveled to Ohio State University to work in the Eight-Year Study Testing Lab. One example comes from secondary mathematics. The reorganization of the subject matter proved difficult for math teachers, many of whom were satisfied with their conventional programs as preparation for college. Educational purposes were taken for granted. As the Eight-Year Study progressed, however, teachers became increasingly interested in designing a unified program of study within which the subject areas would be integrated and made functional and vital to the lives of the students. A Beaver Country Day School math teacher, for example, had developed a course on "practical social mathematics," but her aims were vague and unfocused. She admitted that in assessing her students she relied too heavily on factual information and unsupported judgments of their attitudes and abilities. She was encouraged to reconsider her objectives in preparation for a visit to the Testing Lab where, upon her arrival, she requested specific help in evaluating a teaching unit she had designed on taxation. There she met with Tyler and staff who asked their standard question, "What is your problem?" From this one query, she reported that over the next five days at the Lab she "learned an extraordinary amount about the approach to the solution of such problems and the techniques involved. I learned about entirely new ways to approach the subject matter of the course. . . . I was made more conscious than ever before of the principles and generalizations which underlie my course."[33] Perhaps most noteworthy, she stated that the time she spent in the Testing Lab resulted in better content, a livelier course, and an increased appreciation of the importance of self-evaluation for both student and teacher.

We have found many similar accounts. When members of the Evaluation Staff visited a school and began discussing how to measure achievement and growth instruction changed. A comment from an early Commission document underscores another result: Teachers wanted more and better information about their students than that provided by "traditional tests which usually related solely to knowledge of subject matter."[34] Tyler and his colleagues provided ways of obtaining such information. Between 1935 and 1938 a remarkable collection of tests and appraisal instruments was constructed, over 200 in draft and final form differing quite dramatically in purpose and intent from what is common even today. When designed by the staff, testing served as a means for learning about individuals rather than as a way to separate and sort students.[35]

These tests measured and ascertained "changes taking place in these boys and girls," including their reading habits, beliefs on social issues, abilities to address social problems, interpretive skills, applications of social facts, and many other areas. Assessment was quite expansive. For example, Test 1.4, "Application of Principles in Social Problems," addressed issues of race and class as well as economics and politics. In this test, students were asked to take a position on a specific problem or hypothetical situation pertaining to the use of a new invention (with economic implications), a high school graduation incident with racial overtones, the graduated income tax, and the tension between industrial profit and workers' health. Questions followed the usual elements of test construction, including an introduction, prompt, and response, but the purpose was to ascertain dominant student beliefs and, perhaps more importantly, to identify conflicting values. In fact, prompts scattered throughout the tests were designed to determine whether a student's values were consistent: "Teachers found the tests most useful as a way to detect conflicting and irregular beliefs and actions."[36] Evaluation became a way to facilitate consistency in principled behavior, recognizing that reliable action in social situations seldom comes before the acceptance of a supporting point of view.

As teachers started to view testing as more than a means for determining the acquisition of facts, they began identifying traits that they wished to foster and about which they needed data. Tests 4.2 and 4.3, "The Scale of Beliefs," sought to provide information useful for clarifying students' views on social issues, including militarism, nationalism, racialism, democracy, economic individualism, and labor and unemployment. Test 2.51, "Interpretation of Data," required students to determine whether the evidence presented in test statements was sufficient to make a statement true, probably true, probably false, false, or not sufficient to indicate any degree of truth or falsity. This "gradation of correctness" allowed students to show how well they understood evidence in argumentation. Test 3.1, "An Interpretation of Literature," went much beyond a student's ability to summarize content. Students were asked not only to demonstrate their own understanding of a story but also to recognize another's point of view and to examine the narrative in relation to a philosophy of life and to human motives. The test also ascertained, through a series of questions connected to determining the most logical ending for the narrative, if students were learning to weigh evidence. The scores on these and the other scales clearly had no obvious and direct relationship to a student's ability to complete college-level work; however, when coupled with the professional judgments of thoughtful teachers, they revealed important aptitudes and abilities and said much about the general effectiveness of content-area courses and the school community.

Evaluation also became a way to bring together groups of teachers from separate subject areas as the Aikin Commission continued its effort to integrate curriculum and lessen the fragmentation of the secondary school. Designing the Social Sensitivity Assessment Instrument was but one example. In a 1936 preliminary report prepared by Hilda Taba, social sensitivity was represented by many synonyms: social consciousness, responsibility, concern, outlook, and cooperation. The terms were used interchangeably as teachers charted out what beliefs and behaviors would constitute this objective, thought to be an essential component of democracy and social justice.[37] The concept was all encompassing and easily extended into many realms of democratic citizenship yet too vague to offer any direction for teachers. Tyler's staff formed a (sub)Committee on Sensitivity to Significant Problems, composed of fifteen teachers from various fields and seven staff members, to critique and revise the preliminary report. The term *social sensitivity* evolved into an awareness of "the implications of social phenomena for human values" and took the form of student dispositions, abilities, attitudes, and understandings. The Committee's conversation moved beyond selecting content for testing in specific subject fields to suggesting ways in which such awareness could be experienced in classroom activities. Content specialists began searching for methods to foster sensitivity to significant problems. In mathematics, for example, teachers developed "the nature of proof" in geometry as a way to explore the logic of political speeches and editorials, moving from definitions and

assumptions to conclusions. Latin teachers used classic literature to examine fascism and democracy. As an aim, developing social sensitivity was
considered important for all teachers committed to fostering democratic
citizenship, not merely a goal for history and social studies teachers.

With all of the experimentation in evaluation, students were administered many tests, and acquiring academic knowledge remained a
high priority. For example, Shaker Heights students took fourteen standardized high school tests as well as an array of content-specific assessments developed with Tyler's Evaluation Staff.[38] The Literary Information
Tests focused upon British and American literature (Tests 3.4 and 3.5).
Each ten-page exam included 150 and 160 questions where students
were asked to name authors of specific titles (e.g., *Elizabeth and Essex,
The Faerie Queene, Dr. Heidegger's Experiment, Little Boy Blue*); recognize
characters from specified works (e.g., *She Stoops to Conquer, The Scarlet
Letter*); differentiate quotations by title and author and types of writing,
literary periods, and literary terms (e.g., denouement, masque, son-
net); identify authors from biographical clues and writing excerpts; and
respond to other questions specific to a course of study. As these tests
were being used, Tyler's group also developed accompanying forms:
Test 3.3, "Literature Questionnaire: Free-Reading," and Test 3.6, "A
Questionnaire on Reading Interests and Reading Outcomes," in which,
in contrast to Tests 3.4 and 3.5, students were informed that there were
no "right" answers. The ninety-five questions from the Free-Reading
form probed students' reading patterns, for example, "Do you ever
recount to other people any scenes, incidents, or ideas encountered in
your reading which you have found especially interesting?"; "Do you
ever modify your own practical behavior with regard to certain personal
or social problems directly as the result of your reading of a particular
piece of literature?"; "Do you ever try to explain to someone else how,
in your opinion, certain unacceptable elements in a particular piece of
literature (which on the whole you have liked) could be improved?"

While the Free-Reading form was considered a test, in some ways
it was more similar to a survey or questionnaire. For teachers, such
information had clear and direct curricular implications. The Reading
Interests/Outcomes form, a six-page, thirty-five-item questionnaire,
probed deeper into reading outcomes than the Free-Reading form.
Perhaps seeming naïve today, the Reading Interests/Outcomes questionnaire examined how literature influenced students and from where
information arose (i.e., from newspapers and news magazines or from
full-length books). Students were asked for simple "yes, no, and uncertain" responses; however, with each "yes" reply, they were asked to identify specific sources. Questions were rather specific: "Have you ever read
any of the novels of Hawthorne, Cooper, Scott, Dickens, Eliot, or

Thackerary, aside from those specifically required in schoolwork?"; "In the past year have you read one or more of the best sellers among the new books?"; "Do you have a collection of books of your own, not counting schoolbooks?" And, of course, since the test designers were attempting to ascertain "influence," certain questions were general and divergent: "Have any of the books that you have read given you a better understanding of the depression and its effects?"; "Have any of the books that you have read given you a better understanding of the problems in the lives of [African American] people in this country?"; "Have any of the books that you have read given you a better understanding of the significance of science in everyday life?" For all questions, the response elicits, "If your answer is yes, write the name of one such book here." Other test responses were even more open-ended. Test 3.7, "Critical-Mindedness in the Reading of Fiction," presented short stories and then posed questions for which students were asked to agree or disagree. Their responses, which were compared to those of a panel of teachers and professors, permitted students to be assessed as "judicious, hypercritical, uncritical, or uncertain." Obviously, Tests 3.6 and 3.7 sought not to determine how literature impacted understanding or to appraise a student's cognitive abilities with any degree of "reliability" in a professional sense but instead to assist teachers to make appropriate decisions about their teaching and their students' programs of study.

Ultimately, the work of Tyler and his staff members went well beyond the experimental sites associated with the Aikin Commission. Other schools looked toward the Progressive Education Association in the hope of finding solutions to their particular assessment problems. Tyler once expressed uneasiness, feeling he was caught between either promoting the Eight-Year Study or developing new techniques for testing and measurement. He was told that the General Education Board supported him in order to develop new tests.[39] The GEB's investment was well returned. By 1937, eighty-seven tests and appraisal instruments constructed by Tyler's staff were used by 285 schools and by several hundred teachers outside of those working directly with the Eight-Year Study. The resource materials generated by the staff and distributed to schools on request exceeded 1,500 pages and offered countless opportunities for teachers to adapt and develop their assessment forms.[40]

Conclusions

What has the Evaluation Staff accomplished. . . . The most far-reaching effect upon schools generally has been the development of a theory of evaluation which is extending rapidly to schools throughout the country. This theory of evaluation as it is accepted makes appraisal an integral part of the curriculum, gives the teacher an important place in testing and test construction, places greater attention upon the pupil, and gives a tremendous leverage to curriculum reorganization. (Herbert Hawkes, et. al., 1937)[41]

Three years after the Revolt of 1934, Hawkes, in his report on the activities of the Evaluation Committee, identified its leading accomplishment as quieting the fears of an alienated group of schools and developing a positive attitude toward evaluation.[42] This is a remarkable accomplishment made even more amazing when viewed in the light of current trends that cause many educators to live in dread of standardized testing. In his 1934 conference presentation, Tyler encouraged educators to enlarge their conception of evaluation, and many Eight-Year Study school faculties met this challenge. Evaluation and curriculum became closely linked in positive ways, and assessment was seen as a means for curricular improvement rather than a determinant of the program of study. No longer used merely for sorting students, evaluation was returned to its etymological roots: the process of drawing out values and of examining and reconsidering what should be educationally important. Ongoing discussion now proved to be an integral and important aspect of evaluation, and extensive discourse about values naturally led from the "testing of students" to the "evaluating of programs." Tyler placed this responsibility for assessing school programs on teachers, willingly accepted by many because of a lively commitment to and concern for the future of their students.

Tyler believed in systematic inquiry as a means for school improvement. Successful experimentation required valid data, and appraisal represented the process by which such information is obtained. He also maintained that experimentation should be site-specific and situational and that generalizations should always be understood as tentative and uncertain. Teachers' actual problems, not hypothetical situations, dominated his interests and guided the work of the staff: "Teachers have many such problems to solve, real problems, perplexing problems. Many of them can be partially if not wholly solved by means of similar investigations carried on by teachers themselves."[43] Recognizing the value of formal (traditional) educational research, he acknowledged that there would always be an important place for studies seeking to control variables and to test hypotheses, yet he was convinced that such work was necessarily constrained. For Tyler, establishing validity rather than both validity and reliability was most important, since he understood that teachers work in specific classrooms and with individual children and that their primary concern is to ameliorate problems specific to this work and context.

When Tyler stood at the podium at the Third Annual Conference on Testing in the autumn of 1934, he could not have imagined a faithless time like ours—a time when teachers are seen by policy makers less as sources of solutions to pressing educational problems and more as impediments to improvement, a time when curricular creativity is conceived merely as replicating programs from site to site. Tyler fully recognized the complexity of teaching and learning and knew that many individual teachers failed to measure up, but he maintained an essential faith in school experimentation throughout his career, asserting that thoughtful educators, when provided the requisite resources and possessing good data, could develop fruitful experiences for their students and, through ongoing assessment, engage successfully in a process of continuous educational improvement. Further, he affirmed that school experimentation could succeed, even with "no indubitable proof." To him, the task of appraisal and evaluation served to assist educators in this quest, to provide solid data that would enable good educational decisions, not to punish or embarrass teachers or students.

(The authors wish to express their appreciation to Lorin Anderson for his insights into Ralph Tyler's primary interest in validity.)

Vignette

Understanding Ralph Tyler (1902–1994)

Ralph W. Tyler, photograph, 1932, Ohio State University Photo Archives

Combine a superb memory, the ability to organize one's thoughts very quickly, and keen analytical ability. . . . Over time such a person [Ralph Tyler] can bring a wealth of experience to solving problems. (David Krathwohl, 1996)[1]

Ralph Winfred Tyler was once described as Mr. Fix-it, a moniker that seems especially amusing as a way to depict the stoic statesman who many consider one of the most important educators of the twentieth century.[2] We wish not to make too much of this description but as we examined his early work we have come to realize the importance he placed on fixing and solving problems. From before his involvement in the Eight-Year Study through the 1949 publication of his renowned treatise, *Basic Principles of Curriculum and Instruction*, his career was based upon helping others formulate solutions to complex situations. Tyler seemed less concerned with developing a distinctive ideology or theory. He did not join the Eight-Year Study intent upon reconstructing secondary education or determining how the high school could serve youth more effectively. His participation with the Aikin Commission was, in one sense, merely another research project and another set of particular problems to address, in this instance with a group of twenty-nine research sites scattered about the United States that he visited regularly by way of "a heavy foot in a fast car."[3]

No problem, as described by Tyler and his colleague, Douglas Waples, in *Research Methods and Teachers' Problems*, appeared too great or too insignificant, and all solutions seemed situational—a resolution at one site might not be appropriate in another, a problem here could become an answer there. Tyler would never embrace any approach that promulgated predefined programs or predetermined solutions. While many of his step-by-step procedures began with the identification of objectives, problems became the all-defining motif and helped orient aims, outcomes, and social constructs. This is one of many points we have come to see during our reexamination of Tyler's writings. While familiar with his work, our recent review uncovers many perplexing questions. In fact, Tyler's career now seems almost as complicated as the Eight-Year Study. Both have become mythlike and larger than life. Both are dismissed at times with a scoff by some, while for others both represent all that is good in American education. For someone who lectured and published widely and who generated voluminous amounts of personal correspondence, there is much more to learn about Ralph Tyler: those tense interactions with colleagues, moments of administrative acquiescence, and stress in his personal life. Much more is suggested than what arose during his many interviews.[4] We know that he withheld certain facts about the Study, and we enjoyed our own game of triangulation as we posed questions among Tyler and his 1930s colleagues. Ultimately, our respect and puzzlement is intensified when we remind ourselves that Tyler was "a kid" as he entered a project that was on the verge of imploding. His role would transcend individual school problems as the Eight-Year Study established him as a spokesperson for new forms of assessment that would alter our most basic views of educational evaluation, curriculum, and instruction.

I

They interrogated me all morning and then I had lunch with them. They went into executive session in the afternoon while I twitted my thumbs. . . . At 4:00 p.m. they came and said, "We would like to have you be the director of evaluation for this project." (Ralph W. Tyler, 1989)[5]

After the George School Conference in June 1934, the Aikin Commission hired Tyler to bring stability to the Records and Reports Committee. Up to this time Tyler had served (beginning in 1929) as head of the Division of Accomplishment Testing at Ohio State University's Bureau of Educational Research. He would not necessarily have been the first person suggested to coordinate the evaluation of such a high-profile project as the Eight-Year Study. Other better-known bureau directors could easily have accepted the contract and delegated the work to staff, as did Tyler himself, who worked only part time for the Aikin Commission and secured the services of a full-time associate director. While not the most famous test and measurement person, neither was Tyler among the inside crowd of progressive educators, having taken his degree not at Teachers College, the University of California, or Ohio State University but at the University of Chicago. Tyler's "break" occurred when Boyd Bode, a member of the Aikin Commission's Directing Committee and whose office was opposite his at Ohio State, suggested that he should head up the project's evaluation component. Bode's recommendation proved significant.[6]

No doubt a leading factor for the recommendation was Tyler's belief in the role of testing not as a way to sort and select students but instead as a way to examine educational means and ends, a view of measurement that would ultimately evolve into program evaluation, appraisal, and assessment. These latter terms were not common in education at that time; in fact, Tyler maintained that he introduced to the field of education the term *evaluation* and coined the word "assessment."[7] Evaluation involved the discussion of *values* leading ultimately to ontological and epistemological questions. With Tyler's celebrated curiosity and logical mind and Bode's delight in poking at ideas and his analytical wit, little wonder that he would have enjoyed his junior colleague's company. Tyler displayed to Bode the intellectual capabilities and philosophical interest needed to assist the participants of the Eight-Year Study.[8]

Further, Tyler represented a much different approach to evaluation than that adopted by the Carnegie Foundation's staff, another factor for his selection and one that must have been known among the Aikin Commission's members. Tyler cites the work of Dewey as his inspiration, as did Ben Wood, a self-proclaimed progressive in what must be construed as a unique application of the term, who also credited Dewey as a source of insight for his own writings.[9] Yet these two progressive educators' pasts were filled with tension and fundamental differences. Previously, Tyler had been invited by Wood, at the urging of W. W. Charters, to design a science examination for the Cooperative Test Service. In contrast to the CTS's widely used General Culture Test, a form developed by Wood that ascertained students' knowledge of facts that all educated individuals were expected to know, Tyler developed a much different type of examination that called for students to demonstrate their ability to apply principles and to make inferences. Tyler believed that this examination form and his other tests "in due time undermined the Cooperative Test Service."[10] Also, during this period,

Wood and Tyler aired their differences in the professional literature, described by Madaus and Stufflebeam as the "Wood/Tyler debate over the necessity of measuring all outcomes of learning."[11] In what proved to be the seminal essay in his 1934 primer, *Constructing Achievement Tests*, Tyler questioned Wood's findings in *Measurement in Higher Education* (a 1923 publication that had been Wood's dissertation) and used his position somewhat as a foil to articulate steps for constructing achievement tests, a process that transformed later into the Eight-Year Study's General Procedures in Developing the Evaluation Program.[12] Unlike Wood, Tyler recognized that evaluation influenced teaching and learning and believed that no test technician alone, without assistance from a subject-matter specialist, that is, a teacher, could "construct an achievement test which is certain to be valid."[13] To members of the Aikin Commission, Tyler represented a clean break from the past: the Eight-Year Study could now emphasize aptitude balanced with achievement, higher levels of cognitive and affective mental processes, and a clear, organizational pattern for evaluation that placed teachers at the center of test construction.[14]

II

> At the initial meeting of a project staff or steering committee, and thereafter, invariably his efforts to clarify the purposes and the procedures of the project would become apparent. He was not content to have his own private views of the aims and techniques of the project. (Ralph W. Tyler, 1953)[15]

While this passage describes W. W. Charters, much the same could be said of Tyler. Charles Judd, George Counts, and Charters were important to Tyler during his one-year residency at the University of Chicago and beyond; yet, we have come to see Charters exerting much more influence than the others and substantially more than we had originally sensed. Judd served officially as Tyler's doctoral advisor; however, Tyler's dissertation, *Statistical Methods for Utilizing Personal Judgments to Evaluate Activities for Teacher-Training Curricula*, represented a component of Charters' *The Commonwealth Teacher Training Study*, a massive accumulation of teacher activities ultimately reduced to 1,001 teacher traits (and a project mocked during the late 1970s by the teacher competencies critics).[16] After completing his dissertation in 1927, Tyler accepted a faculty position and assistant directorship of the Bureau of Educational Research at the University of North Carolina for two years, during which time he conducted "service studies," a term he attributed to Charters, for a type of operational research.[17] Charters, director of the Bureau for Educational Research at Ohio State University, brought Tyler there in 1929 as "the curriculum person," where he worked in the Division of Accomplishment Testing and served on the College of Education faculty.

Tyler became one of Charters's "major men," part of an entourage of junior colleagues who worked on soft money projects. Founded in 1920, this bureau maintained strong ties with both higher education and secondary education and sought independent consulting contracts. Charters assisted his clients with clear organizational advice that was seemingly value-free and able "to reach productive amicable agreement" for all involved.[18] In this "for hire research role," Charters was known at times not to say what he believed but instead to express what would be accepted.[19] Tyler, in contrast, stood by his convictions but similarly may not have always disclosed his beliefs in certain situations on the grounds of the importance of maintaining an unfailingly positive, cooperative role. According to his younger brother, I. Keith Tyler, also a staff member at Charters's Bureau, "Ralph learned much from Charters— his stimulator, encourager, and guide for many important co-operative educational projects"—including that one should work within the institutional setting that has already been established.[20] Problems would be addressed, but the true beliefs of the consultant were seldom voiced.

In 1938, Robert Hutchins, president of the University of Chicago, invited Tyler to return as the University's examiner and chair of the Department of Education. Tyler may well have been encouraged to move, since his power and stature within the field had increased dramatically during the Eight-Year Study and he was no longer "under the control" of Charters.[21] He accepted the position and served as examiner and chair until 1948, when he was appointed dean of the Division of Social Sciences, a role he held until his retirement in 1953. He then became the founding director of the Center for Advanced Study in the Behavioral Sciences in Stanford, California, until 1967. Tyler's remarkable influence on people, projects, and the general field of education is all too well known and need not be described here, especially after the release of *Educating America: How Ralph W. Tyler Taught America to Teach.*[22]

III

Tyler had a genius for inventing what appeared to be highly plausible and simple solutions to very complex problems. Indeed, his entire impact on American education has been through this capacity. . . . Of course, there are no simple solutions to the complex problems of education, but those who believe they have invented them do manage to exert influence. (Robert M. W. Travers, 1983)[23]

Much can be said of Tyler's ability to clarify procedures and to state ideas in simple ways. Perhaps due to its clarity, his work has been widely applied but also often misinterpreted, most notably with his use of educational objectives but also with the Tyler Rationale, *Basic Principles of Curriculum and Instruction*, probably the most influential curriculum book of the twentieth century. Often viewed as a direct, value-free curriculum development process, the Rationale has received its share of criticism for embodying questionable values.[24] In a little-known 1970 interview after the release of "The Tyler Rationale: A Reappraisal" by Herbert Kliebard, the strongest criticism brought against the work, Tyler maintained that he never sought to develop a curriculum theory or "theoretical formulation of what a curriculum should be" but merely wished to pose an outline of kinds of questions that should be asked.[25] Answers to these questions were the responsibility of others, not Tyler.

Tyler lore describes a lunch occasion in the 1930s when "Mike" Giles, Hilda Taba, and Tyler were discussing curriculum development and the 1949 Rationale's legendary questions were conceived by Tyler and written on a napkin: What educational purposes should the school seek to attain? What educational experiences can be provided that are likely to attain these purposes? How can they be organized? How can we determine whether these purposes are being attained?[26] Similarly, Giles and the Aikin Commission's Curriculum Associates were charged with formulating "a set of basic principles for the secondary school curriculum," questions important enough to appear on the first page of their 1942 report, *Exploring the Curriculum*.[27] These included: What is to be done? What subject matter is to be used? What classroom procedures and school organization are to be followed? How are the results of the program to be appraised?[28] Both frameworks stressed the use of educational objectives, although neither represents the use of behavioral objectives as we interpret the term today. Tyler's call to "formulate objectives" required educators to reconsider their most fundamental educational goals and, when located within the context of a situational problem, became a way to reestablish "intentions" (which perhaps would have been a better term to have used). Objectives did not represent the confining, convergent dimension that was later popularized in the 1960s and 1970s with behavioral objectives and management by objectives programs. In fact, the Curriculum Associates describe the genesis of educational objectives in relation to the central purposes of education. For Tyler, behaviors meant all types of human reactions at all levels of cognition. Throughout the Eight-Year Study, objectives were developed for nonobservable behaviors: social sensitivity, appreciation, personal and social adjustment. Yet Tyler is now often viewed as the "father of behavioral objectives," even though he stated clearly: " 'behavior' is not limited to 'overt behavior'; what a student feels or thinks is also included."[29] "Human capabilities" became Tyler's phrase of choice when discussing behavior, and he disagreed with the unfortunate outcomes of behavioral objectives when education was reduced to mere training. Two separate 1973 interviews—"The Father of Behavioral Objectives Criticizes Them" and "Ralph Tyler Discusses Behavioral Objectives"— clearly make this point and many others, including his belief that behavioral objectives had become too specific.[30]

IV

The Cooperative Study in General Education, directed by Tyler while he continued to oversee the Evaluation Staff of the Aikin Commission, remains one of the more remarkable yet much overlooked projects of American higher education. A direct outgrowth of the Eight-Year Study, this implementative study conducted between 1939 and 1945 was also funded by the General Education Board. However, the ACE, as opposed to the PEA, served as its fiscal agent. For this particular program, Tyler coordinated the participation of twenty-five colleges that sought to redevelop their general education programs (in contrast to the twenty-nine high schools that were then in the process of redesigning their general education programs). A four-volume report was released in 1947, which included a general overview of the program, *Cooperation in General Education*, along with reports devoted to experimentation in the humanities, the social studies, sciences, and student personnel services.[31] These postsecondary institutions represented a broader cross section of American education—geographically, racially, socioeconomically—than the Aikin Commission high schools. College faculty and staff redefined their postsecondary curriculum and developed educational aims and objectives (including the role of personal-social relations and social understanding). Their use of the concept "cooperation" sought specifically to build democratic communities for the development of educational programs, and the study revolved around annual five-week summer workshops held at the University of Chicago from 1939 to 1944 for staff from the participating institutions. Tyler believed that the Cooperative Study schools progressed more rapidly with their experimental work than the Aikin Commission schools, in part because the ACE asked him "to follow the procedure that worked so well with the Eight-Year Study."[32]

Yet while similar to the intent of the Aikin Commission, Tyler took the Cooperative Study in a much different direction with the development of the primary evaluation instrument. The "inventory," a term selected intentionally as an alternative to "test," represented a form of student appraisal that merged achievement and aptitude tests with surveys of student opinions. Inventories, published and distributed by the ACE's Cooperative Test Service, were similar to the Aikin Commission's "Scale of Beliefs" assessment instruments but took into account (some) knowledge as well as values. Tyler saw the inventory as a way to balance 'the three elements so important in an effective program of general education: the college's responsibility to society, to the student, and to the cultural heritage" (subject matter).[33] Perhaps more significant, the inventory recognized students' roles in the testing process. As Tyler had transferred evaluation from test technicians to classroom teachers in the Eight-Year Study, the Cooperative Study shifted assessment to a collaborative relationship between teacher and student. The significance of this postsecondary conception of assessment is astonishing and remains unexplored to this day.

V

Understanding Ralph Tyler remains as challenging as those many problems he sought to solve. Tyler, representing a complex mix of radical and conservative ideas, has become a lighting rod for dissent, somewhat ironic for such an affable man with a mannered smile, a clever retort, and a penchant for helping others. When Tyler turned his attention to classroom problems, he persuaded educators to reexamine basic, taken-for-granted educational practices and traditions. When he urged the use of objectives, he was offering teachers the opportunity to reconsider their educational lives in classrooms, a setting deeply entrenched in nineteenth century educational practices. And when he advised educators to attach behaviors to outcomes, he was placing the responsibility of evaluation in the hands of teachers and encouraging them to look critically at the consequences of their actions. In many respects, his work continues to justify those activities for educators of the twenty-first century.

Yet with the many accolades, Tyler also worked within the safety of the status quo, within an accepted educational system and already established mores. As facilitator, others—not Tyler—determined ultimately educational practice. In what is certainly an odd statement from one of the most important educators of the twentieth century, Tyler once said, "You can't take responsibility for what other people do, so the only thing you can do when anything becomes a cliché is to get a new word."[34] Martin Dworkin stated that "John Dewey is a figure of *partisan* fiction. Extreme disavowals of his importance are countered by passionate assertions of his greatness. The images of Dewey created in this kind of clamor may say a great deal about American attitudes."[35] In retrospect, the same can now be said of Ralph Tyler.

Chapter 4

Guidance, Human Relations, and the Study of Adolescents

It is beyond question that secondary education has characteristically failed to take sufficient account of the student. (V. T.
Thayer, Caroline B. Zachry, and Ruth Kotinsky, 1939)[1]

Introduction

As the first group of students entered college in 1936, the three Eight-
Year Study Commissions were in place to assist school faculties with
their experimental work. Assessment and cumulative records, rather
than testing, now guided the project as information was collected to
help teachers improve the educational experiences of their students.
Thus the overall charge of the project remained unchanged: to find
through exploration and experimentation how the high school in the
United States could serve youth more effectively. But the focus of the
Eight-Year Study was still emerging with little unified vision or clear
sense of direction. Through these initial years, Commission staff found
that their conversations were directed less on youth and more on the
nature of schooling. Knowledge of adolescence—the period from high
school through college, ages sixteen to twenty-four—was either outdated or nonexistent. Harold Rugg, reflecting back on this time period,
noted, "There was all too little exploration of the actual personal problems of the young people, their egocentric nature, their sense of infe-
riority and defense, the emotional disturbances in their homes, their
anxieties, fears, and frustrations, their manifold unanswered questions
concerning themselves."[2] With the importance now placed upon student records by Smith's Committee on Records and Reports, leaders
believed that more extensive knowledge of adolescents would greatly
improve their ability to create meaningful learning experiences.

Through the next four years, the study of adolescence and human
relations would become as important to the Eight-Year Study staff as

curriculum development and the college success of students. With a twist of fate, funds from the Rockefeller Foundation's General Education Board became available to support this work. Also during this time, the aims of the Eight-Year Study would expand further as its accompanying commissions included vastly different school settings as venues for research—additional public schools, trade schools, adult groups, and even youth work camps. Although these sites were not nearly as involved in experimentation as were most of the Aikin Commission schools, through the Commission on Secondary School Curriculum and the Commission on Human Relations they nonetheless contributed to the overall experimental efforts and, to a certain degree, broadened the implications and impact of the project.

The Thayer and Keliher Commissions brought many important dimensions to the Eight-Year Study, perhaps foremost being the recognition that genuine school experimentation often results in an unexpected broadening of initial plans. The Commissions' staffs found themselves exploring areas that had not been anticipated in 1930. Their research activities took the groups into unexplored domains—depth psychology in education, new forms of educational technology—and into overlooked instructional practices student guidance and determination of needs. Interest in the high school student's life and development expanded dramatically. The Commission on Secondary School Curriculum and the Commission on Human Relations represented a shift—similar to the Aikin Commission's move from testing to assessment—from recording student experience to studying the nature of adolescence. Lawrence K. Frank, GEB staff member, became a central figure in the activities of the Eight-Year Study Commissions, helping to chart directions for both the Thayer and Keliher groups. Viewed by friends and colleagues as "the orchestrator," Frank would bring together an extraordinary group of social scientists and educators to examine aspects of personality and culture in relation to Eight-Year Study schools.[3] Frank's influence was as profound as William Learned's had been during the early years of the Aikin Commission, and while no group of principals staged a revolt as a result, his motives may have been equally as self-serving.

Conceptions of Adolescence

The recognition of adolescence as a particular stage of human development emerged in the late nineteenth and early twentieth centuries from the work of G. Stanley Hall, "the father of adolescence," who published the first comprehensive psychology of adolescence in 1904 and 1905. Hall's conception, however, is now typically viewed as a construction for the middle classes and a product of elite secondary schools.[4]

Characterizing this time in a young adult's life within a conception of German *sturm und drang*, Hall's perspective was substantiated by "scientific observations" of primarily middle-class white males. The next major text on the subject, *The Psychology of the Adolescent*, by Leta Hollingworth, published in 1928, illustrated how dramatically the field had changed in the intervening years. Hollingworth wrote of Hall's earlier work, "The fact is that methods of study and social conditions have been so modified within the twenty-five years just past, that such reference [to G. S. Hall] would seem of historic value primarily, rather than of scientific or practical value today."[5] She came to see adolescence as a period of "transition" with its accompanying unique biological and social challenges from "learning to shave" to "getting away from the family" to finding a place within the larger society.[6]

By the mid-1930s, some could view Hollingworth's research as similarly dated and comprised primarily of a theoretical conception of adolescence coupled with a few select facts to support her normative claims. Hollingworth took into account the adolescent's interactions with society, but the social context was rapidly changing. The Great Depression had a profound effect on schools and on young people who found themselves unable to obtain employment and increasingly dependent on parents for longer periods of time. McGill and Matthews, in their study of New York City youth, summarize the challenge facing American public schooling at the time: "The youth of the 1930s, confronted by a more perplexing world than previous generations have known, had need of greater assistance to prepare them to earn a living, to discharge the responsibilities of citizenship, and to live their individual lives with success. . . . The times have obliged the public schools to assume greater social obligations than ever before."[7]

While the large number of demoralized, unemployed adolescents in mid-1930s America was unnerving, the situation in Europe was frightening. The German Youth Movement was giving new meaning to adolescence and causing the young to appear dangerous. The PEA Commission members were horrified with the growing appeal of fascism and its glorification of youth.[8] Democracy was engaged in a battle with fascism for contemporary youth, and many Eight-Year Study participants were not hopeful about the outcome.

Origins of the Thayer and Keliher Commissions

In 1932, the Commission on Secondary School Curriculum was charged specifically with "a study of fundamental problems in secondary education," but as V. T. Thayer recalled, the group functioned more or less independently of the control of its parent organization, the Progressive

Education Association.[9] The Thayer Commission ultimately engaged in redesigning curriculum, primarily at the secondary school level, and developed "criteria and objectives for this experimentation relevant to the needs of young people in contemporary society."[10] Its work would take two aligned yet separate directions: one generating innovative curricular materials and the other representing detailed research on the nature of adolescence.

The Rockefeller Foundation's General Education Board, soon to become the primary funding source for the Eight-Year Study, was interested in financing experimentation related to its title—general education. While the GEB may be best remembered for its assistance to African American schools in the South, what is often overlooked is the organization's major commitment to general education. Beginning in 1933, the trustees of the GEB organized an extensive program specifically designed to help transform secondary school programs throughout the United States with grants to various organizations and universities.[11] The Commission on Secondary School Curriculum would play a central role.

The first program of the Thayer Commission involved forming subject area committees in science, mathematics, social studies, visual arts, and language—those subjects typically comprising a secondary school general education program—"to focus attention upon the educational needs of all classes of adolescents in contemporary American society, to suggest methods of studying curriculum problems, and to further well-considered experimentation in fundamental aspects of curriculum revision."[12] (The Subject Matter Groups and their six general education reports will be discussed further in chapter 7.) Frank, Thayer, and others, however, recognized that curriculum issues could not be addressed without considering the needs and characteristics of the adolescent student. Since limited information existed, and even that was "based on more or less superficial opinions, and very little on an appeal to more careful observation and study of adolescents themselves," they established the Study of Adolescents Committee.[13] Directed by Caroline Zachry as a component of the Thayer Commission, the Adolescents Study was conducted from 1934 to 1938 "to discover, collect, and interpret such information about the adolescent as is pertinent to the problems of curriculum reorganization."[14] Zachry's staff maintained a very close working relationship with the Thayer Subject Matter Groups, and each content area committee included one member from the Adolescents Study staff. For example, while the Thayer Commission was preparing the *Science in General Education* volume, Zachry's committee was conducting the Study of Science Interests of Adolescents—research involving an analysis of children's science exhibits, a thorough examination of health, school, and psychological records, and personal interviews with science teachers and parents.

Case histories were the primary research method of the Committee, and staff conducted personality, community background, cognitive, and physical studies. Centered at the Fieldston High School where Zachry served as director of guidance, the Study of Adolescents group ultimately prepared case studies for 725 adolescents from ten educational institutions. The researchers accepted their charge to attend to the *needs of all classes of adolescents,* and their research included a cross section of adolescents rather than focusing exclusively upon an upper- and upper-middle-class college-bound group. Adolescents from a Civilian Conservation Corps (CCC) camp, a school for printers' apprentices, New York City public high schools, a teacher training institute, New York City out-of-school youth, as well as students from participating Aikin Commission high schools and colleges were interviewed as part of the study. Five volumes were eventually released by the Zachry Committee, each breaking new ground for the understanding of adolescence and providing ways for Aikin Commission participants to address student needs.

The Commission on Human Relations was established in 1935 to study the problems faced by adolescents. Directed by Alice Keliher, this commission "was charged with the responsibility of helping young people and their parents to understand and to do something about the complex problems of human relations today."[15] To this end, the group initiated three programs: a publications series of books written specifically for adolescents, teachers, and parents; an instructional project drawing upon the relatively new technology of radio; and a film program oriented to help adolescents clarify values and explore human relations. Even more independent of the PEA than the other commissions, Keliher's research team reflected Frank's interest in the developing area of human relations in what would become his psychocultural approach to human development.[16]

In fact, the Keliher Commission evolved from a 1934 GEB-sponsored conference in Hanover, New Hampshire, where source materials were gathered to develop a course on human relations. Organized by Frank, the conference invited seminar participants to spend one month discussing contemporary social trends in human relations and personality development. The Hanover Conference articulated the "culture and personality" approach in American social science as participants—including sociologist John Dollard, child developmentalist Mary S. Fisher, anthropologist Margaret Mead, family researchers Robert S. Lynd and Helen Merrell Lynd, and Frank, Thayer, and others—

met to work on an outline for studying human behavior and relations.[17] Mead described the "multi-front operation" as "pulling together all that we knew about human development as we would want to teach it in the schools . . . [it was] our first attempt to formulate all we knew, using the whole range of human sciences to do it."[18] Vast amounts of materials— 3,500 mimeographed pages—were compiled. The seminar ended before the documents could be developed for use by teachers and students with substantial "raw material awaiting a process of sifting and winnowing, supplementation and adaptation." Thayer, when discussing unexpended GEB funds, asked whether he could assign his Commission staff to prepare the conference materials for classroom use.[19] From this conversation the Commission on Human Relations was formed.

Unlike the Commission on Secondary School Curriculum that was encouraged to develop materials within the traditional subjects of general education, the Keliher Commission was not bound by separate subject distinctions. Curricular material was organized according to its developing perspective of the problems of youth. The Commission believed that such work was long overdue: "Youth, given a hearing, bitterly denounced the education which gives [them] no insight into [their] own behavior, the behavior of those around [them], or into [their] emerging and constantly more difficult sex problems. Of even more significance, though not so evident to youth, the school also fails to give [them] awareness of and insights into the culture which impinges on [their] every decision."[20] While the concept of adolescent needs would lead to great turmoil within the Thayer Commission, the Keliher groups oriented their work around three themes: the family, human growth and development, and human behavior.

The two other projects of the Keliher Commission—the radio and film programs—are generally overlooked in discussions of progressive education but prove to be important and remarkably creative ventures. The Radio Program, first conceived in 1934 and clearly a component of the Eight-Year Study, was not well funded, officially receiving three small grants from the GEB.[21] The project experimented with the educational value of radio documentaries and youth forum discussions in secondary education. A series of 1936 broadcasts, with topics selected and discussed by the students from the Ohio State University School, included the examination of war, the nature of secondary school education, the role of parents on the lives of students, and other issues pertaining to radio and film.[22] The discussions were sophisticated and far ranging, giving young people the opportunity to address issues of great importance to them over the public airwaves. In 1938, the Human Relations Forum, involving a panel of adolescents from the New York metropolitan area and representing a wide spectrum of political and socioeconomic backgrounds, broadcast Monday afternoon radio programs from the American School of the Air on CBS, heard by over 300 school groups.[23] Other radio scripts were prepared to accompany the PEA journal, *Frontiers of Democracy*, to discuss *Science in General Education* (the first Thayer Commission report), and to present excerpts from *Life and Growth* (the first Keliher Commission report).[24] The Commission on Human Relations recognized the then-important role of radio—one high school student estimated that the average adolescent spent "about two and a half hours a day listening to the radio"—and used public broadcast as a way to build extended communities among youth.[25]

From 1936 to 1940, the Keliher Commission's Motion Picture Program produced the Human Relations Series of Films (sixty film shorts excerpted from feature films), conceived to generate "instructive discussion" of human relations problems among adolescents and each accompanied by a study guide containing source material, bibliographies, and suggestions for class discussion. The series could not have been produced if Keliher and others had not initiated negotiations for film distribution rights with the Motion Picture Producers and Distributors of America (MPPDA, also known as the Hays Office) in what proved to help establish film copyright for the twentieth century.[26] Distribution and copyright issues aside, the Human Relations Series of Films represented a remarkable undertaking, bringing an astounding array of innovative curricular materials to high school classrooms. The selections highlighted themes that reflected many of the most troubling social issues of the time as a way to develop knowledge and to explore impact on adolescents' beliefs and values. Excerpts from *Anna Karenina* presented the distortion of values through jealousy; *Fury* depicted the behavior of a lynching mob; *Cavalcade* illustrated war seen through the eyes of a mother; and *Black Legion* portrayed the evils of intolerance toward foreigners. Each selection offered many possibilities for teachers and students to connect academic curriculum to human emotions and personal and social values. Perhaps even more significant was the Commission's decision to use the medium of film that just a few years earlier had been attacked unjustly for its negative influences on youth.[27]

The Human Relations films were field tested in various educational settings, and transcripts were submitted to Keliher's staff where "the discussions were studied for evidence of what the film in question contributed to the study of human relations, how young people are influenced by it, and how films are best used in the study of human relations as an integral part of a more effective general education."[28] When Keliher first approached the GEB for funds, she had planned to use exclusively Aikin Commission schools for the field research and development.[29] Ultimately only nine of the schools were selected as experimental sites, with an additional eleven cooperating "educational entities," each offering somewhat more social class and racial diversity than the Aikin Commission schools. The evaluation program was conducted by Tyler's staff, and human relations surveys and tests were administered to students in order to ascertain changes in their knowledge, attitudes, skills, and behaviors. While the project focused initially upon these individual test sites, by 1941 the Human Relations Series of Films was distributed to over 3,000 school settings throughout the United States, and during the period 1938–1939, Keliher conducted fifty-five regional film workshops for teachers.[30]

Reexamining Adolescence and the Responsibility of Guidance

The Thayer and Keliher Commissions began their studies by redefining adolescence in intellectual, physical, social, and emotional terms as a process with no definite moment of beginning and with no clear break between childhood and adulthood.[31] Individuals matured at different rates among different dimensions, yet they would be viewed not as "abstract fragments but as a real personality talking, feeling, thinking, acting in certain not unrelated ways."[32] The adolescent was seen "as a functioning whole"—and not in isolated emotional, social, and intellectual dimensions. While Zachry and others built their perspectives around the ideals of a unified self, one of the more notable aspects of their view of adolescence was its inconsistency. Thus adolescent study sought to engage teachers continually in understanding individual students, to make allowances for any irregularities and, from "an intensive study of adolescence, [to] show ways for more extensive studies."[33] While the Aikin Commission adopted a continuous process of inquiry for the redevelopment of secondary education, the Thayer Commission simultaneously advocated for the continuous examination of adolescents.

As the Zachry Committee redefined the concept of adolescence, members also altered ways of talking about youth. The GEB staff saw this as one of the most important aspects of the adolescent studies—developing new methods to gather data and to study growth and development.[34] The accumulation of student records led not to a statistical quantification of data, as could have easily occurred under the jurisdiction of Smith or even Tyler, but instead to a discussion of adolescents through individual case studies. In fact, Zachry specifically "abandoned any effort at a very wide statistically valid inquiry."[35] "A small, intensive study was preferable to a broad, loose survey," since, according to Zachry, "most of the material available is based on more or less superficial opinions, and very little on an appeal to more careful observation and study of adolescents themselves."[36]

The case study materials varied from brief interviews to memoir-length documents and from a 100-page chapter on "Paul" in *The Adolescent Personality* to a Teachers College dissertation of over 700 manuscript pages examining sixty-four adolescents from one of the Aikin Commission schools.[37] In certain respects, the Adolescent Study represented an expansion of the work of Smith's Committee on Records and Reports, except that Smith's double-sided, Cumulative Record tagboard card was replaced with volumes of data. Zachry's Committee worked with teachers in developing interviewing skills and conducting observational studies. Large amounts of material were collected from interviews and observations, autobiographies, diaries and creative writing, physical examinations and endocrine studies, intelligence and aptitude tests, "fantasy material," group observations, behavioral records and self-reporting, teacher reports, and many other questionnaires—all to portray the total personality of the individual adolescent. The Committee members were not suggesting such extensive data gathering for every student. Instead, they implied that such activities would sensitize and inform teachers about all students so that instructional decisions could become more responsive and thoughtful. Considering the well-being of students now became a central concern and responsibility of teachers.

Case Study Method and the Zachry Seminar

The acquisition of case materials represented a new research activity for teachers and staff and became a topic for numerous sessions at Eight-Year Study workshops. For Zachry, the purpose of the Adolescent Study was not to predict behavior but instead to help teachers learn methods—called "service techniques"—to better understand student personality by observing behavior. Guided by Frank, the Zachry Committee brought together sociologists, psychoanalysts, anthropologists, and educators to discuss, analyze, and evaluate adolescent trends related to contemporary culture, family, and schooling. In a legendary series of weekly meetings during the autumn of 1936 and into the spring of 1937, the group (many of whom had attended the Hanover Conference) met for a series of presentations of adolescent case studies at what became known as the Zachry Seminar. While the tone of the seminar appeared more in keeping with a psychiatrist's rather than an educator's conversation of cases, activities still addressed how information could be used by classroom teachers to "get a picture of the all-round development, interests, and needs of adolescent boys and girls."[38] The seminar, held at her Manhattan apartment, became a setting for Zachry to explore ideas for her future teacher workshops.

Case study became the preferred form of discourse, involving extensive dialogue as teachers and staff came together to find ways to understand and assist students.

> If faculty and specialists meet regularly in conference, they can pool their insights into the adolescent's striving and difficulties. Each staff member has need of information the others can contribute. In some schools they may have insufficient time for conference on any but troublesome cases. It is, however, manifest that much is to be gained, particularly for a crowded school program, by periodic conferences in which various staff members share their knowledge not only of the student who is unusually troubled but of the boy or girl who seems to be making reasonably satisfactory adjustments.[39]

The cases brought educators together for discussion of a common goal—the well-being of a child.

Due to Zachry's interests, case discussions became increasingly dominated by psychiatric and psychoanalytic theories. Yet as we examined the presentations, we came to see analysis as prompts for far-ranging conversation; participants reflected on and reconsidered fundamental issues that would redefine the nature of teaching and of the school community. For example, one case discussed whether the difficulties in the personal life of the student arose from her relationships to her parents and if so how the educational program would relate to her real needs.[40] Benjamin Spock describes how cases were discussed:

> In the seminar sessions one person, most often a schoolteacher, would describe a problem child in her class and tell as much as she knew about the child's background. Then the case was open—for questions, for speculation about the dynamics (on this topic the leaders jointed in), for listing further information desired, and for suggestions on management. Almost invariably, the first such suggestion would be to refer the child to a psychiatrist or child guidance clinic for evaluation and therapy. And almost invariably Caroline would put the brakes on this suggestion by saying, "Perhaps, at some later point," because to make that decision at the outset would have short-circuited our discussion. . . . Then, on the basis of known facts plus sensible speculation, we would discuss what attitude and what methods the teacher might use to help the child in school, what information from the parents and from last year's teacher about the child's past or present adjustment might throw more light on

the problem . . . and finally whether counseling in the school
or in a child guidance clinic was available.[41]

While presentations represent highly interpretive views of student behaviors and motives, subsequent conversations became occasions for
encouraging resourcefulness and insight rather than for clinical diag-
nosis. The seminars would last for hours and extend into the late evening
as the participants enjoyed Zachry's hospitality.[42]

Depth psychology framed many of these conversations as some
Zachry Seminar participants attempted, ultimately unsuccessfully, to
bring psychiatric discourse into schools. At an April 1937 seminar, Fritz
Redl lectured on a Viennese psychologist's views of neurotic adolescents and latency of inner anxieties. Earlier that year Redl devoted an
entire seminar session to examine the basic concepts underlying Freudian theory. Sometimes the talk seemed absurd and pushed the extremes.
At one session, for example, when discussing a public school case history, conversation centered on a student's vocation: "an individual with
an over-developed infancy interest in the urethral mechanism might
find a satisfactory adjustment through the choice of hydraulic engi-
neering as a vocation."[43] When Zachry and Blos took this material to
the PEA workshops, not all teachers and staff were particularly enthusiastic.[44] Nevertheless, interest grew, particularly in stage theory, and
Robert Havighurst's *Developmental Tasks and Education* as well as his
preliminary work in *Adolescent Character and Personality*, coauthored with
former Aikin Commission worker Hilda Taba, arose from these conversations with Zachry and others.[45]

Defining Human Relations and Guidance

The teacher's role in guidance emerged in the "homeroom phenomenon"—a place and time to unify students' interests and studies—as it
first appeared in the late 1910s, according to Ruth Strang, a founding
figure in the field.[46] While homeroom was still not commonplace in the
1930s, the Thayer Commission assisted school faculties as they defined
new activities for themselves in the guidance area. For example, at the
beginning of the Eight-Year Study, the teachers at the Ohio State University School were expected to take on counseling roles and to begin
the day with a ten-minute homeroom period.[47] Problems quickly emerged
from this assignment, since the need for guidance does not end after
ten minutes. Soon counseling became a part of every teacher's responsibility, and all shared in guidance.[48] Their fundamental position rested
on the belief that the needs of an adolescent often arise from academic
content and that the classroom teacher is the best person to view and

ascertain the development of students. Teachers were assigned grade-level counseling roles, lunch and free-time guidance responsibilities, and homeroom duties. A role remained for the professional counselor, but school staff believed that the teacher—who witnessed adolescents in their interactions with other students and with content—remained at the center of the process, especially after participating in the workshop activities of the Thayer and Keliher Commissions. Along the same lines at Tulsa High School, staff concluded the following:

> Pupil guidance is no longer a thing apart to be handled by an administrator. It is a definite part of the teaching activity—in fact—guidance has become the key to the learning situation. Group discussion of individual guidance problems is a challenge to each cooperating teacher to learn more about his or her pupils and their individual problems. . . . The teacher is no longer the classroom drill master. He is most interested in the personal supervision and encouragement of pupil growth. The emphasis in the classroom is all on the pupil.[49]

Teachers found their roles expanding in new directions, and all aspects of the school community were considered potential venues for social development, not only human relations among students and teachers but also among administrative and custodial staff in settings inside and outside the classroom. The lunchroom, for example, became a place for practicing human relations—cooperation, social sensitivity, and tolerance—as well as a site for integrating experiences within the core curriculum.[50] At the Ohio State University School, high school students were allotted one hour for lunch, during which time they would proceed as a group to the lunchroom and sit in seats assigned by their core or homeroom teacher. Lunch became an occasion for informal conversations concerning ideas and feelings. Coordinated by a knowledgeable teacher, seating assignments situated students so that their interactions with others—students and staff—proved more maturing. Since guidance had not yet become the sole province of a professional staff member as it has today, the teacher's presence became a way to integrate informal activities—lunch, informal reading periods, homeroom—with formal instructional time and to provide opportunities to encourage personal and social adjustment. While seemingly overwhelming in terms of time and emotional responsibility, core teachers acknowledge that the school day became a manageable, more enjoyable occasion of moving from one student community to another.[51]

With their emphasis on human relations and the nature of adolescence, the Thayer and Keliher groups considered subject matter important and integral to their research. Subsequent criticisms of the human relations and life adjustment movements would not always suggest this. In *Emotion and Conduct in Adolescence*, Zachry stated that the chief duty of the school was to help students "make socially constructive adjustments in the course of their growth."[52] Yet social adjustment did not preclude intellectual growth and in fact included cognitive as well as physical and psychomotor and affective functions. Nonetheless, she still maintained that the school is primarily concerned with students' social development. Others working with Zachry, however, disagreed, placing greater emphasis on academic content as a way to foster adolescent growth. For example, the Zachry Committee published a sourcebook for classroom teachers, *Reader's Guide to Prose Fiction*, a teaching method and annotated bibliography for (primarily) contemporary fiction. The guide was organized according to adolescent interests and problems but suggested 1,500 works of fiction related to these topics, including political issues, racial problems, adolescents' need for escape, and economic topics, just to name a few. Certainly the most famous of all reports, the Keliher Commission's *Literature as Exploration*, by Louise Rosenblatt, demonstrated "that the study of literature can have a very real, and even central, relation to the points of growth in the social and cultural life of a democracy."[53] This volume guided the many English teachers who sought to integrate literature and the social sciences, but perhaps more importantly Rosenblatt demonstrated how teachers could assist adolescents with the development of personality and human relations within the context of the classroom by focusing on academic content. Also, the Thayer Commission's Subject Matters Groups concluded their reports with examples—a source unit in genetics, a course in functional chemistry—along with descriptions of an art teacher's way of bringing personality into the classroom, math teachers' method of observing adolescents, and a science teacher's ability to understand students and evaluate their growth. Their emphasis, as with all members of the Thayer and Keliher groups, was quite clear: personal and social development occurred from participation in academic activities.

Conclusions

> To grow up to be a fit and happy member of contemporary society is not a simple process. (Caroline B. Zachry, 1940)[54]

The work of the Keliher Commission on Human Relations and the Thayer Commission's Study of Adolescents was pioneering. Few other efforts in the history of American education so encouraged a legion of teachers to seek ways to know more about their students and to help youth recognize and understand their own values and beliefs. The Zachry Committee provided a rich and detailed portrait of the lives of children that teachers could draw upon as they reworked their programs to respond to the challenges of American society. Innovative curricular materials were developed for teachers and students, and useful guides were written for parents who were concerned about the emotional well-being and social development of their children. New modes of inquiry were created as well as novel professional relationships, where teachers sat alongside distinguished psychiatrists and psychologists seeking insights into how they might better serve young people and their families. Knowledge of students, along with their values and interests, was positioned within larger contexts "to help [students] find themselves anew in their personal, social, and economic relationships, and to develop a working philosophy of values which will give meaning, zest, and purpose to their living."[55]

Examining Zachry Committee's reports can be disconcerting as school staff were almost transformed at times from educational researchers to psychiatrists and from teachers to analysts. Discussions were highly interpretive. Yet the cases, now frozen in time, can be read differently— as thumbnail portraits in an ongoing process of gathering, interpreting, and reporting data. Zachry's work encouraged, perhaps even demanded, educators to constantly gather data on students in order to reexamine and sharpen practice. Labeling of students occurred, but the impressions were constantly changing with the continuous flow of information. This effort was, as Ralph Tyler recalled, an early form of action research with a practical and moral intent.[56] For teachers, the information assembled about students was part of the subject matter of teacher education—to examine and to discuss in group settings—the educational and social experiences of students. As we saw in chapter 3 with student testing and assessment, the discussions of adolescent social development aimed not to separate or categorize young people but instead to help teachers better understand students. Collecting data from interviews, journals, and class papers represented both an act of professional development and a gesture of care and consideration for the student. These activities brought teachers together as colleagues, linking them to students in new and productive ways.

Currently, the field of guidance is no longer the responsibility of the teacher. Guidance counseling, a professionalized study far removed from the role of teachers, now occurs during appointments outside of the classroom and at designated times during the school day. The quest for the professionalization of education has increasingly led to teachers becoming disengaged from learning about students and their parents. Student records of various kinds are still being accumulated but generally not in ways intended to help administrators and teachers improve their curriculum and instruction. The data tend to have other purposes, often political and legal. Further, we see little evidence that counselors are engaged in conversations with students that foster better human relations and clarity of values and beliefs. A 2004 National Center for Education survey found guidance counselors primarily involved with course scheduling and college applications. Any remaining time was allocated to attendance, discipline, and other issues, including record keeping. "Nowhere was there reference to time spent directing the intellectual and moral growth of students or serving as their friends and mentors."[57] In fact, counselors have too often been reduced to clerking, and student records are often of little more than administrative value. This is quite a contrast from those Eight-Year Study participants who maintained as one of their most basic beliefs that "the reconstruction of the curriculum must proceed in the light of knowledge of the adolescent."[58] When contemporary research indicates that just one caring and able teacher can make a positive difference in a student's life,[59] the work of Zachry, Keliher, and their colleagues displays how teachers may obtain rich and detailed information about their students and how this interest in adolescence and human relations culminates in better educational experiences for the young.

Vignette

Alice V. Keliher (1903–1995): Fate, Frank, and Film

Alice V. Keliher, photograph, ca. 1936, New York University Archives

In the spring of 1929 I was awarded the Grace Dodge Fellowship for the following year. . . . This made it possible to join a small group . . . in a tour of children's programs in Europe. I begged and borrowed so I could take with me a movie camera and managed to take motion pictures of many of the centers we visited. . . . This probably was one of those strokes of luck that occur once in a lifetime. (Alice V. Keliher, c 1975)[1]

Alice Keliher's career included other strokes of luck, many stemming specifically from taking this one movie camera to Europe. Her curiosity and zeal for innovative forms of technology, along with much administrative talent and an act of fate, combined for a remarkable career. Keliher, perhaps now best remembered in early childhood education as "the grandmother of day care," represents one of the "dauntless women" of that field who combined a love for children with an interest in psychological development, human relations, depth psychology, and progressive education.[2] We sense that there was little planning in her career; good things just seemed to happen, from leading the human relations movement in the PEA to shaping copyright laws for film and guiding the day care system in the United States to serving as a presidential advisor for Head Start. Another view, however, is that her administrative abilities and dogged determination ensured projects to succeed, qualities important to Lawrence Frank, who acted as catalyst, as the maker of opportunities, for her career.[3] This is not to suggest that she did not have her share of difficulties and disappointments—she was involved in a blacklisting incident in 1950 (reported in both the *New Republic* and the *Washington Post*), and her professional papers include too many unpublished manuscripts for us to believe she was satisfied with her scholarship. But her "passionate career-long effort to protect children from hasty, mechanistic, defeating experiences" and her seeming willingness to complete projects no matter how difficult, along with Frank's touch, took her in many wonderful and unforeseen directions.[4]

I

Alice Virginia Keliher was born and raised in Washington, D.C., where she began her career teaching elementary school. She enrolled in summer courses at Teachers College and later moved to New York City where, after one year of full-time study, she finished her bachelor's degree in 1928. Receiving her MA degree in 1929, she completed the Ph.D. from Columbia University in 1930 with William H. Kilpatrick serving as her advisor. Stemming from her film experience during the 1929 European travels, she was offered a position at the Yale University Psycho-Clinic (later called the Clinic of Child Development) with Arnold Gesell where for the next three and a half years she produced "literally miles" of motion pictures of babies for the naturalistic study of infants.[5] This is when, in 1930, Keliher first met Frank, who was then a program officer for the Laura Spellman Rockefeller Foundation, the funding agent for Gesell's project. From this clinical work, Keliher contributed to Gesell's 1934 publication, *An Atlas of Infant Behavior*, which, among other aims, sought to establish a set of behavioral norms for infant development.[6] She was promoted to instructor in Child Development at Yale University but resigned in 1933, feeling "the chalk dust in my blood," and she took an administrative supervisory position in the Hartford, Connecticut, public schools.[7] Keliher held this post until 1935, when she accepted the full-time position with the PEA's Commission on Human Relations. She reminisced years later that she was quite happy with her Hartford position and would not have left without Lawrence Frank specifically inviting her to develop materials about adolescents that would, in his words, "stop fractionating the child."[8]

Keliher's friendship with William H. Kilpatrick, Teachers College's "million dollar professor" and then the leading proponent of progressive education, did not cause her to accept all child-centered practices uncritically. While serving as a summer lecturer at Teachers College in 1932 and 1933, she was upset with the lack of creativity and free expression of ideas at the Lincoln School. She believed the project method had become too rigid, and Lincoln School teachers were preparing curriculum materials well before knowing the background and interests of their students. For Keliher, this most famous progressive practice at the Lincoln School had almost become as static as the conventional textbook:

> We sympathized with one teacher who had selected a unit about the Hudson River. The children were to read about it, write about it, test it, [marginalia: drink it], sing about it, travel on it, do their arithmetic about it, learn its history, figure its economic value. To get all this done in six weeks allowed no time for other interests, possibly timely events, and we sense that the children felt restricted. Their interest waned.[9]

As an alternative to these practices, she experimented with a more flexible curriculum development program from 1934 to 1938 at the demonstration school of Alabama College. While quite similar to the Eight-Year Study workshops, this summer project began two years before that program was underway. Alabama may seem a somewhat odd location for a New Haven and New York City-based educator to initiate an experimental program, however, Frank and GEB funds supported the selection. Often Keliher would be involved with projects that seemed to defy explanation; yet the common element was always Frank, serving either as a grants benefactor or, as she called him, "the grand gatherer," as he brought together individuals in the social sciences and humanities in his effort to explore culture and personality.[10] In many respects, her selection as chair of the Commission on Human Relations at the rather young age of thirty-three may have been viewed somewhat as a surprise. Some questioned her abilities, but the wishes of Lawrence K. Frank and the funding of the GEB would, as always, prevail.

After five years serving as chair of the Commission on Human Relations, Keliher accepted a full-time professorship in 1940 at New York University (NYU).[11] During her twenty-five years at NYU, she taught numerous courses in human relations, elementary education, and child development, established the New York University Film Library with funds from the Alfred Sloan Foundation, served as vice president and associate director of the American Film Center, and participated in various New York City-related activities focused on child and youth services. Her participation in national and community activities increased greatly after befriending Eleanor Roosevelt, who had rented office space next to Keliher's residence in Greenwich Village. She also maintained interests in psychoanalysis, traveling to London while on sabbatical to observe the work of Anna Freud and serving as an educational director for Margaret Naumberg's Walden School, where she helped develop an integrated core curriculum program. Keliher concluded her career as a distinguished service professor at Jersey City State College and then as distinguished professor at Wheelock College in Boston where once again she was directly connected to Frank, who served as a member of the Board of Trustees.

II

> This looks to me like the kind of job which you and probably you alone could do and therefore, I am writing to ask whether you would be interested in such a venture . . . under the auspices of the Progressive Education Association and which will run for a year or 18 months and lead, it is hoped, to experimental courses in human relations in some schools and colleges. (Lawrence K. Frank, 1935)[12]

So began Alice Keliher's invitation to serve as chair of the PEA's Commission on Human Relations, a position she held not for eighteen months but for the next seven years. This was not the primary reason Keliher was selected to lead the Commission however. Frank was well aware of her impressive organizational abilities. Through the course of one month, shortly after accepting the chair's position and while still completing her responsibilities at Alabama College, they exchanged a flurry of letters in which she conceived, critiqued, and ultimately organized the Commission staff and their activities.[13] Some difficulties would emerge characteristic of any expansive, unstructured program. Yet within the context of this focused yet quite flexible research agenda, Keliher displayed a remarkable ability to ensure the completion of projects and to encourage and assist others to do so as well.

Keliher not only served as chair of the Commission on Human Relations but also as its lead researcher, and her final report, *Life and Growth,* was published first among the six volumes. The connection between the Commission's final publications and the preparation of the Hanover materials (the original purpose of the project), however, is somewhat tenuous. Not all Commission staff had access to the 3,500 pages compiled during the 1934 conference. Louise Rosenblatt, for example, did not recall drawing upon the conference materials when preparing her report and other Commission on Human Relations publications appear quite far removed from the original Hanover documents.[14] Further, the experimental nature of the Eight-Year Study seemed to contradict any notion of Commission members merely editing these conference papers for publication. In contrast, "tentative experimental forms" were distributed to selected readers (teachers, parents, and students) for their review and comments of the draft manuscripts. These forms, actually book-length draft publications, included blank pages with specific questions for the readers to critique each of the chapters. Clearly the comments influenced Keliher and her staff. From the 341-page experimental form for *Life and Growth*, entire chapters were deleted and others were retitled and rewritten, and in preparing *Thicker than Water*, excerpts were selected after the analysis of student discussions.[15] This is all to say that the staff of the Keliher Commission, while originally charged to prepare the compilation of Hanover Conference materials for publication, altered and redirected the nature of the eventual volumes from subsequent research and experimentation.

As with any experimental venture, not all work proceeds smoothly, and this was certainly the case with the Commission for Human Relations. Perhaps most troubling for Keliher were the difficulties surrounding the final publication, *Psychology and Human Living*, criticized for being too advanced for high school students. Walter Langer, who had become especially close to Keliher during their work together, tried unsuccessfully to reorient the book from a psychology of adolescence to a psychology for adolescents.[16] They exchanged many letters in 1937 concerning its re-writing while Langer was in Vienna studying psychoanalysis. Scattered within his spirited letters describing life in Vienna and sessions with Anna Freud were frantic requests for affidavits to vouch for Austrian Jews who wished to immigrate to the United States (for which she sponsored three émigrés).[17] Langer continued working on the manuscript after his return to the United States, and in 1940 the publisher seemed to have given mild approval; however, not until 1943 was *Psychology and Human Living* finally released, five years after the first volumes.[18]

III

The six final reports typically receive whatever little attention is given to the work of the Commission on Human Relations. The Commission's overlooked Human Relations Series of Films component, however, deserves further study.[19] Keliher and her staff produced excerpts from feature films, what were then known as photoplays, as a way to engage students in discussing issues of human behavior in a democracy and in defining themselves in relation to family and society. Three categories of adolescent needs—physical needs, needs for human response, and needs for status—provided the framework for selecting over sixty film excerpts. All of the Human Relations films were edited and framed in such a manner as to elicit questions from students (called "the free entertaining of ideas"), and segments were field tested during a two year period to learn what types of discussions would result. Not only did the accompanying resource materials include the standard film summaries, discussion questions, suggested assignments, and a bibliography of related writings but also interpretations of the film character's motives and behaviors, suggestions for furthering human relations, and transcripts of student comments. Louis Raths, a member of Tyler's Evaluation Staff, served as one of the film series' primary evaluators and later developed materials quite similar in form to the film scenarios for the widely popular 1970s values clarification movement.

Encouraging action among students was, for Keliher, the most important aspect of the Human Relations Film Series: "These solutions and attacks on the issues should involve actually doing something about them wherever possible to prevent either the frustrating feeling that nothing can be done, or the feeling that talking is sufficient."[20] She described students forming a welcoming committee after seeing *Devil is a Sissy*, a film describing the difficulties of an adolescent entering a new school; conducting a housing survey after viewing an excerpt from *Dead End*, which depicted a social-class housing incident; and planning a community recreation center after seeing *Alice Adams*. Unlike later human relations workshops where the intent was often to initiate conversation, Keliher maintained that "Young people need to sense their responsibility for assuming action as a part of their citizenship in a democracy!" A distinct sense of involvement—"activity with meaning"— became the intent of the series.[21]

The Commission on Human Relations was not alone in its experimental research with film at this time. Also active were the Hays Office, National Council of Teachers of English, the Committee on Social Values in Motion Pictures, Schools Motion Picture Committee, and the American Council on Education's Motion Picture Project.[22] But unlike these other film programs, the Human Relation Series of Film staff, selected by Keliher, included a distinguished, radical group of documentary filmmakers.[23] Their views of the role of film were in marked contrast to the conservative "Secrets of Success" program, a character education film project of the Hays Office, developed in cooperation with the Committee on Social Values in Motion Pictures, for which Keliher was also a member.[24] The contrast between these two separate groups is quite remarkable, although not fully articulated in contemporary accounts.[25] While the Commission on Human Relation staff would have been selecting lynching footage from *Fury* and draft evasion themes from *Private Jones* and discussing the significance of incorporating such social issues into classroom discussion, committee members at Secrets of Success meetings would have been discussing the importance of adolescent (Christian) character building arising from student viewing of *Huckleberry Finn, Lucky Dog,* and *Tom Sawyer* feature films. Keliher willingly accepted membership on the Secrets of Success committee in her efforts to help secure copyright release and distribution rights for the Human Relations series in what proved to serve as "the opening wedge in securing the release to schools and colleges of films made in Hollywood for theatrical showing."[26] Without her participation in this remarkably complex and exceedingly difficult negotiation with the Hollywood film producers and the Hays Office, the Commission on Human Relations film series could not have existed nor would schools have been afforded the opportunity to show Hollywood films for instructional purposes.

IV

During the late 1920s and early 1930s, Keliher wrote a number of essays about the misconceptions of progressive education.[27] Little did she suspect that her career would soon become intertwined with one of the most important and most misunderstood programs of the Progressive Education Association. In these early essays, she attempted to resolve many of the more troubling questions: how to reconcile freedom with discipline and how to balance personal development with social involvement. Her resolutions were varied as she both defended and criticized progressive education, but *independence* and *cooperation* offered Keliher a conceptual way to work. Independence embraced both freedom and self-direction when based on knowledge and understanding, and cooperation merged social significance with personal interests and experience. Reflecting the personality of its chair, the Keliher Commission would come to embody both of these attributes. Through the guidance and support of Lawrence K. Frank and from the odd happenstance of dragging a film camera to Europe, independence and cooperation would take "the movie lady," as Keliher was called among Eight-Year Study teachers, and the Commission on Human Relations in many fruitful, unexpected directions.[28]

Chapter 5

The Conception of Needs:
A Dilemma of Progressive Education

> That the curriculum should be appropriate to the needs and
> interests of the learners has been among the most misunder-
> stood issues of education, both by those who have supported it
> and by those who have opposed it. (Hilda Taba, 1962)[1]

The Zachry Committee's and Keliher Commission's research on
"knowing the adolescent student" ran headlong into several serious
conceptual and practical problems. Of these, none proved more vexing
than the struggle to produce a workable "concept of needs," what inevitably becomes a filter for determining the scope of the curriculum.
While the Aikin Commission staff had freed itself from external control
and had finally established a sound administrative structure to embark
on their unique form of implementative research, the conceptual
difficulties arising from determining student needs came close to imploding the project. In fact, as will become evident, a satisfactory
definition never was achieved, and sharp differences remained evident
throughout the life of the Study.

As part of the unsettled legacy of progressive education, meeting
the needs of youth has long been an extraordinarily complex and contentious aim but nonetheless has enjoyed a prominent place in teachers' vocabularies, even today, as a way to justify educational practices.
Then, as now, the concept has a commonsense appeal and attractive-
ness that seems, on the surface, to be an obviously useful educational
concept embraced by educators, parents, and even students. After all,
should not schooling be responsive to the needs of young people and
seek to help them mature into knowledgeable citizens and productive
workers? Beneath the rhetoric, however, many issues lie unresolved:
How are needs to be determined? Why is one need recognized as legitimate and favored over another? Are needs steadfast, or do they change
over time as a student matures and, if stable, can individual needs be

anticipated and planned in advance of instruction? Determining student needs—what is often a forgotten or an innocuous task by today's
educators—raises questions about many of our most basic beliefs and,
in the case of those working in the Eight-Year Study, reveals deep differences about the purposes of schooling, the value of various content
areas and their appropriate place in the curriculum, and the nature of
learning and human development.

Seeking a Middle Position

While the grip of traditional educational practice was tight on school
curricula, simply declaring a faculty free to experiment with secondary
school programs did not guarantee success.[2] The interest of the child
had served up until this time as a fundamental theme for innovations
in curriculum development. Yet when the Thayer Commission staff
came together, conversation did not center upon the importance of
determining the students' interests, what had been the focus of intense
debates around the turn of the century over the proper relationship of
effort and interest in student motivation. In part this neglect reflected
the connection of "interests" with elementary education and the child-
centered faction of progressivism. These educators had been criticized
for undervaluing disciplinary knowledge as well as for celebrating purposeful child activity regardless of the worthiness of the goals served.[3]
Drawing on insights from Dewey, "needs" came to be recognized as
growing out of a "mutually defining interrelationship, a 'transaction'
between individual[s] and [their] surroundings" and thereby seemed
to avoid the taint often associated with student interests.[4] By definition,
children were active and interested (when permitted), a conclusion
anticipated by Dewey, who proposed that the student's purposes—arising from habits, needs, and problems rather than "effort" and "interest"—served as the best guide for determining educational experiences.
Dewey argued that interests were associated with self-expression and
failed to capture adequately the nature of motivation.[5] The Eight-Year
Study leaders thus saw their responsibility as that of identifying student
needs as a way to guide curriculum development. In fact, the Thayer
Commission's purposes altered through the course of the project—
from "examining the fundamental problems of education at the secondary level" to "meeting the needs of young people in a democratic
society of America today."[6] What would tear the Commission apart,
however, became the method in which student needs were determined:
would they arise from an exhaustive empirical examination of adolescent students, or should they be drawn from a normative, philosophical
perspective of the nature of schooling in a democracy?

While the Zachry Committee was accumulating a huge corpus of material describing the lives of young people as a way to help teachers determine student needs, five groups were formed in the fields of science, mathematics, social studies, visual arts, and language to address issues in curriculum development. These committees, known as the Thayer Subject Matter Groups, were expected to work very closely with the Adolescent Study staff and to engage in continual cross-fertilization of ideas.[7] The Committee on the Function of Science in General Education assumed a preeminent role among the other groups by framing the definition of general education and the organizing concept of needs that ultimately provided the conceptual grounding for all Commission publications released between 1938 and 1941 as well as for the Commission's summary volume, *Reorganizing Secondary Education*, authored by Thayer, Zachry, and Kotinsky. For these committee members, the challenge was straightforward: eschewing both extremes of child-centered and society-centered perspectives, how best could a curriculum be formed that proved relevant to life challenges and changing purposes of students while also being academically rich and fruitful for life's future expectations and demands? Needs became the conceptual centerpiece for general education: the philosophical, societal, and psychological justification of secondary school curriculum and a filter for selecting and designing educational experiences.

Science in General Education and the Conception of Needs

The approach to curriculum reconstruction through a concern for adolescent needs received its greatest impetus from the work of the Commission on Secondary School Curriculum and its first published report, *Science in General Education*. (H. H. Giles, S. P. McCutchen, and A. N. Zechiel, 1942)[8]

In May 1935, members of the Thayer Commission met to discuss the early research of the Adolescent Study in relation to the Subject Matter groups' initial charge. The research report included a section on social maturity and adjustment that attempted to connect individual students to their social environment. Drawing on its extensive data, the Adolescent Study had identified tentative stages of individual development moving from infancy through childhood to adolescence. Each stage represented different "basic needs," as Caroline Zachry described them, that could not be rushed without doing harm to the student. For example, "At the adolescent stage there is a reaching out to identify with someone greater than self, to reach out to ideals, philosophies and religion, a need for purpose and an increased sensitivity to social problems."[9] Zachry attempted to relate these needs to the wider social context and to identify how teachers might assist the adolescent to make a successful adjustment, to become socially mature and well integrated in society. Reminiscent of curriculum studies based on activity analysis, she insisted her conclusions arose from the "study of experience" and did not represent a "statement of ideals."[10]

Listening to Zachry's presentation, Harold Alberty felt uneasy. Speaking as chair of the Science Group he said that her comments seemed uneven, one-sided in their emphasis on the individual adjusting to change and fitting into the wider society. Alberty remarked that he always shied away from *adjustment*, since for him the word denoted a passive acceptance of a situation rather than making an attempt to change and improve conditions.[11] Zachry countered by asserting that adjustment was dynamic: "That [the individual] must adjust to society as it is now in order to be able to change it." Later she argued that adjustment is "not to a fixed point but to a growing process [of maturing]."[12] Alberty asked, "Will [the student] be competent to react to change if he is always lagging behind, adjusting to present conditions?" To this comment Zachry responded: "Adjusting to society does not mean [being] satisfied with it. . . . A person who is satisfied with his own present adjustment is a turtle," that is, one who hides from problems and life's challenges. Alberty retorted: "I'm wondering what in this description keeps us from being turtles." Alberty wished to encourage active and reflective engagement with the world, a social involvement that embodied progressive activism. Then V. T. Thayer interjected: "But the goal is not, certainly, passive adjustment to the present conditions; nor is it being radical to the point where you are not living in the present at all." Referring to Dewey, Thayer argued not for a compromise but for a middle position: an organic relationship between the individual and society and "an understanding that the new order is emphasizing certain elements of the present one." The discussion came to a standstill and concluded when an Adolescent Study group member emphasized the importance of clarifying terms.[13] The issue was not merely a matter of terminology, however, but of different ways to understand the work of the school and its place in society. Little had actually been clarified as the conception of needs and adjustment would later return to haunt the work of the group and to cause irreconcilable tensions within the PEA.

Adolescent needs continued to be a regular topic at other meetings of the Subject Matter groups and the Adolescent Study Committee, but a clear definition remained illusive. In addition to the concern Alberty raised about adjustment and the relationship of personal needs and social demands, other issues cropped up, none more significant than the question of the importance of academic content in meeting needs of students, however defined. After one far-ranging and animated discussion at a later gathering, Zachry pressed her position that teachers must concern themselves as much with students' personal and social needs as with specific subject matter. She went on to say, "There are specific needs . . . that subject matter can help to fulfill, but I think it would be exceedingly dangerous if the subject matter groups got the notion that that was all we meant by needs."[14] There were, she maintained, both unconscious and conscious needs, and to meet these unconscious needs required a curriculum that anticipated the direction toward which adolescent development necessarily moved. During her presentation at the May 1935 meeting, Zachry, with her growing interest in psychoanalysis, was supporting a developmental and psychological approach to curriculum building where the sensitive teacher, familiar with students' backgrounds, drives, and ambitions—the stages of development—would be able to introduce content precisely when students were ready and able to respond appropriately to the demands of their personal and social situation and prior to their awareness of need.

Once again, Alberty was present for this meeting. He listened and, perhaps in frustration, remarked:

> It seems to me that one of our difficulties in these discussions is the very broad way in which we use the word "needs." We start in by using needs as a very definite drive on the part of the individual and then later use needs to mean those things which we, as adults in our present culture, anticipate that young people need. I am wondering whether or not before we can really get very far with our discussions, we don't have to settle upon some meaning of this word "need."[15]

Another participant concurred by noting that the word "needs" was being used to describe what a student perceived as wants and lacks as well as what adults wished and expected. Previous discussions had done little to move the group toward a common understanding. As a time-consuming discussion of terminology began, yet another discussant raised a question that foreshadowed later issues: "Should we not start trying to get clear about our philosophy? The idea was that we have to do that searching into our psychological approach, [but] what is the philosophical background of our psychological findings?"[16] For Alberty and others, to decide whether or not student needs should be included within the curriculum presented a philosophical and sociological rather than a technical or psychological problem. Psychology alone could not answer questions of this kind. Essential was a clear position from which needs could be determined—namely, a social philosophy.

Zachry did not see the point, since for her the educational philosophy guiding the Eight-Year Study was straightforward and simple, merely an extension of her view of the PEA:

> Aren't we assuming that we are trying to base a curriculum on our philosophy of education, which . . . briefly is our concern with the development of the individual to meet his present problems, which involves studying him and the present problems of society without, we think, any great need on our part for indoctrinating him in any particular direction.[17]

She believed that fundamental needs could be identified empirically and were the same for any and every adolescent. Values—the researchers', students', teachers'—did not come into play in the determining of needs. Nor did a needs-based curriculum constitute any imposition of beliefs and ideals on the part of the school. Real needs were first biological and how they were fulfilled depended on the wider environment. The challenge for the group, she maintained, became one of generating an "inventory of needs," a listing that would be applicable to all high school students and would serve as a template by which to design the curriculum.[18]

Dissent sharpened. Some participants thought such an inventory unwise if not impossible to generate, fearing that in so doing the emphasis would shift away from concern for the individual adolescent's development and toward a predetermined list of needs. A standardized, predefined curriculum would surely emerge as a result. Once again the question of philosophy was raised as members believed the classification of needs could not take place until a common point of view was adopted. Thayer disagreed: "I think the difficulty is not so much philosophical as verbal." Yet later Thayer pressed for a more sociological position himself, a view that would influence the way in which the list of needs was framed and presented in the various subject area publications, including *Science in General Education*: "I think that if we recognize needs as something that arise out of the interaction of the individual and the environment, defined by both, then we must have an analysis of both."[19]

Thayer's comments pointed to a paradox—that human development is both highly individual and social, arising within the maturing person yet shaped by the limitations and possibilities made available by membership in social groups. For those seeking to develop curricula in response to adolescent needs, ultimately the question of philosophical perspective proved unavoidable and became increasingly insistent de-spite Zachry's resistance. It was recognized that the energy of youth could be directed in many different channels with radically different social and personal results. For example, only from a democratic social theory that embraced a view of general education as involving social adjustment and the "fullest possible realization of personal potentiali-ties" did it make sense to emphasize teacher-pupil planning in the curriculum.[20] The desire and intent of the young to have meaningful relationships with adults and to belong and participate in social groups would find radically different expression in fascist, communist, or demo-cratic states. From a biological and psychological perspective, these needs might seem to be the same across contexts, but clearly they were not.

The final definition that grew out of the early work of the Science Committee placed the personal and social dimensions of needs rather than academic content at the center of the general education curricu-lum. While slow to emerge, this view had multiple effects. Most particu-larly, especially through the work of the Curriculum Associates and the discussions at the first Eight-Year Study Workshop, the focus on needs provided direction to curricular integration already evident among the more experimental of the participating schools. The aim of general education, then, became forging a dynamic balance between the indi-vidual and society; democracy provided the conceptual and contextual bond. But this connection was fragile, requiring constant care and atten-tion. Framing the issue as one of responding to individual needs or social concerns may have been "naive," as Hilda Taba later stated, but was also unfortunate, since the relationship between the two is forever shifting and any balance is surely tenuous. When focusing on the individual or society to the exclusion of the other, democracy inevitably gets excluded.

Thayer Commission's Subject Area Committees

Most of the subject area committee reports would be grounded in the same classification of four adolescent needs: Personal Living, Immedi-ate Personal-Social Relationships, Social-Civic Relationships, and Eco-nomic Relationships. The categories proved helpful to those school faculties struggling to form their educational programs around needs and addressing questions of curricular scope (what will be taught) and sequence (how content will be organized). The Science Committee had finally devised a new way to configure a curriculum that would supplant the rigid college preparatory program: "needs [would] serve as a point of departure in curriculum construction."[21] With this classification in hand, the teachers were now able to focus their individual courses around any one of these themes, each of which was proven to be "psychologically valid and of undoubted significance for young people" by the work of the Adolescents Study.[22] Using the framework heuristically, as "convenient centers of reference," Eight-Year Study teachers could identify needs and related interests worthy of study and could determine what sorts of student experiences were most likely to accomplish desired educational aims.[23] In many schools, courses were designed that emphasized one or another of the categories, while some teachers attempted to integrate the needs represented in all four areas.

Consistent with Thayer's views, the Science Committee recognized that needs evolved in response to a changing social environment and the maturation of students. Thus in contrast to a uniform program developed independent of a particular wider school and social context, it was understood that the actual content of general education would vary from site to site, according to the dynamic relationship of teachers, students, and the school setting. In the Des Moines schools, for example, a Personal Living and Group Relationships course unit integrated content originally included in a former home economics course. This unit introduced subject matter in the areas of foods, clothing, home administration, and family relationships as venues for exploring needs and offered another configuration for the subject matter. Des Moines ultimately organized eight areas of human activity to guide curriculum decision making. Other schools configured the curriculum around different sets of needs. Tulsa selected three and Altoona High School focused on four similar yet different themes. The Denver schools adopted a set of instructional objectives organized around the same categories identified in *Science in General Education.*

The Thayer Commission's Science Committee ultimately took a position successfully reconciling and uniting individual and social needs in each of the four areas; needs became "personal-social in character."[24] Thayer's position was clearly in evidence:

> [Needs] do not exist "under the skin" of the individual or in a vacuum. They arise and work themselves out in living, dynamic events which can only be described as interactions between the individual and the social situation. Thus when we speak of "the need of the student to select and use goods and services wisely," we refer to a want (biological tension) or a desire on the one hand, and the requirements, demands, standards of social living on the other.[25]

Adjustment became the dynamic interaction taking place between the individual, "the already organized personality of the adolescent," and the social environment as the students sought to make their way in society "with the demands of the environment and the standards or ideals which it sets."[26] Yet while the idea of adjustment was accepted, Zachry's belief in developmental stages in human growth was downplayed, reflecting the Thayer Commission's primary interest in the sole stage of adolescence, then understood only rather loosely.

Since adolescent needs were conceived as being personal-social in nature, attention necessarily was given to the wider social context of learning and those personal qualities that were to be developed so that the student would find an appropriate role in society. These traits helped define what were the shared aims of general education in a democracy and included social sensitivity—the ability to recognize consequences of one's action on others—tolerance, cooperativeness, reflective thinking for solving problems, creativeness, self-direction, and aesthetic appreciation. *Science and General Education* presented additional distinctive democratic values (e.g., the free play of intelligence) crucial for creating school programs that fostered these qualities. Such assertions represented just the sort of nonempirically generated ideals and normative philosophizing that Zachry had criticized.

Despite recognizing the importance of democratic values for the organization and content of general education, the connection between democracy and adolescent needs was surprisingly underdeveloped. Rather than operating as a guiding social philosophy, democracy appeared as an addendum and not as an integral part of the Committee's argument. In some ways this is not surprising, since both *Science and General Education* and *Reorganizing Secondary Education* were written "in process"—in the midst of the Eight-Year Study's implementative research—and represented the Committee's positions as school practice continued to change and be refined.

Boyd Bode and an Opposing Concept of Needs

While Zachry's Committee debated the meaning of needs, Boyd Bode was busily at work clarifying his own views. Although remaining on the Aikin Commission's Directing Committee, in 1933 Bode resigned from the Commission on Secondary School Curriculum because, as V. T. Thayer remarked, "he was distressed with the way the Commission proceeded to operate, setting up the adolescent study with psychiatrically trained social workers."[27] Like Dewey, Bode was very dubious about the value of Freudian theory for education and thought the Commission leaned too far toward the extreme child-centered position. During this period he was preparing two brief yet soon-to-be important books, *Democracy as a Way of Life*, released in 1937, and *Progressive Education at the Crossroads*, published in 1938, the same year as *Science in General*

Education. The "concept of needs" would become a central theme in both works. "Any discussion among 'progressive' educators is likely to bring on an early reference to the 'needs' of pupils," Bode wrote. Then his criticism becomes biting as he began distinguishing between "real needs" and "felt needs," for example, a child wanting to strike another. Defining the curriculum in terms of student needs called for a distinction between good and bad—between "real" needs and "felt" needs (student desires). Since, according to Bode, genuine needs could not be determined solely from an individualistic, biological, psychological perspective, a standard was required not only to determine which desires were educationally legitimate but to serve as a means for resolving conflicts among genuine needs. Such differences, he concluded, were frequent and inevitable in life and in education. Developing a standard to judge needs required a comprehensive educational program that attended to fundamental aims. The task was not a matter of making lists, a practice that "often has to do with the discovery of needs which are not recognized as such by the persons concerned." Bode maintained that the "only way to discover a need is in terms of a 'pattern' or scheme of values or an inclusive philosophy of some kind."[28] As a direct challenge to Zachry's Committee and indirectly to the Science Group, he stated the following:

> Studies of adolescence may be immensely valuable as portrayals of the difficulties that beset modern youth. But it is misleading to call them studies of needs, because the needs still remain to be determined after the investigation is completed. The claim that needs are discoverable in this way would have to be rated, not as a scientific truth, but as academic bootlegging.[29]

Toward a philosophy of democracy is where Bode looked for a solution to the problem, concluding that there should be "a moratorium on needs, so that we can get down to serious business and bring to fruition the splendid promise that is contained in the philosophy of progressive education."[30]

Reorganizing Secondary Education, the Thayer Commission's summary report released in 1939, offered Bode the occasion to write a sharply negative review while questioning the importance of needs in curriculum decision making.[31] Thayer was taken totally by surprise and responded to his former teacher and colleague's harsh conclusions with "shock and . . . disappointment." Not surprisingly, Bode had criticized *Reorganizing Secondary Education* for lack of an adequate social philosophy. In response, Thayer asked if by philosophy he was insisting upon a set of ideals and standards to guide the school practice. This, Thayer maintained, was just as misguided as the simple acceptance of needs: "Just as we reject an uncritical identification of a ministering to student needs, so we oppose the imposition of standards and ideals upon both old and young." Bode, Thayer insisted, had misread the book. A more conclusive and convincing refutation would only result from "a complete and sincere reading of *Reorganizing Secondary Education.*" In Thayer's view, Bode simply could not imagine needs as anything other than childish whims and desires, suggesting that he confused needs, as presented by the Commission, with interests, as commonly thought of among child-centered curriculum advocates. Bode's bias was deep, Thayer concluded, and inflexible.[32]

Thayer had a point. But so did Bode, who recognized that the history of needs condemned its further use. Bode found no value in the concept as an organizing principle. In his view, a need is always a lack, an absence, and the best and ultimately only means for gaining insight into what students ought to learn—what they ought to be able to do, feel, appreciate, and experience—arises from an ever-evolving social vision and not from a predefined conception of students' deficiencies, however staged or conceptualized. To be sure, student development has an important place in how educators teach and organize the learning environment of the classroom to encourage student growth, but the concept of needs as a determining factor for curriculum development was simply beyond redemption in Bode's view. He failed to appreciate Thayer's defense: the four categories of needs, balancing both personal and social dimensions, helped orient educators to classroom experiences too often ignored by a school system bent primarily on serving the college-bound student. Bode suspected, and certainly Zachry's views confirmed, that an education driven by needs so conceived would divert attention away from the importance of articulating a clear social philosophy and undervalue academic content as a means for developing the cognitive powers required to make sense of an uncertain and a dangerous social world.

On the surface, Thayer and Bode agreed on two points: "Young people must be helped to cope with cultural confusion as they must gain control over and give direction to social change . . .[and] . . . In order to make a personal dedication to the common good effective, the individual must decide where this good lies."[33] Both wanted to avoid the threat of indoctrination, the inculcation of a fixed social vision, on the one hand, while on the other avoiding a naive relativism arising from an open-ended pursuit of student desires and interests, or those "whims" Bode found so troubling and educationally irresponsible.

Thayer argued that his concept of democracy avoided both pitfalls: "Defining desirable directions of growth in terms of the democratic tradition is not indoctrination in the derogatory sense of the word. It does not mean that the school must serve the interests of the status quo. Change is an axiom in American society, and democracy by its very nature implies change and the reimplementation of its own values under changing conditions of life."[34] Bode agreed with Thayer's view, that the teaching of democratic values did not represent an instance of indoctrination except in a very peculiar sense, inasmuch as democracy requires that a person be taught to critically assess the very values being taught—democracy represents a profoundly self-critical ethos. He did not agree with Thayer's conclusion, however, that the Commission had generated an adequate social philosophy sufficient for guiding action and focusing the curriculum. He had, Bode thought, stepped onto a slippery conceptual slope that inevitably would undermine the very values Thayer wanted most to encourage. Without a proper reference point, only "mischief" would follow the educational pursuit of students' needs.

Bode concluded his discussion of the concept of needs in *Progressive Education at the Crossroads* with the warning that Lawrence Cremin later declared "prophetic."[35] Lacking an adequate social philosophy, the future was bleak for progressive education:

> Progressive education stands at the parting of the ways. The issue of democracy is becoming more insistent in all the relations of life. . . . If progressive education can succeed in translating its spirit into terms of democratic philosophy and procedure, the future of education in this country will be in its hands. On the other hand, if it persists in a one-sided absorption in the individual pupil, it will be circumnavigated and left behind.[36]

Talk of student interests and needs easily merge into one another, and the social dimensions of education—the realization that individuals must be educated to discover their needs against a backdrop of democratic values—are frequently simply forgotten.

During the lifetime of the Commission on Secondary School Curriculum, disparate points of view were softened and in some ways suppressed by a driving commitment to recreate secondary education for the good of youth and of the nation. Within Commission meetings, discussion was often intense and differences lively as members struggled to reach agreement. However, once the work of the Commission was completed, distinctions of the sort separating Zachry, Bode, and Counts reemerged and quickly sharpened. The conditions were ready to pit child-centered and society-centered progressives against one another and to "split the Progressive Education Association in 1942," noted by Hilda Taba, that helped lead to its demise.[37] The balance Thayer sought proved delicate and difficult to maintain. Any hope of achieving equilibrium after the conclusion of the Eight-Year Study was largely quashed with the rise of the much maligned and justly criticized life adjustment movement and the more traditional conception of general education as defined and popularized by the Harvard Redbook.[39]

Conclusions

As we write, a vigorous standards movement has swept the nation. Nowhere in the current discourse about education are individual student needs discussed other than in the sense that all children should be able to read fluently, write with a degree of skill, and understand mathematics and science at some minimally competent level for employment. Ironically, neither the personal nor social aspects of needs, as conceived by Thayer, are present. Absent also are those genuine needs related to social growth and democratic responsibilities. This certainly is not the kind of moratorium that Bode had in mind. Presently, in the rhetoric of schooling, half of the legacy of the concept of needs has been severed and lost, the personal side of the personal-social continuum—that portion linked to discovering and enriching individual talent and developing diverse and creative modes of expression. To be sure, biological schemes of development have found a place within early childhood education, but the central question for educating older children and adolescents, certainly from the middle grades of elementary school onward, is how quickly and efficiently can students be moved along through an established, test-driven curriculum? Speed and efficiency are the primary values, and any conception of needs is now viewed as "student deficits" in relationship to an externally developed, usually narrowly academic, standard of performance. One of the few historical legacies of the concept of needs was the misguided life adjustment movement of the 1950s, greatly criticized and maligned, then and now, and attacked somewhat incorrectly as representative of the program development of the PEA and the Eight-Year Study.

Teachers continue, as they long have, to talk in terms of meeting student needs, and they respond with an often tacit sense of what is correct and proper. Despite the danger of unexamined professional aims, in practice such judgments are often made for good moral and educational reasons. Lacking, however, is any public discussion of educational aims of the sort Bode called for, without which there is no possible way for justifying why one need legitimately has claim on the resources of schools while another does not, other than personal preference or institutional habits. Instead, a desire associated with an aggressive advocacy group comes to be recognized as a legitimate, real need. Once embraced, such commitments tend to persist, and the demands associated with them grow.

Responding to student needs ad hoc may avoid potentially contentious discussions about the mission of schooling, but what is lost is the possibility of producing a powerful, fully purposeful, balanced, and morally defensible education for the young. Many Eight-Year Study staff and teachers, through serious and ongoing discussions about the goals of general education, forged an articulate and a defensible basis for determining the curriculum and for discriminating among "good" and "bad" needs. While there often were disagreements concerning just what the curriculum should contain and what student interests should be studied, the concept of attending to both the current concerns of adolescents and the demands of a dramatically changing society was never questioned. When ends are taken for granted and means dominate educational discourse as they currently do, teachers will rarely be in control of their work, and the reasons given for taking one or another course of action will become increasingly bureaucratic and unsatisfying. Ultimately, by avoiding the crucial yet difficult examination of genuine student needs, the values of vocational training embedded in a narrow educational functionalism (a form of life adjustment) will tend to dominate any effort to consider and discuss the basic mission of schooling.

Vignette

Caroline Zachry (1894–1945): None Quite Like Our Dr. Zachry

Caroline B. Zachry, photograph, ca. 1943, courtesy of Nancy and Stephen Zachry

One of the busiest, most popular, most interesting of our faculty members—Dr. Zachry. We have heard there is one in every college, but there is none quite like our Dr. Zachry who listens patiently to all our troubles and cheers us on to make the best of what we have. (New Jersey State Teachers College yearbook, 1930)[1]

Without a doubt, there was no one quite like Caroline Beaumont Zachry. Benjamin Spock, a close friend and colleague, described her as having a "self-assurance that inspired confidence." Others noted her calmness and charisma, her sophisticated wit and humor "with a nice but never loud laugh," and her gentle sympathetic gaze—this from a Southern aristocrat with "a slightly squeaky voice" whose New York City upper east side apartment would become a meeting place for a remarkable group of psychiatrists, physicians, psychologists, and social scientists—Ruth Benedict, Erik Homberger Erikson, Karen Horney, Margaret Mead, Helen Lynd, Margaret Mahler, and Spock—all gathering to discuss work related to the Commission on Secondary School Curriculum.[2]

Other participants in the Eight-Year Study may be seen as more important: Bill Aikin and Gene Smith were the administrative leaders; Larry Frank and Bob Havighurst provided funding; Ralph Tyler solved

135

problems; Thayer and Alberty helped design curriculum; and Alice Keliher got the job done, whatever that may have entailed. But Caroline Zachry was different—beloved, criticized, and ubiquitous. She "permeated" the Eight-Year Study and inspired a sense of assurance among many of the teachers who wondered whether good would emerge from this massive and unwieldy experimental project.[3] While she appears more central than most other participants, her work was unquestionably the most controversial and certainly the most far removed from current understandings of progressive education.

I

In 1924, PEA President Eugene Smith called for educators to keep pace with the most recent discoveries in child psychology.[4] One may assume that these innovations arose from the American educational psychologists of the time—Charles Judd, E. L. Thorndike, and even John B. Watson. Freud and the Viennese psychoanalysts, however, were capturing the imaginations of many American educators, and the influence of psychoanalysis on the field of elementary and secondary education (and its place within progressive education) must not be overlooked. In fact, the presence of psychotherapeutic work in 1920s and 1930s American educational psychology may be much greater than we have assumed, a position convincingly argued by Stephen Petrina in his examination of the work of Luella W. Cole and Sidney Pressey.[5] Among the Thayer Commission staff, few were more involved in attempting to substantiate psychoanalysis' role in American secondary education than Zachry.[6] Her investigations led to remarkable insights, certain oddities, and a few problems for the Eight-Year Study and the Commission on Secondary School Curriculum.

Alice Keliher was also involved in the psychoanalytic movement within the PEA, yet these two colleagues with their many commonalities kept a cordial but rather distant relationship. In guarded correspondence, Havighurst noted the lack of cooperation between Keliher's Commission and Zachry's Committee, concluding that it was "unfortunate—but perhaps inevitable!"[7] Commission staff members noted the difference between the two: Keliher's political maneuvering and Zachry's reticent, quiet demeanor; Keliher's sharp focus on tasks in contrast to Zachry's unbridled curiosity. Separated by ten years in age (with Zachry being the elder), they completed their dissertations during the same year and both professed great devotion to their doctoral advisor, William H. Kilpatrick. Both befriended Viennese-trained junior colleagues—Peter Blos for Zachry and Walter Langer for Keliher. Similarly, each received substantial help from their mentors—Thayer for Zachry and

Frank for Keliher, with Frank displaying equal if not exceeding affection for Zachry. Their personalities contrasted in such ways that at times we suspect Keliher's invitation to direct and manage the Commission on Human Relations served to complement Zachry's casual leadership with the Study of Adolescents, a committee whose work was intentionally open-ended and exploratory.

II

Although Zachry was a native New Yorker, she maintained an air of Southern aristocracy. Her ancestry included leading nineteenth-century South Carolina families (hence the name Caroline), and her grandfather served as South Carolina's state superintendent of education and later as its governor. After graduating from the Spence School in New York, she taught at the elementary and secondary levels in various New York City schools, including one year at the Horace Mann School and later at the Lincoln School (where certain "troubled students" became subjects for her dissertation work). In 1920, she traveled to England and France before returning to finish her bachelor's and master's degrees at Teachers College. She completed her Ph.D. in 1929, and her dissertation, *Personality Adjustments of School Children*, was subsequently published by Charles Scribner's Sons, an accolade for any young researcher.[8]

In 1926, Zachry had accepted a teaching position at New Jersey State Teachers College, now Montclair State University, and worked with both the education and psychology departments for the next eight years. Also, during the early 1930s she enrolled as a student at the New York Psychoanalytic Institute. Spock described her presence there as a rather bold act, since most of the American psychoanalytic societies at that time, unlike the Viennese, "were opposed to teaching psychoanalysis to non-medical people."[9] She remained at New Jersey State Teachers College until 1934, when she accepted the administrative position with the PEA's Commission on Secondary School Curriculum and moved to the Fieldston School where she also served as director of the Guidance Department.

When the General Education Board's funding of the Study of Adolescents ended, Zachry hoped the teacher training component of her project would become permanently affiliated with either Teachers College, New York University, or Vassar College. Unfortunately, this would not occur.[10] Instead, Vassar staged summer institutes and New York University scheduled courses on personality and social adjustment with her as instructor, but neither institution offered a faculty position. She finally secured a full-time post when an anonymous $100,000 donation to the PEA was earmarked for her Institute of Human Development (also intertwined with the Institute for the Study of Personality

Development). Margaret Mahler described the Institute as a think tank introducing Freudian concepts and practices to schoolteachers, social workers, and school health care providers.[11] Throughout this period she also maintained an active practice as a lay analyst. Zachry led the Institute for three years until 1942, when she left to direct the Bureau of Child Guidance for the New York City Board of Education. Upon her death in 1945, the Institute was renamed the Caroline Zachry Institute, and Frank served as its director until 1950. The Zachry Institute appeared active through the late 1940s, obtaining grants, conducting research studies, and submitting one (somewhat ill-fated) manuscript to Columbia University Press in 1949 but thereafter seems to have faded away.[12]

III

The General Education Board funded many different adolescent studies in the early 1930s and actively guided a "personality and culture" area of study (leading to a focus on social adjustment) through the work of the Rockefeller Foundation's Social Science Research Council. The Foundation viewed this form of research as being among its most significant contributions.[13] The GEB adolescent growth and development program, coordinated by Frank, allocated funds to research centers throughout the country, including Harvard University's Center for Research in Child Health and Development, Yale University's Institute of Human Relations, the National Research Council's Committee on Child Development, Columbia University, and the University of California's Institute of Child Welfare. In 1934, the GEB awarded its first adolescent growth and development grant to the Thayer Commission and a second grant that eventually extended Zachry's Adolescent Study project through June 1940. Of all of the various research programs, Frank seemed most interested in Zachry's work.[14]

Zachry's Committee, while merely a component within the Commission on Secondary School Curriculum, had been an integral part of the planning from its inception. By the beginning of 1934, Thayer describes the purposes of the Commission as becoming "effective only when translated into a study of the adolescent, guidance of the adolescent, subject-matter for educational purposes and educational procedures."[15] He featured the study of adolescent needs as one of its primary goals ("beginning at the earliest possible moment") but seemed not particularly interested in conducting independent adolescent research. This work, after all, was already under way at many other centers and institutes. Instead, the Commission "wove together" adolescent study with curriculum development, first introduced at a spring 1935 Thayer Commission meeting.[16]

Zachry served as one of the original five members of the Thayer Commission (before Rockefeller Foundation funding), and we believe her involvement anticipated an eventual GEB-supported staff post as director of the Adolescent Study Committee. Unlike the Keliher Commission, formed three years later, she was not handed an assortment of accumulated materials to be organized and edited. The Adolescent Study was far from being fully defined and called for an independent, leader-guide who felt comfortable with ambiguity and confident of the project's success. Few others could fulfill such a role.[17] Zachry was strong and independent, willing to enter into unknown realms and unstructured situations, and passionately interested in the problems of adolescence in relation to the dynamics of classrooms.

IV

Zachry believed the case histories gathered by the Adolescent Study Committee provided important materials for in-service training. Teachers would gain "new insights not only into their students but into their proper functions as educators."[18] She implicitly forced teachers to reexamine their own beliefs, since psychoanalysis required such introspection as an act of re-education. Her aim was not to diagnose students. Instead, the cases permitted researchers and teachers to imagine and reconsider ways of interacting with youth. Discussions served as an activity of teacher training—an educational process to introduce psychoanalytic and guidance principles to the participants while adopting a preventive rather than a curative tone.[19] Case studies were drawn from ten sites: three of the thirty Aikin Commission schools (Fieldston, Bronxville, Ohio State) and three of the cooperating colleges (Sarah Lawrence, Cornell, Bennington) as well as the New School for Social Research, the Ethical Culture School's teacher training program, the New York City School for Printers' Apprentices, and a CCC Camp in Maine. She coordinated a group of staff members who, in many respects, were more distinguished than Tyler's legendary evaluation team.[20]

Collecting case study material appears to have most directly guided Zachry's personal work and, as we have noted, the Eight-Year Study leaders applauded her committee for furthering this research methodology and service technique. Publishing the final reports, however, may not have been her highest priority. A 1937 works-in-progress document maintained that the Adolescent Study's contributions rested more with the development of research techniques than with its final reports.[21] In fact, on one occasion Zachry requested grant support to secure the services of editors who would prepare the case studies for publication, similar to what was planned for the Hanover Seminar materials. Zachry appeared as if she wished not to be bothered by the writing. The GEB staff, of course, placed more importance upon these publications and were critical of her inability, unlike Keliher, to meet publication deadlines: "From the beginning the Study has lacked the structure and organization which a better administrator and more logical mind would have given to it. As one result of this, publication of its results has been delayed."[22] Some publications never came to fruition, and all five of the final reports were delayed. While GEB staff believed that Zachry should have better organized her committee, we wonder whether the Study of Adolescents Committee could have ever completed such innovative research if the work had been so tightly organized. Whatever the view of his GEB colleagues, Lawrence Frank seemed quite pleased with Zachry's work and always kept her within his inner circle.

V

The Adolescent Study has the virtues and the faults of its director, Dr. Zachry. (Robert J. Havighurst, 1940)[23]

By the late 1930s and 1940s, Zachry saw herself less as an academic and more as a practicing analyst and teacher whose Adolescent Study research was introducing psychoanalysis to the field of secondary education.[24] Her passion for Freudian analysis would be at times questioned by some Eight-Year Study participants who were less convinced of its value. Robert Havighurst noted antagonism at the Sarah Lawrence Workshop for Zachry's psychoanalytic point of view and a feeling of "utter hopelessness of applying the PEA techniques to the rank and file of youth in the public schools." For these participating teachers, the Adolescent Study Committee was "living in an educator's paradise and making no attempt to face reality."[25] Yet Havighurst, who seemed to disapprove regularly of Zachry's leadership, also expressed great praise for her work. He reported that her speech on the needs of youth at the 1935 Midwest PEA Conference was the high point of the event.[26]

Spock referred to Zachry as the best teacher he had ever known, and her many conference invitations and presentations indicate that her encouragement—her belief that teachers could adopt roles as analysts—was most often well received. She was exploring the implications of new theories, psychoanalysis at the secondary school level as practiced by teachers, and she asked educators to reflect on the motives of students. With her assistance, teachers learned to interpret these behaviors in unfamiliar and at times uncomfortable ways. Yet she continued to believe that it was "possible for psychoanalytically trained observers of young people to understand their individual personality constellations more thoroughly, and to plan their education in the light of their total personalities—not merely in terms of their intellectual needs for the next academic step, but in such a way as to meet physiological, social, emotional, and intellectual needs in their total life adjustment."[27] While we may feel uneasy ourselves knowing that Zachry was urging teachers to apply a highly interpretive framework to understand the actions of students, educators were nonetheless devoting their attention to students rather than allowing themselves to be engulfed in the many administrative diversions of schooling. She extended invitations for teachers to join her in this quest, and her calm, confident demeanor gladly embraced those who were interested and still warmly accepted those who were not. The final appraisal of Zachry's Committee noted that the "Adolescent Study has been remarkably influential through the personal contacts of its director and staff."[28] Complimented and criticized, beloved and belittled, there really was no one quite like Caroline Zachry.

Chapter 6

The Core Curriculum:
Rethinking Curriculum and Instruction

> The tendency to meet new demands by the simple process of
> adding new courses without engaging in any basic reconstruc-
> tion of the curriculum . . . [produces] a curriculum containing
> a bewildering variety of more or less unrelated "subjects." (Boyd
> H. Bode, 1933)[1]

Educational problems are persistent and rarely, if ever, resolved,
except temporarily. One hopes that each generation learns at least a
little from the struggles of its predecessors, but with curricular issues
such optimism is not well placed. Consider the following statement
from *Left Back*, a best-selling book by Diane Ravitch, where core curriculum is panned and roundly criticized: "As conceptualized in the 1930s,
the core curriculum de-emphasized academic subjects and centered on
practical problems of 'social living.' All of the other curricular patterns
were built around various subjects. The core curriculum in the 1930s
was supposed to get rid of academic subjects altogether and put students' experiences and problems in their place, although in practice
this seldom happened except in guidance classes."[2] The images con-
jured up by Ravitch suggest that under the influence of the champions
of the core curriculum, subject matter was ignored, even scorned. If
one accepts her position, then students in progressive schools of the
1930s were allowed to do whatever they wished in classes, studying any
topic that caught their fancy.[3] Further, if the core curriculum at certain
Eight-Year Study schools strengthened the educational experiences of
students, then Patricia Graham dismisses virtually any academic achievements as merely the result of privileged lives of the students.[4] For many
of today's critics, core curriculum was either misguided or meaningless.

As we have argued, the staffs of the Aikin, Thayer, and Keliher
Commissions respected greatly the academic disciplines. When applied
to genuine issues—personal and social—they knew such knowledge

achieved its fullest expression and its greatest value. Grappling with the problems of curriculum revision, these Eight-Year Study progressives never lost sight of the importance of disciplined inquiry "for developing human capacity," nor did they forget how school practice supported a principled way of life. The staff developed versions of core curriculum to attend to both of these concerns and added a third to strengthen curricular integration. They recognized that disjointed programs, that "bewildering variety of more or less unrelated subjects," would undermine the educational potential of schooling and its ability to realize democratic aims. Unfortunately, curricular fragmentation remains a serious issue today, weakening the influence of schooling on the young and diminishing the importance of the disciplines.

Faculties of the Thirty Schools developed innovative configurations of the secondary school curriculum for both the college- and non-college-bound student, some of which proved successful while others did not. Their programmatic designs took on many different names—unified studies, general education, stem courses, and common learnings—but they are best remembered simply as "core." In fact, perhaps there was no aspect of the Eight-Year Study so well known and so commonly criticized—then as well as today. We do not endorse all of the curricular practices of the Aikin Commission schools, nor do we see ourselves as the defenders of a term encompassing many peculiarities. "Core" has long had its critics, perhaps the best known being Arthur Bestor who, in *Educational Wastelands*, also refused to capitalize "Eight-Year Study" while recounting his accusations against progressive educators.[5] The term was described as slang and entirely "unscientific" at the Bennington Conference, and Aikin made matters worse when using core synonymously with general education in the Commission reports, a gesture to the General Education Board but one that also added to the confusion. Nevertheless, while the term had no clear meaning, as both Aikin and Alberty admitted, core programs represented some of the most innovative work initiated by the participating school faculties.[6]

General Education and Secondary School Instructional Practices

In the 1930s, not every educational leader supported the notion of freeing the nation's high schools from college domination as proposed by the Eight-Year Study. Not surprisingly, among these naysayers were Ben Wood and William S. Learned, both of whom argued that secondary school faculties already enjoyed too much freedom. From Learned's perspective, the least able students were setting the educational standard, while the most able were consistently neglected. He believed that the public schools offered a mindless curriculum dominated by a "dummied down" potpourri of elective courses that at graduation added up to little. Separate schools for talented youth, along with rigorous and ongoing diagnostic testing to identify gifted students and to guide instruction, would prove the wisest course for the future, according to Learned. Only the very best students should be admitted to college, and Learned celebrated college control of public high school education. In his 1932 Inglis Lecture, he confidently asserted that schoolteachers wanted to follow the colleges, and many would do so with "great rejoicing."[7]

Learned was deeply troubled not only by the public school curriculum but also by the low quality of instruction. This was due, he believed, to the inadequacies of teachers who, according to data from the Pennsylvania Study, had been the weakest college students. No doubt Learned saw good reason to be concerned by the educational practices of the day.[8] Based on an extensive review of educational research, William Bagley wrote in 1931 that the typical American classroom "has been and still is characterized by a lifeless and perfunctory study and recitation of assigned textbook materials."[9] He found that high school teachers depended more on textbooks and formal recitation methods than did elementary teachers and then, in what surely must have upset Learned, he reported an astonishing research finding: Contrary to expectations, high school teachers who were college graduates, the best educated and just the sort of individuals Learned thought would dramatically improve schooling, were the most dependent of all educators on textbooks and recitation. The preferred instructional practice in secondary schools remained recitation, and a separate-subject curriculum prevailed.[10] In fact, Aikin observed that even at the conclusion of the Eight-Year Study, traditional textbook and recitation practices could still be found in many of the participating schools, a point noted by Cuban.[11] On the whole, the curriculum of secondary education was deeply fragmented and increasingly bloated, a situation that worsened with each passing year as new social demands were met by simply adding new courses.[12]

Initial Plans of the Thirty Schools

The first meeting of school representatives with members of the Aikin Commission took place in March 1933. For two days, in the words of Wilford Aikin, the "schools told what they expected to do with their freedom" to redesign general education.[13] For those participating school principals and teachers, initial planning turned first, if not immediately, to core curriculum. Just three months later at the Bennington Conference, Robert Leigh was able to analyze the still tentative yet already submitted curricular designs of the schools. His assessment served as a benchmark for the Eight-Year Study, since these preliminary plans tended to represent the most basic hopes of the schools. He found the proposed core programs to fall into three somewhat separate categories: cultural epoch core, broad fields design, and students' interest core.

Drawing on progressive practices in elementary education, many school faculties proposed a *cultural epoch core program*, which, Leigh wrote, proved to be the most striking feature of the curriculum designs. This approach rests upon the belief that knowledge must be placed within its proper cultural context, and that the study of ideas should be centered around a cultural period, for example "the nomadic epoch." Information takes on greater meaning when these societal eras are configured in accordance with the developing needs of the individual.[14] Each year, students would study a different cultural period; however, the core did not represent the entire student's school day. Students in some schools would also enroll in a set of required courses, including modern languages or, with the guidance of faculty, selected electives. A single teacher, usually a social studies teacher, would direct the cultural epoch program with various other faculty members playing supporting roles. Literature, English, and social studies were integrated within the selected epoch, along with writing, public speaking, drama, and the arts, if possible.

A second group of plans followed a *broad fields* core where specialized subject areas were reorganized into expansive survey topics (e.g., fine arts and music, languages and literature, social studies, and the sciences and mathematics). This design promised coordination among typically disconnected courses and encouraged greater depth of learning by "looping" students with the same teacher over a period of years. Most of the school faculties, Leigh reported, sought to combine the broad fields and cultural epochs approaches such that work in the various fields would center on a specific era. A third group organized the core around the *students' individual needs and interests*. Once students identified a central interest under the guidance of the teacher, perhaps a future vocation or an academic area of study, a program would be designed to include directly connected course work. Since established specialized courses would remain unchanged, the interests and needs of core initially appeared to represent less a curricular shift and more a change in scheduling and instruction. This conception, that of an adolescent needs core as well as the basic types of programs, would change dramatically through the duration of the Eight-Year Study.[15]

Any reorganization of secondary school curriculum would alter the existing balance among the basic subjects, upsetting some teachers and staff. Reflecting national trends, social studies became a central subject of study in almost all of the curriculum plans, and in most programs students were required to take courses for all three years of senior high school. By examining the tumultuous times in which students lived, social studies teachers made a decided shift toward the study of contemporary problems and issues and away from traditional historical overviews. Even Leigh expressed some concern about the growing prominence of social studies and its displacement of "much older and well-organized [college preparatory] material."[16] The study of English literature and foreign languages would be greatly reduced, while reading and writing would increase, not as separate subjects but as integral parts of the broader study of epochs or fields—a development that was troubling to some English teachers.[17] Science would be given increased standing, sometimes as part of cultural epoch programs, but the place of mathematics would be diminished. After elementary algebra, additional studies became an elective with advanced work linked to various areas in the sciences. Finally, art and music were to be expanded within core programs, and new courses, including vocational guidance, philosophy, and psychology, were introduced into the secondary curriculum.

Enthusiasm ran high during the March and July 1933 meetings. Everything seemed possible, but soon a grim reality set in. The initial plans proved exceedingly difficult to implement, and readjustments quickly became necessary. Principals and teachers were not the only ones who had underestimated the difficulty of educational change. Several months earlier, members of the Aikin Directing Committee had begun to confront the complexity of what they had undertaken.

Providing Assistance: The Curriculum Associates

At the beginning of the Eight-Year Study, many of the leaders believed that simply freeing the school faculties from established college admissions requirements would result in a transformation of established practice. Volunteering their time, members of the Directing Committee would oversee the project, and Wilford Aikin would take care of administrative details as part-time director. Since each school faculty would pursue its own plans, the Committee assumed that an occasional meeting to support and encourage the participating teachers and administrators would be necessary. An explosion of energy was expected to lead to fundamental curricular change. This simple view of school reform gave way to the realization that the job was much too big for the Directing Committee. The schools would need help, but the Aikin and Thayer Commissions were in no position to offer assistance until well after the initial program presentations had been made.

The school faculties struggled during late 1934 and well into 1935 to meet the Evaluation Committee's request for statements of objectives.

Discussion of schools' aims revealed that many of the designs were deeply flawed and some overly ambitious. In fact, Aikin reported that near the end of the Eight-Year Study teachers and staff looked back on the time when they first presented their plans for change, that spring and summer of 1933, with "some amusement and with realization of the inadequacy of their preparation for the hard tasks ahead."[18] The designs lacked clear purpose, and the teachers needed additional help clarifying aims and especially developing curriculum. Up until this point, representatives of the Thirty Schools had gathered for various meetings in what were called "study conferences" to share reports of the work being undertaken, but most of the sessions were held at centralized locations, independent from school settings and somewhat removed from the pressing issues and problems of the actual workplaces.

The limitations in the original curriculum plans proved more serious than even Leigh anticipated. He had not foreseen, nor apparently had other members of the Directing Committee, how the culture of the school and the organization of the teachers' work day could baffle even the most well-conceived and well-intentioned design. The Aikin Commission staff gradually came to realize that curricular change would come slowly, if at all. Plans had been made, but implementation often did not follow or was much less vigorous and consistent than desired. Frustration grew, and at the 1935 Thousand Island Park conference, one of the school directors complained that what he saw within many of the schools was "ineffective 'tinkering' with the traditional college entrance requirements instead of actually [attending to students'] needs as adolescents." Teachers seemed to "mistrust the freedom provided by the new requirements for college entrance" and were hesitant to invest their limited energy and precious time to Aikin Commission activities.[19] Robert Havighurst echoed this assessment when he commented in his diary that "the teachers of the 30 schools have been slow in making curricular changes."[20] Even Alberty noted the limited curriculum experimentation among the schools "after a good deal of fumbling during the first five years."[21] The initial aim of the project proved overly ambitious: by 1936, the year the first graduates of the schools were to enter college under the new admission policies, each of the participating sites should have completely redesigned its curricula.[22] In fact, curricular reconstruction took place throughout the entire life of the Eight-Year Study, and the most significant changes occurred during the final years.

A shift in how the schools faculties and the Aikin and Thayer Commissions worked was in order: requests were made for on-site assistance. With funding from the General Education Board, a curriculum staff within the Aikin Commission was formed in the spring of 1936 to work directly with school faculties as requested. In the four years during which the Curriculum Associates offered their services, nine individuals served as consultants in various subject areas, including foreign languages, English, the arts, science, and mathematics.[23] The Curriculum Associates were led by Harold Alberty, who assisted school faculties to clarify their philosophies, and Wilford Aikin, who helped superintendents and principals explore democratic leadership in curriculum development. During the first year, the curriculum staff visited the actual school sites and met with teachers and administrators to determine how best to serve the school faculties but, similar to the Evaluation Staff, they did not impose any agenda.

In the late summer of 1938, Aikin reviewed the curriculum work of the preceding year and noted that there had been "serious study of the social implications of subjects as usually organized; change in content of subjects in the light of their social bearings; further search for fundamental bases of inter-relationship of subject-matter fields."[24] He went on to say that much of the disappointment with the established curriculum prompted further integration of subjects into broad fields, but no approach proved satisfactory, a realization that helped set the stage for more radical curricular experimentation.

Reconceptualizing the High School General Education Program

> Core may be said to be characterized not by the fact that it combines subject matter, although it does use material from many fields, but rather by the fact that it is a cooperative venture in locating, planning, and solving problems. (H. H. Giles, S. P. McCutchen, and A. N. Zechiel, 1942)[25]

Both Alberty and Aikin came to speak of core curriculum as "the school experiences designed to meet those common, recurring needs of young people which may be best organized without regard to conventional subjects or courses."[26] Neither had any intention of undermining the importance of subject matter; core would refocus and complement that work done in the conventional subjects. This definition stood in contrast to the then-common understanding that *core curriculum* referred to courses or subjects taken by all or nearly all students, such as a textbook-driven sophomore English class. Since so easily confused, the choice of the term to describe a unique educational practice—one emphasizing content integration, student experience, and attention to shared personal and social needs—was most likely unwise. For a time the more accurate but awkward phrase *unified core studies* was used.

The educational burden placed on unified studies was tremendous: to meet individual needs, to ascertain new needs, to strengthen democracy in the classroom while continuing to explore significant academic content. How the Aikin Commission faculties addressed these goals varied dramatically, even from year to year in the same school, and the approaches tended to blend into one another. The schools least prone to innovation held tightly to conventional subject-matter lines and reorganized content within courses. Consistent with the original plans analyzed by Leigh, others worked to reconfigure portions of the curriculum into broad fields. Some integrated English and history. A few schools, most notably the Horace Mann School, developed a cultural epoch program. Resembling the epoch design but lessening the role of chronology, other school faculties developed a contemporary-problems core where a single crucial issue, such as the Sino-Japanese conflict, was studied for part of each school day for an entire year. Those teachers most profoundly influenced by the work of the Thayer and Keliher groups pioneered an "adolescent needs" approach.

Based upon his experience visiting the schools, in 1937 Alberty prepared for the school principals and college representatives a refined definition of core and argued that the curriculum should focus on persistent and widely shared human problems that reach beyond the established boundaries of the disciplines, incorporate a diversity of viewpoints, invite a variety of experiences, and include cooperative planning, learning, and teaching. He then summarized the "common elements of core," attributes that served to define a program: core provides for experiences common to large groups, cuts across subject-matter lines, entails cooperative planning and teaching, requires a larger block of time than a traditional class period, and calls for the exploration of a wide range of relationships.[27] While Alberty would later alter these elements in his own core classification, this summary defined and characterized the innovative development work for the Eight-Year Study schools.

Those core programs following Alberty's common elements worked—and worked quite successfully. Each of the six schools determined by the Evaluation Staff to be the most experimental in the Eight-Year Study implemented a form of core—either adolescent needs, broad fields, or cultural epoch—and together they formed the basis of the Study within the Study evaluation of the Aikin Commission.[28] The 323 graduates from these six schools significantly exceeded their matched pairs in college work and, more importantly, dramatically out performed students from the other twenty-three participating schools. Dalton, Lincoln, Parker, Ohio State, Tulsa, and Denver school graduates achieved higher grade point averages; exhibited greater curiosity; were more self-directing, adaptive, tolerant, and cooperative; and received substantially more academic and nonacademic honors than their peers. The research findings were clear: some core programs, these six in particular, served their students well—academically and socially.

Describing the uniqueness and special qualities of core is, to say the least, difficult. As one teacher said, "You can only wonder how wonderful it was to be among a group of core teachers and to go to school each day knowing that it would be afresh."[29] The Ohio State University School offers an example of faculty struggling to build such a program. Their experience, while unique, was also somewhat typical in terms of the challenges facing program development. Parents were concerned about the well-being of their children, students worried about the nature of their schooling, and their principal was interested yet not fully convinced of the benefits of an integrated core. Within this context, the teachers struggled and ultimately succeeded in developing a curricular design most appropriate for their individual setting and for the needs and interests of their students.

The Ohio State University School: Beginning with a Clean Slate

Founded for experimentation, the Ohio State University School opened in October 1932 in order to participate in the Eight-Year Study. As a demonstration center, this public school hosted thousands of visitors each year.[30] Subjects in the new school would be integrated, yet the first director, Rudolph Lindquist, worried that by developing core curriculum, disciplinary specialists could conceivably be misused and underappreciated. The problem of curricular sequence troubled him too, and he appeared to have been a somewhat reluctant supporter of unified core studies. Still, he vigorously supported reform and experimentation. In particular, he sought to develop a problem-centered and experience-based program that would "challenge the powers of all children."[31]

Lindquist wanted a curricular design that would engage students in what he called "essential experiences"—learning characteristic of the disciplines and representative of a specialist's "way of knowing the world [that] is educationally significant to youth."[32] What he meant by "experience," however, proved to be a source of slight misunderstanding. The art teacher pointed out that one might have an experience without any special meaning and, while drawing on insights from John Dewey, suggested that education takes place only when one has *an* experience.[33] The distinction was not merely academic, as Lindquist recognized. Clearly, as Dewey had argued, to have "an" experience meant that there was both a doing and an undergoing, some sort of processing of events and developments, of forming relationships and connections, that brought meaning and established value. From this view, the curriculum was "the total experience with which the school deals in educating young people."[34]

The faculty had been struggling to achieve a shared understanding of the purposes of the school and the central role of experience and in December 1934 arrived at a working conception: "The purpose of the school is to provide a rich, challenging environment involving actual participation in school living, through which each pupil is stimulated and guided in the continuous reorganization of his experience in the direction of a consistent, ever expanding life program and a responsible role in a dynamic society."[35] But how does a program facilitate the reorganization of secondary education? How would the reconstruction of experience, which is an individual and a private act, lead to responsible citizenship and to systematic knowledge of the disciplines? These were troubling questions for Lindquist and the teaching staff.

While Lindquist held doubts about "consolidated courses," he strongly advocated involving students in planning their programs of study and in practicing self-evaluation. He viewed promoting the reconstruction of experience and offering the teaching staff great flexibility to design their programs as critical components of the core program. The teachers strongly opposed externally developed, expert-driven curricula with the accompanying "problems to be solved [and] solutions to be memorized," but they also wanted to ensure that students learned academic content.[36] Lindquist recognized that curriculum must focus on experience and life problems with genuine involvement of students in planning, even when their participation was carefully circumscribed by teachers, as he thought it should be.

During the school's first year, unified studies began in the seventh grade, involving teachers in English, social sciences, and the arts. Science teachers were added to the core program during the following year. A single teacher would be responsible for two core sections of approximately thirty students each and would coordinate the participation of other teachers as their particular subject area expertise, talents, and personal interests were found to contribute to class studies. Throughout the life of the Eight-Year Study and afterward, the University School teachers continued to experiment with ways to involve others in the core program in order to increase the use of specialists while maintaining reasonable workloads. Without question, the entire faculty worked extraordinarily long hours, and sometimes participation in core was merely an added burden. While greatly strengthening the integration of the school curriculum, core did not mean an end to the problems of curricular continuity and coordination.

Lindquist was not alone in his uneasiness about core. Parents had their doubts as well, and so did the students, at least initially. Pupils were startled by what they heard from their core teachers in their first class meeting. Stemming from their experience at other schools, they failed to see the value in having a "two classes in one" long period. They were stunned when their teachers told them that they "were to do [their] own planning under the teachers' guidance, instead of merely carrying out definite daily or weekly assignments."[37] This was not how students and teachers were to behave. They reported that their new role "was difficult for us at first because we had always been told just what to do and when to do it. We were rather bewildered as to what the future held for us. Imagine us, telling teachers what we wanted to study!"[38] Thus began their participation in core and curriculum development.

Once the course topic was identified, planning began in earnest. Students and teachers mapped out the area of interest and identified major topics that met their criteria for study. For example, civics took several forms, each touching on the relationship of government to citizen welfare, with English, history, science, and the arts infused into the course work. With guidance by the teacher, students chose, planned, and undertook individual research projects, all involving library work and many including observation in the community. As a record of their work, students organized and prepared a final report that became part of their cumulative file.[39] Student records, promoted by Eugene Smith's Evaluation and Recording Committee, proved an important source of information to plan future studies and, for teachers and students alike, to identify areas of individual academic and personal strength and weakness.

H. H. Giles observed that when core programs were effective, teachers and students came together and formed a working community.[40] The metaphor was apt and, at the Ohio State University School, core took hold in the different content areas. Students from the 1938 graduating class, "the Guinea Pigs," in their junior and senior year enrolled in a mathematics class called "Nature of Proof." The two-year course was designed to help them learn to think critically and combined Euclidean geometry with an analysis of arguments embedded in material culture. "In this class geometric material was used to illustrate the meaning of proof, as such material had no emotional content and we were not prejudiced regarding any factors of it. By working out numerous geometric theorems each of us constructed his own textbook.[41] Their texts included sections on terms and theorems as the students examined a variety of materials, from Supreme Court decisions to newspaper editorials and advertisements. They noted that, "we are now conscious of the need for definitions at all times," and resulting from their preliminary work with geometric proof, "a part of our class made still another study which was chiefly devoted to learning how to think critically or rather how to avoid arriving at conclusions without having thought critically. This was a study of propaganda which a group of us undertook in the eleventh grade. Some of the functions of this study were to show the most influential agencies in the modeling of public opinion, how opinions are formed with the benefit of methodical thinking, and the results of the use of propaganda—its effectiveness and its dangers. This study was instigated in our social-science class."[42] Through the course of their studies, the students sought out the assistance of a psychology teacher and wrote to a national institute on propaganda analysis. The students reported: "It might seem that this course does not cover enough geometry to give us a good background. But, in the Ohio Every Pupil Test in Plane Geometry . . . the pupils from our school who studied "Nature of Proof" last year made a median score of 52, or 15.5 points higher than that of the state."[43]

These teachers and students truly believed in their school and in its academic programs, feelings that endured over time, as we now see from the recent accounts and reflections of the University School Alumni Association.[44] Parents were involved and became allies in the common cause of progressive education. Teachers engaged in ongoing studies of curricular practice, and the school became a research site for several master's theses and doctoral dissertations. Teachers shared leadership with students who, as they matured, were given increasingly significant responsibilities for curriculum development and school governance. Lindquist realized, as did his successors during the Eight-Year Study, that committed teachers who drew upon the many available resources of any school community could ultimately design a highly successful core curriculum program.

Teacher-Pupil Planning

Developing core curriculum clearly became much more than a matter of selecting and combining content. Cooperative curriculum development, now forgotten, was typically a central activity, most often taking form as teacher-pupil planning. Although crucially important to core and to each school's commitment to democratic living, this activity generated considerable criticism by opponents of progressive education. Though intended as a method to select course content, teacher-pupil planning entailed much more: providing motivation for teachers and students and encouraging both to extend the range of their shared interests and values. Over time, criteria evolved as both students and their teachers became increasingly sophisticated at cooperative work.

This did not mean that teachers abdicated their responsibilities and allowed students to pursue questionable topics, as critics have charged. Quite the contrary; teachers were expected to be more conscientious than they typically had been in traditional instructional settings:

> [Teachers were] responsible for pointing out possibilities which would otherwise be overlooked, resources and limitations which would otherwise be neglected. The teacher must speak in such a way that knowledge and competence are brought into full play. . . . But always the greater experience and ability of the teacher will have most influence on the learning of the pupil as it contributes—through questions and classroom arrangements—to stimulation of pupil thinking.[45]

The following example is typical: Prior to the first class meeting, teachers conducted a preliminary survey of pupils' backgrounds. They reviewed cumulative files to learn about abilities and interests as well as about past academic experience, and they discussed the previous years' work with a view toward program continuity. Preplanning involved carefully anticipating possible topics and projects for study, surveying available instructional materials, and devising ways to evaluate the completed work. Larger school aims were always kept in mind as were students' individual needs. All of this work took place behind the scenes. What followed was often time consuming: a two-month unit might take two full weeks to plan, as time was spent identifying salient topics (often the most difficult problem), assigning group and individual projects, and deciding on common experiences and determining how ideas would be brought together, shared, and evaluated. During the process, revisions would be made as needed. Planning was as much a part of the learning experience of students as was the execution and evaluation of the designs themselves, each a component of the "use of intelligence as a method [of] reflective thinking."[46] Was this easily accomplished? "The skillful teacher, one who has a real understanding both of children and of the treasured wisdom of the ages, has no difficulty in helping children to choose wisely from among their interests those about which a vitalized curriculum can be built, a curriculum vital to boys and girls because it has both genuine meaning and rich content."[47] A typical example, revealing strengths and some weaknesses in the curriculum, comes once again from the Ohio State University School Class of 1938:

> Our tenth-grade schedule set aside three hours a week for science. Under the guidance of two teachers, we chose the modern scientist's conception of the physical universe for the year's

study. Through lectures and charts made by the teachers, we all got a brief survey of how scientists believe the universe was formed. . . . We were then able to line up a long list of individual problems dealing more in detail with the study of our solar system and its operation. Each one of us was able to choose from this list the topic in which he was most interested. After about six weeks' work, largely in the library, on these different problems, we came together again as a class. The following two months were spent listening to individual and group reports. Different forms of reporting were used. One striking demonstration involved a walk from one corner of our campus to another. This walk was to try to show us the size of our solar system. Along this walk two girls had laid out our solar system to scale. This unquestionably showed us, in a way we will not forget easily, how small the world really is.

An examination made it possible for each one of us to rank himself in comparison with the class median of achievement. We all thought that the two months spent in reporting was too long a time for this and should be cut down in the future. This system of individual research and reporting was felt to be an inefficient way of getting the scientific information. It seemed desirable, however, as it taught us to seek out the material for ourselves, to compile it into a written paper and finally to present, orally, the most important facts to the whole class. These skills were deemed highly worth having, much more so than the few scientific facts we may have lost by this method of study. The last month of the year, we decided to undertake a study of our earth's structure and how it had been formed. This was mainly a lecture course. . . . An examination on the material covered in the last unit ended the year's work.[48]

While the students' description may appear somewhat romanticized, many Eight-Year Study teachers have made a point of mentioning to us the satisfaction they received from engaging in this type of work.[49]

Looking back over their secondary schooling, the 1938 Guinea Pigs observed that teacher-pupil planning was one of the unique features of their education, and nearly every course included this method to some degree. One striking dimension is evident in an anecdote told by one of the core teachers, William Van Til, who described a talk given by H. H. Giles on the method. A critical question was posed by a member of the audience who doubted the wisdom of involving students in planning and distrusted their ability to make important educational decisions: "Mr. Giles, in this 'Teacher-pupil planning,' which is more important, the teacher or pupil?' Mike [Giles] memorably responded, 'The Hyphen.' "[50] Just as core curriculum represented much more than the act of merging content, teacher-pupil planning as a form of instructional discourse went far beyond a series of choices. The hyphen represented a working conception of cooperation and democracy in the classroom.

Developing Resource Units and the Thirty Schools

To teach a core class required that instructors be broadly educated and that they maintain a lively interest in current issues and events. Core teachers were typically a unique group, simultaneously generalists and subject area specialists, who could move across the content but also maintain their respect for the disciplines. Additionally, they were individuals who recognized their own limitations and thus willingly sought to involve others in their classrooms. The scarcity of such individuals was one reason core programs were difficult to maintain and even more challenging because the work was all-consuming. Yet at times we wonder if core teachers were merely unknown rather than scarce. Alberty, as the second director of the Ohio State University School, would often receive comments to the effect that with such an excellent teaching staff any school would be outstanding. His usual retort—"your staff may have been just as exceptional; our school allows the teachers to become outstanding"—suggests that many others could have fulfilled and enjoyed core teaching positions if given the opportunity.[51] To teach core provided unparallel opportunities for a teacher's own learning and growth.

Effective core teachers could not rely on textbooks, however, and there were no ready-made instructional programs that could be easily adopted. Curriculum development thus became a responsibility of those who required assistance in initially facilitating teacher-pupil planning and in identifying and organizing useful instructional materials. Teachers also needed help finding the "hyphen" mentioned by Giles—the illusive fulcrum point between the rigidity of predetermined content and the unpredictability of pupil choice. The "resource unit" proved to be the solution, an inventory of ideas and materials for teaching rather than a specific, printed, detailed course of study.[52] Resource units usually included a preliminary analysis of the selected classroom topic to show its relationship to the recurrent problems of youth as well as to their interests. A list of activities and experiences with potential for meeting needs and achieving desired educational aims followed, sometimes without any particular order. Often a bibliography of useful materials was included, along with recommendations for evaluation.

After the 1938 Rocky Mountain Workshop, resource units found an important place in the curricular work at many of the Aikin Commission school sites. The previous year had been frustrating for Des Moines core teachers, who had been trying to develop (predefined) units of work for their classes that would link the student needs categories developed by the Thayer Commission to the " 'respectable subject matter" of a fully integrated or "fused" history and English course.[53] The concept of a "unit of work," still relatively new to secondary education, even well after being popularized in Henry C. Morrison's *The Practice of Teaching in the Secondary School,* made no provision for including students in classroom planning.[54] Teaching units were set out in advance of instruction. For the Des Moines staff, there "always arose the double-barreled conflict between predetermined units and pupil participation in planning, on the one hand, and on the other, the immediate nature of student needs and the deferred values of content based on the social demands of adult society."[55]

To resolve their dilemma, the Des Moines teachers generated their own list of categories that seemed to offer more promising avenues for joining established subject area content and student needs. Plans were made to create resource units rather than prescriptive and detailed subject packets, enabling them to link their categories to recognized subject matter. In this way the concerns of parents for legitimate academic content would be largely satisfied. Using a curricular design that centered on contemporary problems, they established a scope and sequence that distributed the categories across the three years of senior high school. From the perspective of the Curriculum Associates, the struggle at Des Moines schools revealed the potential value of resource units to address the problems confronting core teachers. With these materials in hand, the group could prepare to teach in advance by anticipating potential learning categories and activities and yet provide room for choice, flexibility, and genuine teacher-student planning.

The message was not overlooked by the Curriculum Associates: When education, not training, becomes the aim of the school, variability and unpredictability are inevitable elements in all curriculum planning, even when determining scope and sequence. The most useful resource units proved to be those designed by groups of teachers and planned with their own students in mind. By reviewing course materials created by others, the teams were also given access to a range of ideas and activities potentially useful in designing programs with their own students. But creating their own resource units, sometimes with surprising educational possibilities, proved powerfully educative.

Conclusions

> While current renewed attention to interdisciplinary curriculum is certainly consistent with approved practice of the curriculum field, it is not without its problems. One of these is the failure of many recent proposals to draw from past interdisciplinary initiatives. Periodic reinvention of the wheel not only is an inefficient approach to solving curriculum problems, but it militates against the possibility of building upon existing professional knowledge. (William G. Wraga, 1997)[56]

The conditions and contexts of education are constantly shifting, yet the problems of schooling do not go away. To describe educational change as simply a matter of a pendulum swinging between extreme positions of child-centeredness and subject-centeredness is a damaging distortion, even when applied by critics of core curriculum who tend toward the subject-centeredness side. The result, as we have shown, misrepresents core, at least as practiced by teachers at Des Moines, Tulsa, Denver, and Ohio State schools. Serious academic work was not neglected but embedded in problems and issues during part, not all, of the school day. These teachers sought a middle position that simultaneously honored a dynamic psychology of learning, seeing humans as purposeful, meaning-making beings, and recognized the disciplines of knowledge as proven means for realizing human purposes. Locating and holding this position—"standing on the hyphen"—made them vulnerable to criticism from both sides of the educational divide. An additional concern was often expressed: teachers at the most experimental schools were exceptional, and there were simply not enough good ones to sustain such programs. The Coalition of Essential Schools movement has been a partial response to this criticism. Every school has exceptional educators on its faculty, yet teachers require opportunities to fully develop their talents for the benefit of themselves and those they instruct.[57]

Reviewing the Ohio State University School publications—student yearbooks and literary journals as well as the memoir by the Class of 1938—raises many questions. Surely material of this quality is within the reach of most young people when they share their in-school hours with dedicated and well-educated teachers and work on projects that reflect burning issues and fundamental concerns. In the simple-minded rhetoric that currently often dominates educational discourse, there is no place for student participation in curricular decision making. Rather, as roundly criticized by leaders of the Eight-Year Study, students are thought to be passive recipients of teaching—a position that views teaching merely as transmission of knowledge—which is as false and impossible to sustain as it is socially and morally unwise.

One final point: in the most experimental of the Thirty Schools, core curriculum was lashed securely to the aim of providing students with opportunities to practice the virtues of democratic citizenship, including the ability to engage in intelligent, reflective, and socially sensitive problem-solving endeavors. There is no evidence that maintaining a sharp focus on subject matter produces decent citizens, but everywhere we see the results of a society that largely ignores responsibility for cultivating even the most ordinary obligations of citizenship. To encourage development of civic virtues among all students, citizenship became an explicit aim for many of the school programs, not only the core classes but the specialized courses in mathematics, English, languages, the arts, social studies, sciences, and physical education, as well as the various and diverse school activities from the lunchroom to the school play. Students learned about democracy by living democratically, and core curriculum stood at the center of this effort.

Vignette

Harold Alberty (1890–1971) and the Quest for Core

Harold Alberty, photograph, 1940, Ohio State University Photo Archives

Harold Alberty's participation in the Eight-Year Study decisively affected his career, and in many ways he helped determine the direction of the project. After the completion of the Study and for the rest of his life, he championed an adolescent needs-based and problem-centered core curriculum, a form of general education that he was instrumental in developing during his tenure as director of the Ohio State University School and as a curriculum associate with the Aikin Commission. He could not have known that his name would become so intimately connected to core. This association was strengthened by his extensive consulting work and through the three editions of *Reorganizing the High School Curriculum*, the final edition co-authored with his wife, Elise Alberty.[1]

Originally Alberty had not intended to become an educator. Perhaps stimulated by his father's love of Sherlock Holmes, from an early age he wanted to become a lawyer. In 1913, having simultaneously completed his undergraduate studies at Baldwin University and legal studies at Cleveland Law School, he was admitted to the Ohio Bar and planned to join the firm of one of his law instructors. His future seemed assured when suddenly his teacher died, and he found himself searching for employment. Since he had previously taught eighth grade, he decided to return to teaching and to his surprise became increasingly interested in education and in the problems of learning. Promotions came quickly, and soon Alberty was appointed superintendent of the village schools (assistant county superintendent of the Cuyahoga County School District in northern Ohio). Although he did not plan to abandon his law career, he began graduate studies in school administration at Ohio State University in 1920. While working on his master's thesis, he enrolled in a course taught by Boyd Bode. Up until this time, Alberty had been deeply influenced by activity analysis and the writings of W. W. Charters, whose book, *Curriculum Construction,* became his "bible." Bode's course proved an "upsetting" experience, one that affected him profoundly: "Each day I would climb out on a limb—only to have it sawed off by my beloved professor."[2] Bode's influence grew as Alberty gave up his dream of practicing law and decided to devote himself to the study of educational issues. Yet diverting his legal career did not mean that he set aside his considerable analytic skills. In education, these abilities were put to good use, particularly in seeking to make sense of the confusion surrounding the concept and practice of core curriculum.

I

Students sometimes referred to Alberty in his presence as the father or perhaps the grandfather of the core program. "If so," he would retort with some levity, "it is an illegitimate child." (Victor B. Lawhead 1996)[3]

Curricular integration was becoming an important theme for the Aikin Commission schools as early as 1933, when Robert Leigh first categorized the various approaches to program development. Unlike Leigh, however, Alberty wanted not only to map current practice but to develop a logical scheme that would assist educators to clarify their thoughts about the purposes of core curriculum. Eventually, he settled on five general education designs that appeared in *Reorganizing the High School Curriculum.* Each curriculum represented a different approach to the problem of general education, those educational programs "specifically geared to the task of providing educational experiences to meet the *common* problems and needs of the student, and to develop the values, understandings, and skills needed by all for effective democratic citizenship." Alberty contrasted general education with specialized education, which focused on the "cultivation of the uniqueness of each citizen."[4] General education was seen as that portion of the secondary school curriculum that would engage all students; core curriculum in one of many forms came to represent general education.

Integration became the ultimate quest of general education, unlike specialized education, which emerged "at the point where special interests can no longer be effectively dealt with in groups organized primarily in terms of common concerns."[5] These two concepts—general and specialized education—provided a starting point for Alberty to respond to a set of persistent issues in curriculum reform: Which is more important, content breadth or depth? How does one integrate the curriculum, softening disciplinary boundaries? What is the purpose of general education? He was convinced that the demands of democratic citizenship required focusing the strengths of the disciplines on common problem solving and calling for citizens to understand the complexity of the world. For this to occur, he argued, the curriculum must become interdisciplinary, a move away from overly narrow disciplinary orientations toward engaging genuine shared problems and concerns.

To facilitate an understanding of general education, Alberty developed a conceptual framework composed of core curriculum types. The five core designs were placed on a continuum representing ever increasing divergence from the traditional subject-centered, general education program. Each core, Alberty maintained, was "regarded by some people as being the most effective plan of providing common preparation for democratic citizens."[6] A Type 1 core program reflects a *separate subject design*, with the general education program consisting of a set of independent courses or fields of knowledge, sometimes taught by the same teacher but typically involving other content specialists. Under this model, by far the most common then as well as today, students enroll in English, history, science, mathematics, the arts, and physical education courses and fulfill a set number of Carnegie units. Type 2 core involves the *correlation* of multiple subjects, most often English and history. Within this design, instructors responsible for two or more required subjects emphasize interrelationships among the content fields. For example, students studying the American Civil War in their history class might read *The Red Badge of Courage* or *The Killer Angels* in their English sections. To facilitate instructional planning, sometimes an "overarching theme" might be selected, such as "the sorrows of war." In a Type 2 core, the subjects are taught at separate times and in separate classrooms, but teachers would make links whenever possible, similar to today's Arts Infusion programs.

For Type 3 core programs, two or more subjects are *fused*. Originally, social studies represented this design where history, economics, political science, and sociology were intertwined; however, social studies has now taken on a disciplinary designation in its own right and is considered a self-contained subject rather than an integrated program. A more current example can be seen in "hip-hop curriculum" in which traditional subject lines are softened, sometimes obliterated, and a new scope and sequence involving the unified subjects are developed. Those traditional basic content areas, such as English, math, and science which defined Type 1 and 2 core programs, are discarded as an organizational framework for a Type 3 core, but subject matter from these disciplines is consciously retained and balanced.

A Type 4 core is configured around a *problem areas* design. While still drawing heavily from the traditional disciplines, the Type 4 core determines its basic direction from the common needs of the learners. Subject matter is selected based on problems rather than on balancing a predetermined amount of content, as would have occurred in Type 1, 2, and 3 core programs. The Type 4 core is also grounded in a fundamental belief that general education should assist young people to identify and meet their common needs and directly confront their shared problems. Academic content was central to meeting these aims; however, no predetermined amounts and proportions were designated. In essence, while the instructional setting of a Type 3 program blended stipulated, predefined content, Type 4 programs determined educational experiences from students' designated needs rather than from an academic rationale. Of the five program types, the Type 4 core was Alberty's preference at the secondary level, becoming a focus for much of his professional career. The Other Ways program, described by Herbert Kohl in his memoir *The Discipline of Hope*, characterizes a recent example of this type of core.[7]

Type 5 core represented a final and logical extension of the framework. Alberty found Type 5 core programs limiting, but the design attracted champions among the 1960s' "romantic critics." The curriculum is built around teacher-student planned activities without "reference to any formal structure." Problem areas and other organizational forms give way to the plans set by the teacher and students, and the curriculum unfolds as interests develop and opportunities present themselves. In practice, Type 5 core design usually involves some cooperative effort to establish standards for determining worthwhile topics or units for study. Afterward, when a schedule is examined of what had been done during a term, the program of study would be revealed, and not before.[8]

When discussing general education, then as now, Alberty's core types help frame the purposes of common learning and locate the role of the disciplines in realizing those aims. Traditional curricular questions of scope and sequence must be addressed, as well as the more innovative progressive issues related to the quality of relationships existing between a teacher and her or his students. Alberty's broad use of the word *core* prompted criticism, however, since his framework allowed for programs to be based upon separate subjects. Holding a more ideological view, Faunce and Bossing, for example, argued that "freedom from subject-matter patterns [is] one of the distinctive aspects of the core curriculum."[9] Inclusiveness and comprehensiveness were the goals of Alberty's framework: all conceptions of general education were represented, from crossing disciplinary boundaries to maintaining traditional subject designations and from extending class time in order to explore issues to improving conventional Carnegie units-based courses in standard periods. Core teachers could be unified in their efforts for curricular reform, even though the degree of curricular integration would vary substantially across programs.

II

Alberty's interest in curricular balance underpinned his dissertation, *A Study of the Project Method in Education*, published in 1927.[10] In his study he criticized perhaps the most popular of elementary school progressive practices, the project method, which William Heard Kilpatrick tirelessly promoted as a general teaching method.[11] His critique underscored how he stood between the extremes of child-centeredness and subject-centeredness—between the psychological and logical organization of subject matter—and valued both. For him, these were not antagonistic or antithetical positions. Reviewing Kilpatrick's work on this popular form of instruction, he concluded that the method was hopelessly confused and impossible to tell what was and what was not a project according to Kilpatrick's definition: a "wholehearted, purposeful activity, proceeding in a social environment."[12] This approach tended to overrely on incidental learning, to dismiss the educational value of the logical organization of the disciplines, and to downplay the importance of continuity of experience in learning (i.e., the direction toward which learning was headed).

There was a danger that activity rather than learning would dominate teachers' attention, a concern that led to sharp criticism of informal education in the 1960s. Once, upon returning from the Holtville School, a famed "project method" program, Alberty described a core unit involving children setting up a small canning factory to preserve vegetables that they had grown on their school farm. Alberty mentioned watching for an extended period of time Holtville students canning tomatoes. Later he asked his students and University School colleagues, "How many cans must children can before they have reaped the full benefits of the experience?" To Alberty, the correct answer was "one"; any further canning was time wasted and miseducative and represented a mindless obsession on student activities.[13]

Foreshadowing his later work, Alberty tried to clarify the meaning of the project method by offering his own definition and set of criteria to guide discussion. He saw genuine possibilities in the teaching practice as a means of *indirectly* acquiring knowledge but, he said, careful consideration must be given to the "direction in which the educative process should move. That is, the goal which we hope to achieve when we afford children the opportunity for education."[14] Under Bode's influence, this direction embraced the "moral ideal" embedded in the concept of democracy.

III

After completing his dissertation, Alberty accepted a position at Ohio State University, where he would serve primarily as professor until his retirement in 1959. For a period, he served as university school director, a position that enabled him to experiment with core curriculum and practice democratic administration and supervision, a concept he and Thayer discussed in *Supervision in the Secondary School.*[15] As director of a public laboratory school, he increased the faculty's involvement in school decision making and encouraged curricular innovation that resulted in extending core from the junior into the senior high grades. Alberty also appointed a "Needs Committee" that through its research profoundly influenced the conception of core, serving to define a Type 4 design. Not only did he support greater involvement of teachers in school governance, Alberty increased students' participation as well: initiating the secondary student's evaluation of teaching and strengthening the role of student government in the school. He also added to the number of available scholarships so the student body became even more representative of the wider society. Democratic citizenship was articulated as "threads of continuity," experiences underpinning all school practice and producing a sense of wholeness and purposefulness to the school culture.

To the faculty, the threads of continuity linked learning experiences to the philosophy of the school. Democratic citizenship entered every phase of school life—from students engaging in debate and learning to respect divergent points of view to groups working together to examine issues of importance for contemporary society.[16] Teachers of specialized courses as well as core instructors sought to make certain that every class was conceived and taught in ways to further social sensitivity, cooperativeness, democratic living, and self-direction. In math classes, students analyzed newspaper editorials and learned how arguments were made and evidence marshaled through "the nature of proof." Social studies courses embraced cooperation and self-direction as students and teachers studied their community as a laboratory for examining social class issues and the effects of industrialization on health and well-being.[17] To what degree "democratic citizenship" was manifested at the University School really can never be fully determined. Under Alberty's guidance, the issues were taken seriously by faculty and students. Involvement in the wider community was extensive, students became more responsible for their education, and their attitudes toward others and their world deepened or were changed to reflect values more consistent with a democracy struggling to survive in what was a hostile world.

IV

Once Alberty said to one of his students, "If educators would only take the idea of learning as the reconstruction of experience seriously, a revolution would follow."[18] In his own teaching, he took this concept seriously, anticipating the rise of constructivism. One student maintained that he brought "great discovery" to education: "He showed me that a successful teacher must create situations wherein students would be passionately jarred into the realization that there are critical unresolved problems in democracy, and he further showed me that a good teacher will create an equally passionate desire to find some conclusions."[19] He understood that reconstruction does not come easily, and as a teacher his commitment to his pupils' learning was unbounded. He supported students in a variety of ways—lending money, providing hospitality, listening to troubles, and generously and frequently quoting their work in his publications. But as gracious and generous as he was to colleagues and students, he could also be sarcastic and sometimes biting when engaged in a battle over ideas. Like his mentor, he pushed students hard and was impatient with sloppy thinking and conclusions too easily reached.

Throughout his career, Alberty sought broad and far-reaching curriculum reform and invited educators to engage with him in middle-range theorizing, bringing practice and social philosophy into intimate interaction. At present, curriculum design work in local schools is sorely neglected. Talk of curricular integration seems all but forgotten, while textbook publishers go about their business and policy makers quietly dictate the curriculum. Curriculum theory has splintered often into subcategories of identity politics, mostly of marginal interest to elementary and secondary school educators. For teachers, instruction has subsumed curriculum. In such a context, Alberty's core curriculum types could play an important role in educational renewal and highlight the importance of revitalizing conversations and providing a language for conceptualizing and planning educational experiences.

Teachers and administrators currently involved in curriculum reform will likely be well served by revisiting Alberty's editions of *Reorganizing the High School Curriculum* and that of specific Eight-Year Study core programs as described in the Aikin Commission's final report, *Thirty Schools Tell Their Story*. After a period of relative silence, curricular dilemmas have re-emerged in slightly new forms to perplex educators: What is curriculum integration? What organizational principles or patterns ought to guide integration? These issues were familiar to participants in the Study, but to a new generation of educators they are novel and certainly problematic. Without concepts useful for deliberation about the design of integrated curricula, educators currently tend to struggle to make sense of what must be done, lacking a place to begin. Efforts to "connect various disciplines in some way" have become a kind of courageous trial-and-error foray into the unknown, an experience of stumbling along toward an uncertain but compelling educational vision. As Alberty's core types invited all of his contemporaries to gather and examine similarities and differences, his framework extends an invitation to educators of the future and offers possible solutions to many of the most basic issues of curriculum design.

Chapter 7

The Importance of Social Philosophy: Democracy as a Way of Life

Democracy must be reborn with each generation, and education is its midwife. (John Dewey, 1916)[1]

When George Counts spoke at the February 1932 PEA annual
conference in Baltimore, he hoped his words would lead to action, to
a fundamental shift in the Association's priorities. His comments were
sharp and unforgiving as he sought to arouse members to recognize
their own class biases and to confront through schooling the serious
economic and social issues of the day. The keynote address, "Dare
Progressive Education be Progressive?," served as a pointed reminder
that the PEA had not clearly articulated a set of social aims and that
traditional political and economic interests remained unquestioned,
reflecting the values of the "liberal-minded upper middle class who
send their children to the Progressive schools."[2] This point may have
been self-evident to Counts but not to the large numbers of PEA delegates who at first sat in stunned silence. Subsequent discussions threw
the conference into pandemonium as sessions were cancelled and
members stayed into the evening to discuss the implications of the
charges. For Counts, "The conscious and deliberate achievement of
democracy under novel circumstances [was] the task of [his] generation," a point made during speeches delivered later that same month
to the Department of Superintendence of the National Education Association and the National Council of Education.[3] He urged educators
to look toward the American democratic tradition for direction and to
strive for "genuine equality of opportunity among all races, sects, and
occupations [and] transform or destroy all conventions, institutions,
and special groups inimical to the underlying principles of democracy."[4] Education represented much more than preparing youth for
jobs or devising child-centered curricula. Shortly after his Baltimore
speech, Counts was appointed to chair a PEA committee where he

continued to challenge the membership. The Committee on Social and Economic Problems' report, *A Call to the Teachers of the Nation*, released in 1933 and written primarily by Counts, asserted that "Teachers . . . cannot evade the responsibility of participating actively in the task of reconstituting the democratic tradition and of thus working positively toward a new society."[5] Only two years earlier the members of the Aikin Commission met to initiate the reconstruction of secondary education. Now they were being called upon and charged with remaking American society.

The story of the growing appreciation of school philosophy among Eight-Year Study participants is at first a tale of indifference and resistance that eventually gave way to interest and concern. For many of the participating schools, an educational philosophy only existed on paper and was in no way connected to Counts's challenges or, for that matter, to their curriculum programs. The issue was not whether teachers should build a new social order (and whether this would constitute a form of indoctrination). Instead, many of the educators merely asked whether they needed to articulate a social vision for their school. Similar to today, educational aims were seldom discussed and, as Aikin recognized, "Democracy was taken for granted."[6] On the surface, the high school faculty and staff acknowledged the schools' important role in strengthening democracy, but there was little agreement on exactly what this meant once platitudes were set aside. Then, as now, the case had to be made that social philosophy was profoundly important and should serve to guide educational practice. Slowly they would come to realize that determining educational aims led to rich, lengthy discussions about what type of community they wished to build for themselves and for their students, and arising from these conversations would emerge a social philosophy that centered on democracy as a way of life, a way of living most supportive of human growth and the development of personality. No other aim would prove more important to the Eight-Year Study.

"Let's give no more time to philosophy"

The schools were slow to accept the challenge of thinking through the social purposes of their work. For the first few years of the project, other matters were of greater importance to the teachers and administrators. Remarks made following an October 1935 session devoted to the "search for the meaning of democracy" nicely capture the feeling of the majority of participants. Aikin reported that several school principals responded by saying, "This has been very interesting, but let's give no more time to philosophy. What we need is discussion of the practical job of curriculum revision."[7] Educational means dominated conversation, while ends were accepted as already fixed. Further, those teachers at the elite private schools associated with the Aikin Commission saw little reason to change their long-term commitment to traditional liberal education. Maintaining hard-won reputations of academic excellence proved paramount, and any other educational philosophy or social aim seemed far removed from this dominating concern. Why, when their academic programs were highly respected, would faculties from these renowned institutions want to reconsider their purposes?

The more experimental schools faced a different sort of challenge. As Edmund Day of the GEB observed: "As long as progressive education was largely an attack on existing educational organization, its forces could act effectively with no clear statement of positive purpose. . . . [The] time has come for progressive education to indicate its primary aims much more explicitly and systematically than it has done thus far."[8] Day argued that progressive educators had to declare explicitly a positive social vision, one the schools could use to guide decision making, to judge the quality of their programs, and to inspire commitment among teachers, students, and parents. They could no longer be comfortable simply opposing traditional educational practices and representing a "movement of revolt." They needed to stand for something constructive and progressive.

Several efforts were undertaken to encourage representatives of the Aikin Commission sites to critically examine the aims of their work. The first general attempt to articulate and review their underlying philosophies took place at the Bennington Conference. Harold Rugg presided at a session to discuss the philosophy of what was then being called the Secondary School Experiment. He charged the participants "to ask themselves what kind of education they would like to have" and then described basic expectations for the schools: that the curricula must not become dominated by the textbook and that "every one of these schools" must develop activities based on what youth desire and need to know of the world about them.[9] Any school, he said, that refused to meet these expectations should quickly withdraw from the experiment. There is no record of how his comments were received, but his session marked only the beginning of what was to become a week of serious discussion about differences over the direction of the project.

Ultimately, Rugg maintained that the success of the Eight-Year Study would be directly related to the ability of the participating schools to clarify what kind of society was wanted, and this would require that each faculty become actively involved in the analysis of the current social situation in America. Yet during another conference session, when Counts's Baltimore address was discussed, teachers feared that they were being asked to prescribe a social vision that would indoctrinate their students.[10] While most of the participating schools would later center their social philosophy on the importance of democracy, remarkably, there was little evidence of this orientation in any of the session minutes, although much discussion occurred about the proper link between school and society. The Bennington meeting and the subsequent 1934 George School Conference led to little progress in determining social visions and common aims for the participating schools, but at least conversations were starting to take form.

The work of Ralph Tyler ultimately caused teachers to begin to examine their school philosophies. In the autumn of 1934, the Evaluation Staff stressed the importance of determining clear aims for initiating and guiding experimentation. Inevitably, as faculty discussed objectives, they confronted questions relating to the wider social purposes of schooling. Talks were far ranging, often intense, and very serious. Tyler insisted that the school faculties clarify aims, and the Evaluation Staff help teachers in the lengthy process of revision. Looking back on this time, Aikin commented that with the encouragement of Tyler's staff, objectives were revised over and over again, and through this process the teachers began to discover the "direction in which they should travel."[11] For some, lists of discrete objectives formed a larger social vision—not just specific ways of behaving but ways of living. At other schools, educational goals cut across the disciplines and constituted broader shared aims intertwined with a democratic way of life. The mere listing of goals, however, did not constitute an educational philosophy. Anticipating the fate of school mission statements in our time, Boyd Bode commented on the tendency of educators to compose long and impressive lists of objectives but then to pay little attention to what they actually meant or to how they would influence practice: "I have read pages and pages of objectives, and in them I find such things as cultivating open-mindedness, citizenship, and so on, which everybody can subscribe to, from Hitler up or Hitler down. Now, there is something wrong when we agree thus readily, and the reason is that those objectives cease to be objectives—[they] simply become statements."[12] If objectives were to become meaningful, then they must make a recognizable difference in educational practice and activities of the schools. True then, and true now, education in a democracy should in some fundamental way be quite different from schools operating under other social systems.

An Initial Formulation: The Briarcliff Memorandum

At the 1935 Thousand Island Park Conference, the third and final gathering of the participating school faculty and staff, Burton Fowler urged participants to assess their own programs to determine if a common understanding of purposes was being achieved. Clearly, the Aikin Commission staff believed that the schools' educational aims were unfocused and that some position on social philosophy was necessary in order to generate discussion. They proceeded to draft a memorandum as a means for better focusing their experimentation.[13] Receiving mixed reviews when released at the headmaster's conference in Briarcliff, New York, the initial statement reconsidered the aims of secondary education and sought "to make changes in our schools to achieve those objectives more effectively and completely."[14] What became known as the Briarcliff Memorandum begins with a brief description of "the American tradition" followed by a list of eleven educational statements, each serving as a preliminary standard for evaluating programs. The implications of the memorandum were far reaching, suggesting changes in accepted patterns of school organization, curriculum, teaching practice, and student, teacher, and administrator roles and responsibilities.

For example, one plank redefined the process of educational change by maintaining that "the fundamental purposes can be attained only to the degree that the members of the school staff help to formulate and understand the objectives, desire their achievement, are willing to analyze them into their essential elements, participate in the planning, and cooperate in putting into effect such procedures as contribute to carrying them out." Another standard—that "the students be given the opportunity to make their school an example of successfully working social life, the school and community a laboratory of intelligent citizenship"—urged a greater degree of involvement from students.[15] Taken seriously by a school faculty, these statements invited wide participation in curriculum decision making, including teacher-pupil planning, and altered traditional teacher and administrator roles to include regular consultation with staff and students. Ongoing discussions about educational aims and their assessment would become a central activity, and citizenship moved to the center of the school program rather than being seen solely as a responsibility of the social studies teachers. These proposals promised dramatic program changes and no doubt were seen by many as threatening long-established and valued practices.

Slightly revised in January 1936, the Briarcliff Memorandum remained a general orientation, a point of departure for discussion, rather than a detailed answer to Counts's challenge or, as suggested by Rugg, as a "credo to which everyone must subscribe."[16] Initially, some faculties did not appreciate that they would have to work out their own statement of aims and instead criticized the document for lacking specificity and clarity. As discussions of the memo continued, signs of frustration with dawdling school principals arose. One year after the Briarcliff

Conference, Edmund Day told the headmasters and Aikin Commission staff that while he was not interested in forcing a particular formulation of social aims on the various schools, he saw no excuses for delay: "[It] does seem to me," he said, "important at this stage . . . for every school that seriously regards its responsibility to American society to undertake some formulation of its own purposes." Determined to press the issue, he posed a heavily loaded question: "To what extent, and under what circumstances, is a school justified in declining to state its educational philosophy?"[17] In Day's mind, no such justification existed, but for many school staffs, larger educational aims were still being taken for granted. Educators had yet to make a connection between their daily lives in classrooms and any larger social ideal for secondary education.

Articulating Aims and Making Progress

Bode and Frederick Redefer, among others, had traveled to a progressive education conference in Cheltenham, England, in the summer of 1935. During their time together, Bode stressed the importance to Redefer for the PEA to clarify its purposes and link educational aims to the future of democracy in America. A social philosophy was needed that teachers could use when making curriculum and instruction decisions, and the Eight-Year Study offered a promising venue for the PEA to experiment with the relationship among democracy, social philosophy, and school practice. Redefer, as executive director, supported the basic tenets of progressive education; however, he could not have been seen as a particularly strong proponent of the project, even at that time. Yet Bode's arguments proved convincing, and Redefer, who during their travels noticed the ominous signs of the growing power of communism and fascism, claimed that Bode convinced him that the "next job of the [PEA] was to make democracy meaningful to the American people." In his memoir he wrote, "When I returned from the European trip . . . I was full of a new crusade. . . . We must give democracy a meaning to young people."[18] Democracy could not be, as it had so often become, merely an educational afterthought—if acknowledged at all. To become vital, democracy had to become a way of life and a basis for educating the young, the central driving force behind all that was done in the school. Redefer came to agree with Bode that the school must represent the embodiment of the democratic idea and, indirectly, the Aikin Commission schools would become the laboratory within which to develop and test this emerging commitment.

Under GEB sponsorship during 1937, the PEA staged eight experimental conferences on the philosophy of education.[19] The question of the social aims of education would be considered by the school faculties, and Harold Alberty, trained primarily in administration and curriculum, was appointed as one of the Aikin Commission's Curriculum Associates with the specific responsibility to help teachers recognize the social significance of their work and to connect school philosophy to educational practice. An outgrowth of Alberty's role was the formation of a set of criteria to help participating school faculties assess and think more clearly and critically about their social philosophy. This was not a standard to be enforced but instead a series of questions that arose from what he judged to be the best activities and practices taking place in the schools: (1) Is the announced social philosophy of the school the product of group thinking on the part of the entire teacher staff, the pupils, and the parents? (2) Is the social philosophy of the school in the process of continuous reconstruction and revision in the light of changing conditions? (3) Does the social philosophy of the school provide a sense of direction in all areas of school life? (4) Does the social philosophy of the school serve as a basis for integrating school-community attitudes and practices? (5) Does the social philosophy of the school aid the pupil in developing standards for determining beliefs, attitudes, and plans of action concerning personal problems of school and community life? (6) Is the effectiveness of the school's social philosophy being systematically tested by available means of evaluation?[20]

Taken together, these questions represented a set of principles consistent with an emerging and increasingly shared understanding of democracy, now moved to the center of educational activities. Further, the questions emphasize the expectation that each school faculty would develop its own philosophy based upon an understanding of democratic principles. Students and parents would now have a significant role in designing educational programs and would join teachers in determining what kind of school community and what sort of education and school life would be forged. Given a rapidly changing society, social philosophy would evolve over time and would not become fixed. The discussion of the aims of education would be viewed as an ongoing, essential part of school life and a basis for students to explore personal values and social commitments. Every aspect of the school program, curricular and extracurricular, would be justified by its contribution to achieving established social aims. In addition, philosophy would serve as a basis for strengthening ties between the school and the wider society and would provide a focus for bringing together diverse communities to consider ways of extending the range of interests they held in common. Alberty also insisted that education programs were evaluated to determine if the social aims enabled more intelligent and effective planning. According to Aikin, 1937 was a turning point for the Eight-Year Study. A consensus was emerging among the faculties that "the high school in the United States . . . should be a demonstration, in all phases of its activity of the kind of life in which we as a people believe. . . . Everyone recognized the need of a sound philosophy for the reconstruction of American secondary education."[21]

Discussion of the social purposes of education intensified throughout 1938. The faculties of many of the Aikin Commission schools became increasingly critical of their own practice, and a sense of urgency was evident in the meetings. H. H. Giles, during his 1938 visits to the schools, came away deeply impressed with the "extension of democracy in many—not all—of these schools. It is democratic to attack problems through group thinking rather than to make a solitary game of it—no matter how brilliantly one plays. . . . Democracy is painful, not least because it is the long way of doing things, but it seems to many schools to be worth suffering for. . . . Increasing efforts to create a partnership between pupils, teachers, administrators, and parents, however, testifies to the realization that extension of democracy through practice of it is of ultimate importance."[22] The PEA philosophy of education conferences, the Eight-Year Study workshops, the efforts of the Curriculum Associates, numerous Commission-sponsored meetings and discussions, and, importantly, events in the world all converged to alter long-held opinions about the proper aims of education. Unfortunately, while many of the Eight-Year Study sites were engaged in fruitful conversation about school purposes and exploring the educational implications of democratic values, the same could not be said of the PEA.

Throughout the 1930s PEA membership had become increasingly fractious. Two committees had been appointed, one in 1936 and another in 1938, and charged with articulating the aims of the Association. Both failed. The first committee accomplished very little. As best as we can determine, the report of the second committee was never formally adopted.[23] By trying to cut a pathway between advocates of extreme child-centeredness, most of whom were concerned exclusively with elementary education, and the social reconstructionist wing of the PEA, the committee only succeeded in alienating both groups.

While the PEA failed to achieve agreement on the purposes of progressive education, the faculties of the Aikin Commission schools made steady headway. For many of them, by 1938 the task had become concrete and practical, not a venture into meaningless abstractions. Where PEA leaders sought a single and shared statement of purpose, Aikin Commission staff encouraged participating school faculties to vary their programs as necessary. Differences in guiding philosophies were not only inevitable but desirable; no single all-encompassing statement was necessary. A few schools made little headway, a point that would later be of great concern to Bode when the occasion came for reporting final results, but others produced remarkable documents that proved their value in practice.

Democracy itself suggested that differences should follow honest and open deliberation among faculty about educational aims. In fact, from such discourse, understanding of the social purposes of education and the unique challenges of teaching and learning in a democracy evolved among the Eight-Year Study participants. Also, perspectives were broadened by the concerted effort to link the examination of educational aims to Aikin Commission-sponsored conferences, workshops, and meetings. That the discussion of aims proved a valuable form of faculty development was a welcome but unanticipated outcome.

Social Philosophy at Work: The Tulsa Schools

The philosophy of education must discover and ally itself with the social forces which promote educational aims, as well as uncover and oppose the vested interests which nullify and reduce them to mere flourishes or to phrases on paper. (John Dewey, 1933)[24]

In Tulsa, four junior high schools and three high schools participated in the Eight-Year Study. When deciding how to implement the project, two educational programs were run side by side in nearly every building—one represented an experimental school-within-a-school project, collectively called "little schools," and the other corresponded to a traditional school curriculum. Although tensions sometimes arose between faculty members working in the two curricular strands, there was, on the whole, a remarkable level of faculty support. A broadly representative Steering Committee oversaw the experimentation in the Tulsa schools, and during the period 1936–1937 this committee produced a statement of purpose that was eventually approved by the entire secondary educational staff and the Board of Education. The preamble to this document included an assertion of faith in the value of the democratic way of life, and aims were listed with accompanying experiences as a way to link social goals to curriculum and instruction.

After two revisions, the Steering Committee members defined democracy as "a way of living so that all individuals and groups feel responsible to provide for the maximum development of all," and they endorsed two broad purposes: (1) to develop "a fundamental faith in the American ideal of democracy and to develop those attitudes, skills and understandings which will enable the individual as a member of the social group concerned to become a positive force in the process of its achievement" and (2) to develop "an effective personality through

an understanding of self and through an appreciation of the importance of the aesthetics and the spiritual in human activities."[25] To achieve
these two ends, a set of more specific aims was identified, each suggesting the kind of educational experiences recognized by the Committee
to move students along toward achieving these purposes. Thirteen aims
were associated with the first purpose and five with the second; each
was understood to be an "obligation of the school."[26] Examples included to develop an understanding of, and a desire to use, the democratic method as a way of solving economic and social problems and to
foster the courage to face intellectual opposition and to stand for one's
own convictions against popular clamor and material gain.[27] Serving as
"threads of continuity," the aims gave the entire program coherence
and direction. Additionally, specific activities were suggested to assist
the teachers in their planning. While these statements might be dismissed as platitudes as being either too general or impractical to guide
decision making, the influence of the accumulating experiences, one
following upon and adding to another, convinced the teachers—if not
provided the courage—to confront the inherent weaknesses of the traditional, fragmented, and separate subject curriculum.

The Steering Committee's "Aims of Education" generated continuous discussions of social philosophy in what became an integral part of
self-assessment efforts. The Final Report for the Tulsa schools noted
that as "time passes attitudes and understandings are becoming clearer."[28]
Using these statements as a basis for conversation, each school faculty
eventually produced an individual, somewhat distinctive statement of
philosophy that over time evolved in response to changes in the wider
social and school context. Faculty and administrators at Will Rogers
High School, for example, forged consensus around eleven objectives
each used to guide instructional, curricular, and administrative decisions. From these statements, the high school staff formed school governance committees, service groups, voter registration programs, and
other community activities. The school philosophy came alive in the
experiences of administrators, teachers, and students and was not filed
away to gather dust in a district office.

Tulsa's 140-page final report to the Aikin Commission—in which
each of Alberty's six criteria is apparent—presents a description of educational innovation under extreme financial limitations. New forms of
school organization were developed, including changes in schedules, to
allow teachers greater planning time and to enable correlation of subjects—English, social studies, mathematics, and science—to be taught
in extended blocks of time. Although in general "each school . . . developed its own program as those concerned have been able to make

adjustments in schedule and personnel," innovations were tested, sometimes comparisons made across sites, and then extended to other schools.[29] In the junior high schools, grade-level themes were chosen to focus the work in general education. Moving away from standard textbooks, resource units were developed by teachers around persistent life needs of young people. In some schools, teachers and students stayed together for more than a single year. Teacher-pupil planning was widely adopted, and team planning was common. Administrative roles changed to give others—teachers and parents—greater involvement in and responsibility for decision making. Students engaged in studies of the local community, and efforts were taken to strengthen school and community ties: "Student Councils began to function as working organizations rather than as 'rubber stamps' for faculty thinking."[30] For the faculty, staff, and students, this array of activities was not the result of the sort of curriculum planning normally thought to be the purview of teachers but instead the outgrowth of a firm, schoolwide belief in realizing a set of social purposes all their own.

Other Aikin Commission sites made similar advances. In Denver schools, the commitment to democracy expressed itself as a "widening participation among [individuals] in the solution of their common problems."[31] This belief was grounded in a two fold faith: first, in the dignity and worth of all individuals; second, in the ability of otherwise common persons to cooperatively solve their problems through the "free play of intelligence."[32] Specific behavioral characteristics were identified that would increase each young person's ability "to share in democratic living" and, as in Tulsa, each teacher and subject area faculty was expected to contribute to their development. Among the characteristics were social sensitivity, a disposition to think clearly and critically, and the ability to work through problems in the light of their social consequences. Recognizing that growth always occurs in some direction, success was determined by students gaining a fuller understanding of and participating more effectively in a democracy society. Other schools produced similar lists of characteristics and likewise worked to design programs that provided consistent and abundant opportunities to engage in activities that would enable the practice of democracy.

School Philosophy, Democracy, and Discourse

> Democracy can be made unutterably wearisome and wasteful if the whole group undertakes to make every decision and to perform every function which had previously been centralized. (Margaret Willis, 1940)[33]

As the Eight-Year Study Commissions came to understand, instituting democracy takes time and forging a school philosophy is difficult and often frustrating work yet essential to the formation of democratic communities. The Horace Mann School faculty members viewed clarifying their social philosophy as a way to unify and invigorate the entire school. They acknowledged that some staff thought the undertaking almost insurmountable, others anticipated disagreements, and still others saw the practice "so filled with compromises that it would have little value."[34] Nonetheless, guided by Alberty's criteria, the staff posed five broad questions that served to coordinate their curricular and extracurricular activities.

At the Ohio State University School, faculty and staff came together before the opening of their first school year to discuss educational aims. As one teacher said, "Fine plans were being shaped for hypothetical children. When school opened with real children a vast amount of new planning had to be done in very short order."[35] The staff continued to meet regularly during its first and subsequent years to talk through educational beliefs and to explore promising practices, and while working in a fully operating and very active school, no organizational structure was set up in advance of a perceived need. Guidelines, rules, and regulations evolved: "How the faculty lived through the first few months is still a mystery, but somehow the sense of working together at something important carried us through," one teacher recalled. The discussions were not *pro forma* but involved genuine differences of opinion and lengthy, heated exchanges as educators attempted to forge a shared vision for the school. Speaking of the work done during that first year, faculty believed the time was not wasted: "Endless faculty meetings, evaluating, criticizing, planning" brought forth a commonality of purpose.[36]

The Ohio State site illustrates what became a common activity for many teachers associated with Eight-Year Study schools—participation in an ongoing examination of practice in relation to social and educational consequences. School philosophies were dynamic, not fixed or static, pronouncements of intent common to mission statements. This spirit is nicely captured in the final report of Radnor High School:

> One of the most significant developments [of the Study] seems
> to many of us to have been the gradual growth in our under-
> standing of the purpose of the school and of our part in the
> achievement of this purpose. A philosophy for a group of
> teachers is neither born nor made—it grows. It is not (or
> ought not to be) the result of administrative fiat; it is never
> finished; it is never equally acceptable to all; it recognizes that
> some of the group would hurry along toward a dimly outlined

goal, while others are inclined to question the direction, and still others—most of us apparently—move more cautiously but steadily toward a nearer more clearly defined three-quarters-of-the-way marker.[37]

In recognition of the diversity of philosophies eventually produced by participating school faculties, Bode argued with the Aikin Commission's Directing Committee for the final summary of the project to reflect "not just differences in procedure, but also differences in ideas and viewpoints in order to suggest the social philosophies emerging for guidance of secondary education."[38] He especially did not want all of the schools "lumped together," warning that to do so would mean that important differences would be obscured and lost. A quick review of the Aikin Commission's final report, *Thirty Schools Tell Their Story*, underscores the importance of Bode's argument. There one sees the diversity of programs, each representing the best effort of faculty and staff to articulate the kind and quality of life they wanted to live within the school and with students, its best thinking and honest inquiry into what they most valued and who they were as people. Their message is clear: There are many good answers to the fundamental questions of education, but developing such responses requires evidence, open argumentation, and a sincere desire to live more richly and productively together.

Conclusions

We have been nominally democratic for so long that we presume it is our natural condition rather than the product of persistent effort and tenacious responsibility. We have decoupled rights from civic responsibilities and severed citizenship from education on the false assumption that citizens just happen. (Benjamin Barber, 1998)[39]

We share Benjamin Barber's belief that schools are "the workshops of our democracy."[40] This was precisely the view held by those Eight-Year Study leaders who realized, as was stated in the first sentence of the Briarcliff Memorandum, that "Some philosophy of government, of society, and of life inheres in every educational program." They recognized that this philosophy—democracy as a way of life—must be made explicit in schools and then examined and reexamined in the light of changing circumstances. Discourse was extensive and continuous and, gradually, ongoing discussion of aims came to be seen not as an indulgence but as a fundamental part of what free people must do to remain free. As Dewey said, "Democracy begins in conversation" and must manifest itself not just in beliefs but in action—in voluntary reading programs, teacher-pupil planning, shared curricular responsibilities, student government that enjoys a measure of influence and power, and in ongoing and open-ended discussion of why one or another decision is made.[41]

Democracy as a way of life requires a unique and distinctive form of education in the classroom. Despite common conceptions, democracy is not merely a matter of choice or synonymous with capitalism, a consumer's dream of endlessly expanding options and of unbridled rights. Nor is it easily exportable, as some politicians and corporate leaders seem to suggest. Reaching beyond politics and economic systems, democracy becomes a way of being with others and represents an ethical ideal embedded in fairness: justice becomes shared vulnerability, human intelligence serves as a means for resolving problems, a faith exists in discourse and engagement, and there emerges a profound respect for human relations and diversity in all of its many manifestations. Democracy entails learning to become comfortable with uncertainty and demands humility, even from those holding formal institutional power, principals and teachers alike. As Bode knew, if democratic means were used, there was no reason to worry about educational ends. "What is required of progressive education is not a choice between academic detachment and adoption of a specific program for social reform, but a renewed loyalty to the principle of democracy."[42] When taken seriously, democracy demands great courage of teachers: Authority shifts, modes of discipline necessarily change, and power is diffused. Democracy also requires faith—faith in the capacity of "the common person"—colleagues and students alike—that they each may make positive contributions to the development of a greater good. Such a way of life represents an open invitation to conversation about the future coupled with ongoing criticism of the present, requiring sacrifice born of the elevation of common over specialized interests. This was just the sort of interaction that came to characterize the work of several of the school faculties associated with the Eight-Year Study, most especially with the more experimental schools.

Vignette

Boyd H. Bode (1873–1953): Philosophy Brought Down to Earth

Boyd H. Bode, photograph, 1926, Ohio State University Photo Archives

Prior to 1930 John Dewey and Boyd Bode were almost alone in considering democracy an important factor in determining educational objectives; afterwards the word democracy began to appear in education treatises with growing frequency. (E. E. Bayles and B. L. Hood, 1966)[1]

In October 1938, *Time* magazine published an article on the progress of progressive education written to commemorate the PEA's twentieth birthday. Boyd Bode was prominently featured. No doubt he was simultaneously pleased and probably more than a bit embarrassed by the attention he received. As one who did not join groups, Bode thought of himself as a friendly critic of progressive education who stood some distance from its center. Certainly he blushed when reading these words: "Recently Progressive Education's No. 1 present-day philosopher, Ohio State's gaunt Professor Boyd Henry Bode, in a book called *Progressive Education at the Crossroads*, declared that nothing but chaos could result from exclusive attention to children's individual needs, interests and learning. Progressive schools, he insisted, must lead their pupils to oppose dictatorship and make democracy "a way of life," and he defined democracy as "continuous extension of common interests."[2]

No one who knew Bode as a young man could have imagined that these words were being said of the modest, studious, and dutiful son of the Reverend Hendrik Bode. Steeped in Calvinist traditions by his immigrant minister father, most of his contemporaries likely thought Bode would one day join the ministry. But instead of studying theology, Bode studied philosophy—then not so far removed—graduating from Cornell University in 1900 with his faith mostly intact, as he assured his worrying parents in frequent letters home written in colloquial Dutch. A decade of prolonged personal struggle followed that culminated in 1913, when he proclaimed himself to his friend and former student Max Otto, a "confirmed pragmatist."[3] By rejecting absolutes, by having thought his way out of idealism, as Otto maintained, Bode took his first steps toward becoming a champion of democratic principles—of an open universe where truth arises only from human experience.

With his embrace of pragmatism—to which he would make significant contributions—Bode turned toward education as a place where philosophy had important "work to do."[4] Reflecting on his years teaching philosophy Bode concluded that formal logic was nothing more than "horse sense made asinine." What he wanted was a philosophy that made a difference in human affairs—"philosophy brought down to earth."[5] And so, like Dewey before him, Bode found himself increasingly interested in and involved with education-related issues.

While teaching at the University of Illinois, Bode began to wrestle seriously with education. The then-idealist Bode obtained this academic post from extraordinarily strong recommendations by William James, James Hayden Tufts, and Dewey.[6] Encouraged by his colleague, friend, and fellow Cornell graduate, William Chandler Bagley, he became a regular participant in the annual high school conference sponsored by the university. No doubt his participation provided an occasion to reconsider his brief experience in 1892 as a nineteen-year-old teaching in a one-room, rural school. Later Bode began offering a course in educational theory and soon was publishing on a variety of educational issues. He had come to believe, as Dewey argued, that the "most penetrating definition of philosophy which can be given is . . . that it is the theory of education in its most general phase."[7]

I

In *Fundamentals of Education*, Bode's first book in education, philosophy and democracy are given central place. The two are inextricably linked, but he felt compelled to argue for the importance of each to education separately. Respecting democracy, he wrote:

> To be truly democratic, education must treat the individual himself as the end and set itself the task of preparing him for that

intellectual and emotional sharing in the life and affairs of men which embodies the spirit of the Golden Rule. In proportion as common interests are permitted to outweigh special interests, the individual is becoming humanized and the successive adjustments of life will be made in the direction of democracy and in accordance with the needs of an expanding life.[8]

Not surprisingly, while the book gained much attention from educators, Bode, like Dewey, found that professional philosophers had difficulty taking his interest in education seriously. Nevertheless, these words set the agenda for the rest of Bode's professional life and led him away from academic philosophy, although he claimed he never really left.

II

In 1921, Bode became chair of the Department of Principles and Practices of Education at Ohio State University, a move that was as shocking to some as it was delightful to others, particularly in Columbus. Bode once wryly wrote of his shift to education, "I found [upon my arrival in Columbus] everybody all dressed up, but with no place to go. It was just the right kind of situation for [me] even though it did involve listening to an incredible amount of bunk from pedagogs (sic) who should have stayed with dad on the farm to look after the cows. But at that, it was no worse than listening to disquisitions on epistemology and symbolic logic by a person whom I would hesitate to trust with cows if the cows belonged to me."[9]

Bode's appointment to the Directing Committee of the Eight-Year Study seemed quite appropriate. In 1927, the widely adopted and critically acclaimed *Modern Educational Theories* was published, and two years later *Conflicting Psychologies of Learning* was released, a book that was, according to Harold Rugg, the best writing on learning, showing how conceptions of mind profoundly influence educational practice.[10] A witty and beloved teacher, Bode was an accomplished and popular speaker at PEA-sponsored conferences. He was widely recognized as a gadfly who could, through his critical abilities, help others think more clearly and broadly about their own work and locate where dangerous consequences might lie. To Bode, the Eight-Year Study provided an opportunity to further his own interest in the Ohio State University School, which he hoped and expected would become a laboratory for testing his ideas and, perhaps more importantly, would provide opportunities to influence the participating schools to think carefully about their social purposes, another extremely important place to bring philosophy down to earth.

Throughout the 1930s, Bode continued to press the cause of democracy within the Eight-Year Study and with a growing sense of urgency. His concern was evident as he spoke in 1937 at the annual meeting of the PEA. As one audience member reported, "Dr. Bode is frankly worried about conditions. He feels that democracy is fighting for its life. . . . He notes a great confusion in our social patterns and in our ability to develop any coherent, consistent viewpoint with regard to our cultural heritage."[11] Bode understood the ineluctable connection between democracy and education—democracy is a theory of education—and his own experience confirmed the power of this conclusion. But it was not until Americans sensed the rising fascism in Europe that his message was widely heard and understood by many educators, such as Frederick Redefer. Bode completed *Democracy as a Way of Life* while in Germany and wrote in anticipation of war:

> The contention that a program which encourages every normal person to engage in an independent reconstruction of experience will lead to unity in thought and action has the appearance of paradox. But paradox, as someone has said, is truth standing on its head in order to attract attention. Like every other program in this field, the democratic program of education is an adventure in faith. It rests on the faith that if the reconstruction of experience goes hand in hand with sincerity and careful self-criticism, the basis of understanding among men will be continuously widened. . . . [Democracy] stands or falls by its faith in the common man.[12]

This was the message Bode brought to the participants of the Eight-Year Study and tirelessly presented to members of the PEA, a message that he continued to share until his death in 1953.

III

For Bode, a democratic frame of reference for education represented a unique point of departure and involved "an attitude of generous give-and-take, or reciprocity and sharing [and an] intellectual outlook . . . a clear recognition that common interests have right of way over special interests."[13] There is, then, a peculiar and particular democratic social ethic or ethos that is self-critical and stands in stark contrast to other ethical systems, including all those grounded in one or another absolute—religion, fascism, or communism. The particular challenge of general education in a democracy was, according to Bode, to "cultivate both this attitude and this outlook" and, in order to do this, young people needed to understand democracy as a set of principles and internalize a set distinctive attitudes, values, and emotional habits indicative of living a unique way of life. This way of life would and should be practiced and also criticized in school: "Teaching democracy in the abstract is on a par with teaching swimming by correspondence."[14] Because of this belief, he concluded that a "democratic social order which understands its own character and purpose is bound to have a distinctive system of education."[15] That he was likely looking down on the streets of Munich as he wrote these words helps explains their tone: "The school is, par excellence, the institution to which a democratic society is entitled to look for clarification of the meaning of democracy. In other words, the school is peculiarly the institution in which democracy becomes conscious of itself."[16] At a time such as the present, when the importance of citizenship seems to have disappeared from public discourse about education—despite there being no shortage of chatter about schooling—and the future of public education is in doubt, such a vision invites a serious reconsideration of the purposes of schools.

Chapter 8

Staff Development:
Teacher Workshops as Personal
and Professional Growth

Improving the quality of teaching has long been a pressing issue and remains so today. Under federal legislation, the goal to place a highly qualified teacher in every classroom is a worthy aim. But definitions of what constitutes "highly qualified" are sharply contested as they have been for generations.[1] Despite a century-long move toward increasing standards, at present a rather simplistic conception of outstanding teaching is predominant among many policy makers and politicians: to be a highly qualified teacher merely requires a college subject area major and some degree of verbal fluency. From this perspective, expertise is defined in technical ways, often by classroom behaviors, and the ultimate proof of good teaching is determined by high scores on students' standardized achievement tests. Many educators realize that much more is involved. Few disagree that teachers require ongoing instruction in order to remain effective in the classroom, but debate becomes intense over what kind of education, or training, is most valuable. In particular, sharp disagreement exists concerning the respective value of content area versus pedagogical studies and activities in pre-service and in-service teacher education.[2]

Standing back from these differences, all agree that teachers should have strong academic backgrounds and possess specific skills demonstrated to promote learning. These values were also important to leaders of the Eight-Year Study; however, there was another area of concern, one that is seldom mentioned in discussions today: "To be a good teacher one must be first of all a good human being."[3] Being a "good human being" is not a precise designation either, of course, and consistent with the Aikin, Thayer, and Keliher Commissions' spirit of experimentation, this end was never seen as fixed or static. The beliefs and values of teachers were considered very important, as were their academic knowledge and instructional skills. But Commission members understood that the humanness of a person—the thoughtfulness, the kindness, the inquisitiveness of the teacher—profoundly influenced not only how content would be presented but also how well students would learn.

Educators who participated in the Eight-Year Study came from many different personal and academic backgrounds—from small liberal arts colleges to large universities and from specializations in science and mathematics to degrees in elementary education. In fact, the Aikin Commission's Curriculum Associates applauded the diversity of experiences among the participating teachers, especially those who had previously held blue-collar jobs and maintained dramatically different interests.[4] At the same time, these teachers shared qualities and dispositions—a deep curiosity about the problems of teaching and learning, a robust commitment to improving school practice, and a strong belief in themselves as learners—commonalities that seemed to emerge from discussions at some of the participating schools.

Certainly such traits were embraced and promoted, since the project's success rested ultimately upon the abilities of teachers to implement educational change. Yet these traits do not just appear. Teachers cannot be "trained" to accept values, nor do certain beliefs— the importance of school experimentation, for example—evolve naturally. In fact, one principal, in attempting to explain her staff's modest attempts at experimentation during the initial years of the study, remarked, "We have come to love our chains."[5] Many of the teachers needed assistance to reimagine themselves as scholars and academics and to change habitual ways of thinking about instruction and learning. Their faith in experimentation and their confidence in themselves and others as being capable of directing reform would have to grow. Through a series of planned experiences—all oriented toward fostering discourse, examining ideas, clarifying values, and attending to consequences—teachers and staff were able to come together and reimagine themselves and their work as educators, that is, good human beings maintaining faith that positive outcomes would result from conversation and community. Commission leaders learned that one of the most significant factors for improving schools was straightforward but profound: "When a group of teachers dealing with the same students begins to talk about human beings instead of subject matter, changes begin."[6]

Typically the Eight-Year Study is viewed as a curriculum project but, as previous chapters have shown, expanded to become much more. In this chapter we explore one of the more neglected aspects of the experiment: in-service teacher education designed for the growth of teachers broadly understood involving more than content knowledge and teaching skills and instead drawing upon a full range of human potential. "Teacher growth" and "capacity building," now common terms in the professional literature, became an integral part of curriculum development and gradually emerged as major responsibilities of the Commissions' staff. In fact, the growth of teachers constituted one-fourth of the Aikin Commission's publication *Exploring the Curriculum.*

Becoming a Teacher in the 1930s

The task of improving the existing pool of teachers was daunting and in some parts of the country seemed hopeless, since significant numbers of educators held lifetime certificates with no obvious incentive to improve. Throughout the 1930s, teaching jobs were scarce and turnover was very low. Unqualified individuals were employed due to political connections or the necessity of meeting the district's meager budgets. Each year, new teachers entered a glutted job market, gaining certification either through examination or studying at one of 800 institutions of higher education—normal schools, teachers' colleges, and universities. While state legislatures increased initial certification standards and tightened course requirements, great unevenness in the quality of instruction challenged the workforce. In 1937, only five states required four years of postsecondary school education as the minimum standard for elementary school teaching and most required only two years of education beyond high school. Certification standards for secondary schools were higher; but even among these teachers, great variation could be found in their educational background and preparation, especially between those in urban and rural settings. Few states required practice teaching, and most provided very little, if any, pedagogical training. Teachers frequently were unprepared for their assigned subjects, and matters were made worse because junior and senior high school teachers typically were assigned to instruct in more than one subject area, often three or four in rural settings. Across the nation in small secondary schools enrolling fewer than 125 students (what constituted more than 50 percent of all high schools), less than 10 percent of teachers taught in their major areas of study.[7] In-service education offered little help in improving the knowledge and skills of those several hundred thousand teachers already employed.

Other than personal study, summer schools and correspondence courses were the most common means of continuing education. Summer programs, which were widely available, were especially important for teachers who held certification that required additional schooling for periodic renewal (about 40 percent of renewable certificates) or who sought a different kind of certificate, perhaps in a specific area of study or level of teaching. Requirements for renewal, however, were modest: usually only about eight semester hours of course credit.[8] At the time, supervision of teachers in their classrooms was thought to be the most important means for improving teaching and increasing student learning.[9]

Influenced by industrial practices, however, the supervisor's traditional role had been to inspect schools and to manage teachers. Research, teacher training, and guidance were added to these responsibilities, and supervision became a specific area of academic study, not just a part of the everyday work of the busy school principal. Some administrators were trained specifically as supervision specialists, and leaders in the field sought to create a science of supervision, centering on empirical techniques for improving teaching. Yet with all of these differing conceptions, "scientific supervision" remained largely "inspectorial."[10] A teacher had good reason to be wary when a supervisor, notebook in hand, dropped by for a classroom visit. As Cuban has noted, supervision conflated two aims: teacher development and evaluation.[11] Rating systems varied and, much like their students, teachers were often graded.[12] In 1932, then-PEA President Burton Fowler proclaimed, "The old idea of a supervisor as a whip-cracker is out of date. What is needed in supervision is a very large amount of self-direction under expert guidance."[13] At this, however, Fowler may have been overly optimistic.

Even among many progressive educators, the use of the phrase "under expert guidance" captured what appears to have been the commonsense view that teachers needed to be guided, to be led. William Burton, one of the more influential exponents of "democratic supervision," viewed teachers as having no right to participate in educational decision making unless they had received "advanced training" specific to the task at hand.[14] Social efficiency demanded nothing less. The leaders of the Eight-Year Study, however, expected something quite different from the participating teachers and principals: they hoped that together they would reconceive and recreate secondary education. While the proposal seemed radical, there were indications that such an undertaking could be successful. A decade before the project began, for example, Denver schoolteachers had taken major responsibility for improving the curriculum. The Commissions' staff recognized that the success of the project rested with the ability of teachers to cross established role boundaries and to take on new and expanded responsibilities.

There were lingering doubts, however, that teachers could meet the challenge, especially in the larger public schools, where work conditions were discouraging. Even the leaders of the Denver schools, looking back on the first three years of the Study, wrote, "Seldom have teachers and pupils been given such opportunities and responsibilities ... it remains to be seen whether teachers can realize the new opportunities for their own growth which progressive education offers them."[15] As the project unfolded, the Aikin Commission staff came to realize that teacher education needed to be added to its agenda.

Changing Teacher Roles and Improving the Growth of Teachers

> In the course of the Eight-Year Study there has been opportunity to see such faith [in values] transform teachers from persons who were merely "going along" into eager, active individuals who showed unsuspected powers. (H. H. Giles, S. P. McCutchen, and A. N. Zechiel, 1942)[16]

As the Eight-Year Study progressed, teachers and administrators found their roles changing and expanding in many different ways. Of necessity, they became guides and counselors, researchers, philosophers, analysts, community activists, and apologists for innovative educational practices. Some were not ready for these new responsibilities; others embraced them eagerly. Teachers became increasingly involved with core programs that dramatically altered their work "from guide of a conducted tour to guide of a group of explorers."[17] Instruction became simultaneously more complicated and, for some, much more interesting. With the move toward curricular integration and cooperation, those who assumed responsibility for core found themselves—some for the first time in their careers—heavily dependent on others for their own classroom instruction. Course content could no longer be fully set out in advance, and adjustments were required all along the way. Flexibility and foresight were essential, and traditional patterns of evaluation were swept aside. In the more experimental schools, authority was decentralized, and teacher study groups and curriculum councils became increasingly more influential in establishing school policy.

Since textbooks no longer represented the basic curriculum, teachers were forced to confront the need for new materials as well: "The accumulation of 'refrigerated packages of educational content of standard size and value,' known as credits, have lost their pedagogical force. Stripped of his erstwhile goads to learning, the teacher faces an awesome world."[18] This became a daunting and sometimes overwhelming challenge. An occasional visit from a Commission staff member or a visiting dignitary would do little to help teachers meet their new responsibilities successfully. New forms of in-service education were needed if they were to "experiment successfully with the curricula in these thirty schools without harm to the students under their charge."[19]

Reflecting the basic belief that democracy involved the "maximum development of individuals and groups" and trusting that teachers could assume leadership for curriculum improvement, the Aikin Commission staff approached in-service education in nontraditional ways.[20] Learning environments were created to provide opportunities for teachers to grapple with problems of both personal and professional interest. The staff recognized that university training and the organization of a school day offered teachers little time to discuss and otherwise confront the challenges of teaching. To reconceive in-service teacher education, they looked outside of the universities and schools and planned an experimental setting to nurture teachers: the workshop.

Reconstructing In-service Teacher Education: The Workshop

The exact origins of the PEA workshop are not completely clear. A general, traditional PEA summer Teacher Institute was first staged in 1929. Organizing summer sessions for "retraining" teachers in progressive secondary methods was discussed as early as the spring of 1933, but nothing came of the proposal except, perhaps, suggesting the idea.[21] The Eight-Year Study staff realized that during the school year they lacked sufficient time to consult with the participating teachers who, in turn, knew that their regular duties left little occasion to engage in program development. During discussions between Ralph Tyler and GEB staff, "the suggestion was first made that a portion of the summer might be used to give the staff an opportunity for intensive work with teachers from the thirty schools."[22] Tyler believed the new venture—a workshop—would be successful only if financially independent from the regulations of university summer school courses. Their criticism of traditional graduate education was quite pointed, concluding that summer courses were characterized by "the formal, mechanical scheduling of courses, the hit-or-miss methods of grouping in classes, the lack of a sense of responsibility on the part of one faculty member for the continuing guidance of these students-with-problems, the habit of looking at a student through the screen of single courses."[23] The Curriculum Associates even mocked the "Great Professor" of the university (Professor Brilliant and Dr. Hairsplitter) and felt teachers should not be placed under any external pressure for such superficial results (grades and papers) as they would during the summer course at the university. Tyler wanted something different— a time and place where teachers could discuss their problems in depth and where they would be given the "opportunity to work in small groups on large problems."[24] Such gatherings would not be an occasion to merely listen, nor would they be limited to a single weekend; solutions to large problems called for extended time. For Tyler, a workshop would be a place for teachers to *work*—to be totally immersed with the problems and issues of schooling that concerned them.

The Eight-Year Study workshops began as an experiment "to test the hypothesis that a group of teachers can work with each other and the members of a highly accessible staff upon problems growing out of their separate situations."[25] The first program was held for six weeks during the summer of 1936 at Ohio State University. Thirty-five teachers were selected to participate, most of whom came from the fields of science and mathematics, since the Thayer Commission's Committee on the Function of Science in General Education also sought their critical comments. Teachers were recognized as having expert knowledge essential to the success of the Commission's work, and participants critiqued materials for *Science in General Education*. While the workshop theme detracted from the time and attention that could be given to participants' individual problems, an occasion to think through a new adolescent needs-based approach proved to be engaging work. In addition, teachers worked closely with representatives of the Evaluation Staff and "developed a deeper understanding and some ability to guide the work of evaluation in their schools."[26] The first workshop, considered highly successful, confirmed the Commission staff's faith that teachers could come together for an extended time and engage in fruitful activities for the Eight-Year Study, for their individual schools, and for themselves.

Teachers were enthusiastic for a second summer program, and through a grant from the GEB, a workshop was scheduled at Sarah Lawrence College to run from the beginning of July to the middle of August 1937. Similar to the first gathering, this six-week session was planned for teachers of the thirty schools, and faculty were drawn from the Eight-Year Study Commission staffs. But unlike participants of the Ohio State workshop, the 126 teachers represented a wide range of subject fields. Several school systems sent teachers for the purpose of addressing specific problems, and the expenses of many were paid with school funds. Denver, Des Moines, and Tulsa public schools sent the first "delegations," and teachers attended expecting to work on the core curricula within their respective schools.

Events at the Sarah Lawrence session profoundly altered future workshops and changed how leaders of the Eight-Year Study thought about in-service education. As with the Ohio State meeting, planners set aside a considerable amount of time for review of the Thayer Commission materials, now much farther along, particularly the report of the Committee on Science in General Education. These teachers, however, attended the workshop with specific problems and expected to make genuine headway toward finding solutions. They objected when their topics were relegated to a secondary position and judged less important than concerns of the staff. This was not what they understood a workshop to be. A "friendly rebellion" was staged.[27] In response, the staff reassessed plans and agreed not to introduce materials unless directly useful to the teachers. Although the 1937 workshop focused on educational aims and curriculum development, nearly half of the participants ultimately became involved in the construction of tests that would be used to assess their programs.[28]

Another important outcome was equally unexpected. The Sarah Lawrence campus was relatively secluded, and all participants—faculty, staff, and teachers—involved themselves in workshop activities from early morning until late at night as a form of staff development as total immersion. Everyone lived and dined together on campus, and leisure hours encouraged informal as well as formal discussions. Participants came to realize that "learning was taking place at the breakfast table as well as in the conference room or library and that the variety of associations was adding to the enrichment of the personal as well as the professional life of the student."[29] A community of learners formed during this six-week period, when boundaries separating staff and teachers collapsed and new friendships formed. Accordingly, subsequent workshops placed significant emphasis on creating conditions for informal interaction, leisure activity, and involvement in the arts. The legacy of the Sarah Lawrence session was apparent the following year when at the Rocky Mountain workshop 75 percent of the participants felt that the strongest feature of the program was the "unusual opportunity for personal contact."[30]

In addition, the Sarah Lawrence gathering revealed the value of having teachers from the same schools attend the workshops. Such delegations enabled dramatic progress to be made on specific school problems, and these teachers returned as leaders and spokespersons for school experimentation. For example, the six teachers from the Denver public schools who had attended the workshop formed a committee that visited each high school in the district to speak about what they had learned about evaluation and classroom practices: "Their enthusiasm spread to other teachers so that when the first Denver workshop was formed in the summer of 1938 the attendance from Denver was large, sixty-seven in all, including both junior and senior high school teachers and administrators."[31] A few of the teachers became staff members at later workshops and increasingly assumed leadership roles within the summer programs.

The Summer Workshops Expand

GEB funds supported a third round of workshops for the summer of 1938: one returning to Sarah Lawrence College (the "Eastern Workshop"), one at the Colorado Woman's College in Denver (the "Rocky

Mountain Workshop"), and one at Mills College in Oakland, California (the "Western Workshop"). Teachers from outside of the Aikin Commission schools requested the opportunity to attend what had become PEA-sponsored events, and the expansion to three sessions allowed for wider participation. In addition to teachers working outside of the thirty school sites, a group of twenty-three college and university faculty members was admitted, thus recognizing the importance of arts and science faculty in teacher education and in school reform. A total of 500 teachers was selected to participate in the workshops—"those who were at a point in their professional development at which they could profitably devote an entire summer to a professional problem of local significance."[32]

The aims of the 1938 workshops went beyond attending to those specific problems brought by participating teachers. Topics addressed the lives of individual teachers, including engaging in the arts and recreational activities: "The whole physical set-up of the workshop [was] designed to facilitate free association among students and staff members unhampered by the formal administrative arrangement common in large summer schools."[33] Reviewing the results of the Eight-Year Study, the Aikin Commission's Curriculum Associates concluded that "the first requirement for growth of teachers through any means is that they work under conditions which are favorable to their growth as persons."[34] Ultimately this matter of personal growth became an important goal of the workshops; however, professional problems—curriculum, assessment, and instructional practices—still guided the programs. Each of the 1938 workshops invited specialists in a variety of areas, including adolescence and guidance, literature and language arts, social studies, mathematics, sciences, the arts, assessment, and evaluation of radio materials in the social sciences. Additional groups formed at the Eastern Workshop to focus on the liberal arts college; at the Rocky Mountain Workshop to work further on the core curriculum, home economics, and foreign languages; and at the Western Workshop to develop additional resources in physical education and health.

Of the three workshops, the Rocky Mountain program was designed primarily for teachers from the participating Aikin Commission sites. C. Leslie Cushman of the Denver schools led the gathering. Over half of the 190 workshop participants came from the Denver, Tulsa, and Des Moines school systems, and in response to the proposed problems for study, special attention was given to developing core curriculum, engaging in art activities, and examining problems of educational administration. The latter topic addressed organizational challenges related to school reform. The workshop day was organized into three periods, with morning sessions devoted to meetings for subject area specialists and school delegations with an occasional general session. In the afternoon, work focused on creating resource units and participating in activities in the art studio. For one evening a week, a general session presented research useful for addressing the small group problems, and the other evenings were set aside for group recreation and musical performances.

Much was accomplished professionally by the participants during the summer; however, we wish to describe the "human" side of the workshop, the aspect that strengthened a sense of community among educators who came to Denver from twenty-three states throughout the country. We begin with an account from one of the participants: On the second day, one of the Curriculum Associates was "expounding a great idea about personal and social needs, and all of us were doing a great deal of talking, one of us broke out in a witty little tune; before he could be put out, another began shuffling a cowboy dance under the table, and a third pulled out a piece of moist clay from his pocket and began to model."[35] At first the workshop staff was surprised by the mischievousness of the teachers, but they also must have recognized the long and tiring day, working in heat and humidity and in tight quarters. On this and many other occasions, the teachers needed something more than talk: they needed to play, to celebrate being together, and to take risks that would further both their own development and the work in which they were engaged. Quickly staff members met and adjusted their plans for "living the joyous life." They realized that time would have to be set aside for participants to "sing and dance and write poetry and feel clay under our fingers, throw the shuttle through the opening warp, mass bright colors, and sweep a mural onto a convenient wall."[36]

Art became central to the celebration. Several artists were in attendance and helped the participants build a studio "in a large room that looked from the third floor windows across the [Colorado] prairies." Looms, oil paint, water colors, brushes, paper, different types of clay, chalk, an easel, and leather and metal working tools comprised a "glorious studio" where teachers "doffed our dignity and restraint and dared to do what we had never done before, dared to express in clay, paint, and chalk, ideas which we had never before let anyone know we had. . . . [There] was no tenseness, no strain; only freedom and good fellowship."[37] In addition to developing forty-four core curriculum source units during the course of the workshop, participants composed and sang songs, took photos, prepared theatre scripts, wrote poetry, and performed dances.

These activities were not mere diversions. In fact, for Aikin they caused the Rocky Mountain program to become the most significant and important "experience we have yet known."[38] In addition to strengthening a sense of community that reinforced shared commitments, each activity in some way developed source units and addressed serious educational issues. One participant, for example, wrote a short but powerful defense of the arts for children and a lamentation of the effects of budget cuts on school programs. A spirit of openness and intellectual honesty characterized the work of the groups and the relationships among staff members, and the teachers felt comfortable and confident enough to poke fun at the nationally recognized notables on staff.

The power of the workshops was profound. After sixty years, Paul R. Klohr, former director of the Ohio State University School and then a young teacher, vividly recalled his participation as an important moment in his professional career:

> [There was] a pervasive spirit among the participants. They came to view themselves as real professionals who were capable of creating curriculum and experiencing democracy in practice. . . . An informal setting was created in the dining room which had become the work place with room for the assembled books and periodicals. . . . A central focus was on the development of resource units, or "resource files," collections of teaching materials/resources that tended to cut across several disciplines. . . . However, the most pervasive aspect of the entire workshop was the experience of "democracy in action." The workshop participants ate together at mid-day and attended planned trips at points of interest on the campus and the city. [All] promised to share their newfound curriculum development skills with their colleagues.[39]

The sessions were more tightly linked to the work of the teachers than adult summer camps and much more demanding than the typical university summer school course. Many of the participants traveled long distances and obviously made substantial sacrifices to attend. Also, as mentioned by Tyler, the teachers were put to work. For six weeks, they researched topics, edited curriculum materials, prepared reports, constructed evaluation instruments, created resource units and, most time-consuming, forged a shared understanding with their peers of the basic aims and purposes of American secondary education. They did not receive graduate course credit for their attendance nor were they paid to attend. The workshop participants were simply dedicated and hardworking educators captivated by an idea.

A Shifting Focus for Summer Workshops

During the summer of 1939, eleven PEA-sponsored workshops were planned with thirty institutions applying to become hosts. Earlier programs proved remarkably successful such that demand far outstripped the ability of the PEA to adequately support them. Overwhelmingly, teachers and administrators who attended the sessions judged them far superior to university summer courses, and as a result administrators considered the possibility of workshops becoming a PEA "program for the advanced training of teachers."[40] Evaluations consistently supported their worth as a promising new form of in-service teacher education. For example, over three-fourths of the 1939 Teachers College participants believed their workshop was more valuable to them than summer school.[41] Tulsa teachers found much that was praiseworthy. Workshop participation, they wrote, "Causes growth through contact with teachers from various parts of the country." Participation increased their sense of pride in being a teacher, helped them rethink their approaches to teaching, and strengthened their desire to design programs more responsive to the needs of adolescents. From the workshops, they concluded that the "teacher brings back a changing viewpoint" about education.[42]

With such positive reactions, it is not surprising that the summer of 1940 saw a dramatic expansion of programs promoted under the "workshop" label; however, not all met with the approval of those who had pioneered the idea. Recognizing the allure of workshops to attract students, universities began offering summer programs that were not connected to the Eight-Year Study or to the PEA. Some Commission staff questioned the intent, quality, and methods of university-sponsored programs that, although becoming quite popular, embraced few of the elements that made the Eight-Year Study sessions so successful. The PEA leaders feared that workshops, if taken over by universities, would lose value. Cushman worried for the future of the idea as well: "There is danger that the name but not the spirit of the workshop will be maintained in our educational practice."[43] After visiting ten summer programs, Carson Ryan expressed concern that three of the most important factors contributing to success—the focus on adolescent guidance, "creative arts" of the sort that blossomed and helped build a sense of community, and the "experience of living together"—would be lost under pressure to lower costs.[44] Despite their widely shared fears, Commission members recognized that without significant external financial support they could not continue to stage workshops.

While this form of in-service teacher education was considered one of the most successful GEB-aided projects in the general education program, the PEA withdrew completely from sponsoring workshops. In the fall of 1940, the Association transferred the remaining funds to the American Council on Education's Commission on Teacher Education, an organization also receiving GEB support. With this transfer, a new era in the development of in-service education began, one that for a brief time strengthened the initial trend toward involving not only teachers but also administrators, supervisors, and university faculty in workshop programs. By 1942, the original concept of the workshop had been totally transformed. The Commission on Teacher Education compiled a directory of 114 summer workshops "planned for a minimum of four weeks." The Commission noted, "To be sure, the term [*workshop*] is very loosely used in educational circles and applied, without necessarily much change in method or emphasis, to many offerings that used to be called clinics, institutes, working conferences, and the like."[45]

Conclusions

> [Teachers] must have faith that their job is important to individual human beings and to society; the teacher amounts to something—occupies a worthy place in society. . . . Teachers with such faith will live their professional lives creatively and devotedly. The next question is: how does such faith get its start? (H. H. Giles, S. P. McCutchen, and A. N. Zechiel, 1942)[46]

The Eight-Year Study workshops dramatically affected most participants, not only professionally but personally, and proved to be a productive means for encouraging the growth of teachers and changes in schools. Those who designed the workshops aimed to create conditions favorable to participants' growth as persons, not just as teachers, and to offer an opportunity to direct their own studies. This conception of in-service education represented a deep and respectful understanding of adult learners and intimate knowledge of the various contextual challenges teachers faced, from large class sizes to limited resources. Remarkably, recent research on effective professional development emphasizes the value of this approach. Garet and his colleagues conclude that in-service education involving active learning and "collective participation" (for groups of teachers from the same school in activities of sustained duration) is powerful and most likely to improve education. In addition, programs that give a "greater emphasis to content and that are better connected to teachers' other professional development experiences and other reform efforts are more likely to produce enhanced knowledge and skills."[47]

All of these conditions were met in the in-service programs of the Eight-Year Study. The workshop activities reached across the entire academic year and were continuously supported by the Commissions' staff. Teachers were actively engaged in learning, and many came to the workshops in groups to address problems of significant concern to them and to the faculties they represented. The programs were carefully planned and purposeful yet also flexible and responsive to shifting needs and interests. Workshops were intense and sharply focused often on specific content areas, as in the first gathering, when science in general education was the major topic. Teachers left the summer sessions feeling renewed and energized by what they had learned. Finally, the participants experienced great joy from playing, living, working, and learning with other educators, including some of the highly recognized leaders in American education and in the social sciences.

Ironically, the Eight-Year Study was initially undertaken to free secondary education from the constraints of university admissions requirements. In the end, the grammar of university-based teacher education co-opted the workshops and limited their educative potential. It is this danger that makes the aim of "simultaneous renewal" of schools so very difficult today. Yet while the Commissions' workshops may have seemed destined to be engulfed by university summer school practices, their significance remains, lingering and ephemeral, but still present. When Ralph Tyler was asked in 1976 why the project did not have more impact, he responded, "You must remember that education is a vital thing, it's a human enterprise . . . human beings who carry it on."[48] The power of the workshops, those intense and focused gatherings that inspired "total immersion" and the building of democratic communities, forged a dynamic group of leaders whose influence extended across two generations of educators and beyond. This accomplishment underscores why determinations of impact are so difficult. Programs may end but what is learned along the way continues, and so it was with the workshops, to the great benefit of young people and teachers across the nation.

Vignette

Margaret Willis (1899–1987): And Gladly Would She Learn

Margaret Willis, photograph, 1942, Ohio State University Photo Archives

Miss LaBrant: We did two things after class last night. We had the questions mimeographed for you. Miss Willis rearranged them so that the questions that went together were put together. . . . We knew we could not handle all sixty-two of you at a time, and Miss Willis has the list of those who belong in each of the groups.

Miss Willis: As far as possible we followed the preference of those who had a preference. There were a few people who did not listen to what was said and handed in a problem which they wished to follow after the two or three weeks were over. One person handed in a preference, but forgot to sign his name. Before I read the groups I want to call attention to the difficulties we are going to be laboring under. (Ninth grade core course transcript, 1934)[1]

This concluded the second session of the 1934 ninth-grade core class for a group of students who later would write a book about their high school experience entitled *Were We Guinea Pigs?* Margaret Willis, along with Lou LaBrant, William Van Til, and others, served as their core teachers. The transcript depicts many of the mundane realities of classroom instruction, even at an innovative progressive school. Willis informed the students of which rooms could be used during their 1–3 p.m. class period. She read names of those pupils who would be working within four designated groups—local and city government, state government, national government, and the United States among the nations—alongside their English, social studies, and science instructors. Teachers were asked to speak louder; students were told to be quiet. Willis added background information to the discussions. On one occasion she informed the group of a new book that had been received by the school library during the summer. Such was the exchange of an active core classroom of lively students and teachers in 1934.

Margaret Willis repeated—gladly—these same core program customs for thirty-six years. She lived a gratifying career, remaining in the classroom without ever taking on administrative roles and devoted to one specific institution: the Ohio State University School. She arrived as a member of the first faculty in 1932 and retired in 1967 with its closing after three years of protest against the decision to discontinue the school and just one month before the final high school commencement exercises. The career of Margaret Willis, although not representative of all Eight-Year Study teachers, demonstrates how one person made meaning for herself and for her students within a progressive classroom.

I

I am satisfied ... when I am living for the present in a daring and adventurous deed. . . . I think that life tends to become sluggish, too comfortable, unchanging because of too much thought and no action. (Margaret Willis, 1931)[2]

Margaret Willis' educational background was not uncommon for women who emerged as academics in the early part of the twentieth century. Following her graduation from Wellesley College in 1919 with a BA degree in history and economics, she spent two years in Japan as a governess for an American Embassy staff member. Her appointment was arranged through the Wellesley College placement bureau, and although Willis did not view herself as an educator, teaching offered the opportunity to travel. In 1921, uncertain of her future, she returned to her home in Mount Vernon, Washington, and taught history at the local secondary school for the next three years. Recalling this experience, she wrote, "I learned something and the children something, but none of us very much. When it got to be too monotonous, I resigned."[3] The use of the term *monotonous* is noteworthy; Willis's ultimate embrace of progressivism, her social activism in local and national communities, and her never-ending interest in travel attest to a desire for intellectual adventure.

Willis enrolled at Columbia University in 1925 and, after completing her MA degree in political science, she moved to Maryland State Normal School (Towson State). Willis described her interview for the normal school position by explaining "how little I knew about education and educational theory, and when the director persisted in offering me the job, I accepted out of sheer amusement."[4] After two years, she left for Istanbul, where she eventually taught at the Constantinople Women's College for Girls for a four-year period, returning in 1931 to teach at the Bennett School in Millbrook, New York. No doubt Willis could have continued moving from one institution to another for the variety that would provide her with a satisfying educational career. She was offered, however, a teaching post at the Ohio State University School, an experimental demonstration school that would provide countless new experiences for the next thirty-six years.

Willis described her abilities as a teacher prior to her employment at the University School in rather self-effacing terms. Of her two years in Japan, she admits that her teaching "was pretty mediocre and that it is an understatement to surmise that I learned more than the children did."[5] This all changed with her arrival in Columbus, Ohio. In 1940, she mentioned to Wilford Aikin that her teaching career had been largely accidental and pretty haphazard before the University School and, though rich with many interesting experiences, she had engaged in little reflection.[6] During her participation in the Eight-Year Study, however, Willis became swept up in the seriousness of the progressives' endeavor, the life of teacher and learner, and the camaraderie of colleagues and students. She found a venue in which new abilities and interests could flourish: "When [Eight-Year Study] teachers conceive of teaching as a creative art, based upon scientific method and knowledge, they are transformed from routine workers to creative adventurers."[7] She embraced the secondary social studies program in this unique school, best known for its integrated broad problems core program. Social studies and language arts were closely linked at the secondary level but, interestingly, not integrated on superficial grounds or merely because these subjects could be correlated. In fact, Willis objected to efforts to merge needlessly these fields. She recalled with "special vividness a June meeting of the Thirty Experimental Schools about 1934 or 35 at which a spinsterish lady of uncertain age spoke glowingly of the happiness which had resulted in her school from the marriage of English and social studies. They have never been married in the University School. . . . English and social studies work together where their aims are best realized by such cooperation, and . . . work separately where their objectives are distinct."[8] Willis's "middle position" supported curricular integration; however, she would not conduct classroom experimentation at the expense of content knowledge and would not participate in interdisciplinary activities just for the sake of being "progressive."

II

Willis's career, somewhat similar to Keliher's, balanced independence with cooperation as she defined democracy in the classroom. This was not a democracy of "forms and election ritual," as she once said, but one of independent thinking in concert with community. While she believed in the importance of discourse, she was far from being long-winded and at times actually seemed quite gruff. She typically changed topics impatiently with the phrase "we can't go any further with this." Many stories have been told of her edginess and restlessness. For example, in the 1950s, the parents of a graduating high school senior objected to their daughter being escorted by an African American during the commencement processional into the amphitheater. Since the class included two African Americans, one male and one female, the parents requested that those students be paired and that another male student be assigned to walk next to their daughter. Willis was called to the meeting in which the parents explained their concerns. She looked at them, replied "nonsense," and then stood up and walked out. The meeting concluded with no further comments, and the processional pairings were not changed.[9]

Despite her straightforward demeanor, Willis also displayed great compassion as she embraced the ideals of democracy. Yet she was not content to nurture merely the individual needs of students. Margaret Willis, who "suffered no fools," prized disciplined intelligence. She expected and assumed that all would join her in the academic journey, and most apparently did. Although she was never described as charming, she embodied kindness and humaneness even as she was nicknamed "the goose" by students. Willis was tough and gentle; her interests, however, remained focused on learning and teaching and seeking intellectual experiences for her students, her colleagues, and herself.

III

Independence and cooperation among teachers and students distinguished the University School from most others. A project by its students on behalf of themselves, their teachers, and their school ultimately proved unique. The graduating class of 1938 (fifty-five students) published a work entitled *Were We Guinea Pigs?* about their six years at the

University School and participation in the Eight-Year Study. As the first group to have completed its entire middle school and high school years, the students stated, "We feel that it is important for us to examine and evaluate our six years' experience. We are becoming more conscious of the principles behind all that we have been doing."[10] Other faculty members may have been more directly involved with the project, yet Willis became most beloved and best known as their teacher, a feeling that has stood for seventy years.

The students remark in their opening paragraph that they had completed all of the work themselves: "No teacher was even present at the final revision of the manuscript." Yet what proves more interesting is their sole reason for writing: "Our school is often misunderstood. We have been criticized and opposed because we are 'progressive.' So many attacks are made."[11] Throughout 300 pages they describe, in remarkable detail, fortunately made possible by the school's cumulative records, their many diverse intellectual and personal experiences. The emphasis, however, was not on themselves but on the quality of teaching during their school years: "We feel that our faculty is one of our greatest assets. . . . We are fortunate in having teachers with a wide variety of backgrounds and opinions. . . . We enjoy talking with the teachers because our interests are similar. Our discussions are usually frank and open-minded."[12]

Any educator who has been closely involved with a group of pupils inevitably asks, "What happened to my students?" Willis took the initiative to find out. Coincidentally, she mentioned in 1936 two of her professional goals: to write about the laboratory school and to maintain contact with this particular group of students (then the tenth grade, the graduating class of 1938).[13] Her hopes would be more than fulfilled since, in 1968, she would publish a follow-up study, *The Guinea Pigs After 20 Years*. This work, reviewed in *The Saturday Review* as well as in various educational journals, explored the impact of the class of 1938's secondary education: "The thesis of this study is simple. If basic high-school curriculum reorganization is worth the effort, it should have results which are apparent in the adult living of the students who experience it. This follow-up attempts to look at all the "guinea pigs" to find out how successful they are in their living nearly twenty years after high-school graduation, and to see what connection, if any, can be established between the nature of the high-school experience and the kind of adult living discovered."[14]

Willis acknowledged the difficulties of defining "success in adult living" and recognized the many variables that cause one to hesitate in claiming direct causal relations between school and adult outcomes. The project, however, expressed the school's commitment to experimentation and, in its own way, brought a more logical form of assessment to the idea of future success. Unlike the Follow-up Study of the Eight-Year Study, the guinea pigs were not compared to other students according to their college grade point averages but instead to their own conceptions of success after twenty years, which included living an educated, socially involved, and culturally active life.

When the guinea pigs were interviewed in 1988 at their fiftieth school reunion, they stated that if a follow-up study were to be undertaken, they knew Margaret Willis would be the researcher.[15] She conducted interviews with all of the students, traveling to their homes throughout the United States and asking them to spend hours filling out questionnaires. "Only for Margaret Willis" was the comment many of them made when asked to participate. Willis stated, "To see what kinds of men and women yesterday's boys and girls have become is a dream of every teacher."[16]

IV

Willis expressed strong views about the preparation and selection of Eight-Year Study teachers, and she valued traits often different from today's most prized competencies: "All successful (teacher) applicants demonstrate qualities of resourcefulness, personal balance, open-mindedness, ability to take criticism from 'inferiors' as well as 'superiors,' and a kind of intellectual curiosity and awareness which squeezes meaning out of every experience. One of the poorest criteria would be that an individual has been so happy and secure in a stereotyped learning situation that he wants to go on perpetuating it."[17] This sentiment reflected her view of teacher development as a way to break from monotonous and often stereotypical learning. She described the satisfying yet exhausting nature of teaching at the laboratory school, affirming that "it was not the weariness of meaningless routine. There was routine, of course, but unless it served some educational purpose, it could be discarded. It was not the fatigue which comes from frustration [and] it was not the nervous drain of petty bickering and backbiting."[18] For this reason, the many years of experience often proudly touted by teachers never impressed Willis. Experience was not valued in itself, and she would criticize, rather strongly, those teachers who were having "one year's experience repeated fifteen times."[19] As she stayed at the University School year after year—viewed as the leader from the beginning—she ultimately grew into the role of the "tribal elder." When asked why Willis never became the director of the school, one former student commented, "Because she didn't want to take a demotion."[20]

V

To many we were a strange pair, two women tourists traveling in summer heat in a land whose beauties and marvels aren't suggested for summer visiting. We were a rarity, two women tourists traveling alone, interested in everything and apparently suffering from nothing—heat, inconveniences, flies, cats, nor contaminated water. We endured them all, let none be deceived. But this was our vacation, and we were going to enjoy Iran. We were not going to pass up this opportunity to see as much as we could—weather or no. (Margaret Willis, n.d.)[21]

Margaret Willis was one of the many common, unnamed, progressive teachers whose entire life was spent in the classroom, yet what a life: "interested in everything" and continually engaged in adventures with students, staff, colleagues, and friends. Willis's story is also uncommon in the way that she emerged as a leader who enjoyed no formal position of authority as she gladly taught at the University School for thirty-six years. Progressive education has taken many hard hits—then as well as now—for focusing on the needs of students, for "frivolous" life adjustment programs, and for blatant signs of anti-intellectualism. These criticisms are no doubt accurate in certain self-styled progressive schools. Yet Willis was so intellectually alive and the University School placed such importance on academic content that such accusations seem somewhat superfluous. Staff researchers of the Eight-Year Study noticed the striking changes in attitudes not only of students but of hundreds of teachers. The Commission staff attributed the differences to "the discovery of the possibilities of personal growth through teaching, the discovery of a new faith in democratic ideals and the place of education in achieving them, and the assurance of a modicum of freedom and security."[22] Willis and her colleagues discovered possibilities for personal growth through teaching as they engaged in a life of learning that could bestow the same joy to their students. Her adventurous company included all learners—students, colleagues, and friends—and among these companions she emerged as a crusty and tough leader with a head filled with wonder.

Chapter 9

Reexamining Secondary Education in America

There's never a time when you can sit back in your chair, put your feet up on the desk, and say, "Thank God that job's done!" If we are educating youngsters for efficient participation in a democratic society, we must always consider them within the framework of a social background which is constantly changing. So our schools must be constantly changing; and the processes of bringing about change must be constantly under way. (A. N. Zechiel, 1964)[1]

A. N. Zechiel, curriculum associate with the Aikin Commission, joined his many colleagues at the Goddard College Conference on Current Educational Issues twenty years after the completion of the Eight-Year Study. H. H. Giles, Harold Alberty, S. P. McCutchen, Hilda Taba, V. T. Thayer, Katherine Taylor, Alice Keliher, and others gathered to reminisce and to reconsider the work of the Commissions in relation to the then-current practices in American education. After witnessing the educational and cultural developments of the 1950s, one would have expected the conference presenters to lament the lack of impact of the Commissions' findings. Expectations for this project had been great; merely thirty years earlier, John Dewey wrote, "If [the Eight-Year Study] works it will probably do more than any other one thing to reconcile the public to the fact that change and experimentation are needed in education."[2] Yet the Carnegie unit remained firmly entrenched, a separate, tracked curriculum for the comprehensive high school had been established, and the formation of the Educational Testing Service (in 1947) ensured that standardized testing would guide college admissions for years to come. The conference proceedings, however, show great hope among the presenters. Few actually bemoaned the Study's "modest outcomes," while all acknowledged that its many influences had been diffused throughout American education. The

Follow-up Study was placed in proper perspective, and the "sustainability" of the project was seen not as perpetuating a static model or curriculum mold but instead as recognizing that "the processes of bringing about change must be constantly under way." In fact, rather than questioning the degree of impact, Alberty stated that the project had actually taken on "an aura of holiness" that he felt was somewhat unwarranted.[3] Not dismissed as an outdated, failed example of educational reform, the conference participants discussed the many innovative practices and seemingly countless insights that arose from the study. For them, the Goddard Conference continued the work begun by the Commissions. The process of bringing about change was continuous and constant, even though the Eight-Year Study and the Progressive Education Association were no more.

As we conclude our examination of the Eight-Year Study, we too are left feeling cautiously hopeful. Our comments about the Study, however, cannot summarize all that is important. Nor will we try. Instead, we are left to determine how to engage those many opportunities for school experimentation that will arise during the upcoming years. Similarly, we ask you to consider the same, for whatever historical lessons emerge from the experiences of the Aikin, Thayer, and Keliher Commissions, we concur with Herbert Kliebard that insights arise from the process by which issues are treated, adapted, and interpreted for specific contexts rather than from historical solutions.[4] The Eight-Year Study progressives, with their theoretical practicality and reasoned balance in relation to changing needs and discoveries in the field of education, offer no answers to today's questions. But with their trust in the ability of teachers and with an essential faith in school experimentation, they suggest many viable approaches to the persistent problems of improving education.

I

We recognize that maintaining trust in teachers and faith in school experimentation may be quite unnerving given the current state of educational affairs. No Child Left Behind legislation and the growing standardization and depersonalization fostered by various testing and certification programs seem to undermine possibilities for school innovation. With the rise of high-stakes testing and the threat of federal punishment, administrators and teachers are frightened that their schools will be declared failing based on standardized test scores disaggregated along various demographic lines, not showing continuous, year-after-year, improvement. A fearful conservatism now exists, avoiding practices not consistent with current fashions or state and federal mandates. School innovation has become merely demonstration, a quest for replication, of some so-called "Texas miracle" or some other seemingly successful project.[5] The national debate about education indicates little sense of the adventurous, of the experimental, of pushing boundaries to discover what might be possible for young people through schooling.

Further, we acknowledge that merely believing in the value of the Eight-Year Study may prove equally difficult today. We are the first to admit that detractors will continue to criticize the Aikin Commission's work, defined as the Follow-up Study, as being nothing more than an inquiry into the educational experiences of a fortunate few students. Any impact on the schools' programs is dismissed as a result of social-economic class privilege reflecting a "homogeneity of [student] experience."[6] Our attempts may seem fruitless to expand an understanding of the Commissions' research and to articulate the belief that teachers can, in fact, make a profound and positive difference in the lives of young people and that schools do not always reproduce social inequities or confirm privilege. While we have shown that the demographics of student populations were quite varied, especially at the participating public secondary schools—Altoona, Denver, Des Moines, Ohio State, Radnor, and Tulsa—this fact means little to today's critic of progressive education. We are reminded, however, of John Dewey's remark: "What the best and wisest parent wants for his own child, that must the community want for all its children."[7] Even though many of the schools did not include the student diversity that we would wish, in large measure their programs represent a type of education we would want for all children and more importantly point to the importance and value of supporting school experimentation as part of every educator's professional life.

While we wish not to romanticize the Eight-Year Study, secondary school exploration and experimentation represented by the Aikin, Thayer, and Keliher Commissions still thrives hidden away within classrooms and in numerous educational settings throughout the United States. In its various and often unsystematic forms, the teacher researcher movement carries forward many of the values and practices of implementative studies, as does action research, a connection noted by Tyler, where dedicated teachers and administrators seek to solve problems to improve their practice. Certainly not as comprehensive as the Eight-Year Study and not as formal as today's research-based initiatives, the results are still shared with other educators in lunchrooms, faculty lounges, and in-service meetings. Such research is conducted through thoughtful reflection and by establishing relationships between actions and outcomes along with a working conception of validity within a specific context and typically without regard for generalization. Often professional hunches function as hypotheses rather than the search for "indubitable proof," and what counts as data becomes expansive. While such current-day implementative research does not seek replication of results, this is not to say that comparisons across sites cannot be made, only that such contrasts are tenuous, even when fruitful, and that programs are inevitably adapted and evolve as teachers, students, and contexts change. More importantly, however, inquiry becomes an ongoing part of the everyday work of schools. Many such examples exist today where experimentation has become an integrated aspect of life in schools.

Today's research sites are, of course, much different from those schools that participated in the Eight-Year Study. Yet the spirit of experimentation becomes the province of all educators who seek to provide better educational experiences for the young. Supported by the Bill and Linda Gates Foundation's "small school" initiative, teachers and students at the Minnesota New Country School stage a variety of interdisciplinary projects that not only represent serious academic work but provide opportunities to address the genuine needs of youth.[8] Another Gates-supported school, the Urban Academy in New York City, is organized around centers of inquiry where students in the social sciences, for example, enroll in a Nature of Proof-like course that addresses controversial topics and includes critiquing one's own and others' work. Graduation requires students to demonstrate academic proficiencies as well as to engage in local and Urban Academy community activities. El Puente Academy for Peace and Justice in Brooklyn offers a type-four integrated arts and social problems core program for developing in students leadership skills for peace and justice.

In Salt Lake City, the City Academy seeks to build a democratic learning environment—a "laboratory for democracy"—where justice is "restorative." With a curriculum more rigorous than the district public schools, collaborative learning is emphasized, and a project-based curriculum is organized around "essential questions," involving teacher-pupil planning and authentic assessment. The Little Village School for Social Justice, affiliated with the Small Schools Network in Chicago, has developed a secondary school program centered on project and problem-based curricula addressing issues through the perspectives of race, gender, culture, economic equity, peace, justice, and the environment. The Big Picture High Schools of Chicago embrace aspects of teacher-pupil planning as well as an integrated core based upon personal-social student needs with an emphasis on social reasoning.

In addition to the many progressive education-based high schools, regional and national organizations are working to encourage and sustain school experimentation. In San Francisco, the Bay Area Coalition for Equitable Schools supports the development of "high-achieving and equitable small schools" that echo the spirit of the work undertaken by the Aikin Commission's Curriculum Associates. The League of Small Democratic Schools, supported by the Institute for Educational Inquiry, provides a venue for educators to develop programs that emphasize the growth of students within a democracy society. The work of the National Network for Educational Renewal centers on an Agenda for Education in a Democracy that includes acculturating the young for participation in a social and political democracy. And the Coalition of Essential Schools, originally guided by specific practices from the Eight-Year Study, has developed a set of ten principles, including modeling "democratic practices that involve all who are directly affected by the school." These are but a few of the many examples of curricular innovation occurring today, each reflecting active engagement in the challenge of building a culture of inquiry and experimentation.

II

With standardized tests now guiding the curriculum, the Eight-Year Study must not be dismissed as a naive experiment before the advent of evaluation. Students attending the Thirty Schools were also administered a substantial number of conventional tests. The Revolt of 1934 did not occur because the principals were opposed to assessment but rather because they feared the aims of their experimental efforts had already been determined. The role of the Carnegie Foundation in those early years is now played by state departments of education operating under tight legislative directives. Local control has dramatically eroded over the past few years. Yet there are signs of a new revolt brewing but of a different order and of a vastly different magnitude than that of 1934. Socially and politically conservative state legislators find themselves in a puzzling situation: on the one hand, they have championed school choice, while on the other they have supported a dramatic expansion of federal control over educational policy through standardized testing. Recognizing the inconsistency, some are beginning to press for change—adjustments in federal law—but few address or question the value of standardization, accepting or not realizing that reliance on externally mandated testing establishes taken-for-granted aims of education.[9]

The Aikin Commission school principals believed in evaluation and assessment because they knew that better and richer information about students—extensive cumulative records to appraise student progress—would permit more thoughtful educational decisions. Further, they recognized that the teachers could develop these forms of assessment themselves—without explicit concerns for reliability—and that their participation in evaluation was worth the fight with the test technicians.

Cumulative student records, having met their expectations for validity, permitted teachers, students, and parents to examine changes in learning over time. Reliability thus became even less important since, for Tyler and the Evaluation Staff, learning represented growth, that is, the continual change in behavior broadly conceived to include skills as well as understandings, appreciations, and interests. Ultimately, the more experimental school staffs embraced an expansive view of assessment where testing was directly connected to the production of information of most use to teachers. Rather than lead to greater standardization, evaluation, so conceived, actually promoted curricular differences and more responsive programs of study, just the sort of development now called for as schools face the challenges of rapidly changing student populations.

This is where the Aikin Commission's 1934 Revolt speaks most forcefully to the present situation, lending support to Rick Stiggins's argument that if school improvement is the aim of educators, then assessment of learning must be balanced with "assessments for learning . . . [in order] to provide teachers and students with the kinds of information they need to make decisions that promote continued learning."[10] Currently, test results often arrive too late for making programmatic adjustments and have little if any value for curriculum decision making. Improved practices should follow the wise use of cumulative records focusing on student development and including information of various kinds, such as students' interests, abilities, and accomplishments, with descriptions and accounts by students, teachers, and parents. This represents assessment *for* learning. Ultimately, the need is for more, not less, data, information of a different kind and quality than that which now dominates educational practice.

III

At first, many of the teachers associated with the Eight-Year Study were overwhelmed by all that was expected of them. Only slowly did the Aikin Commission leadership come to appreciate that not only did long-established instructional habits impede innovation but that the working conditions and the depersonalizing organization of schools limited even the most committed teacher's ability to engage actively in curricular change. As a recent study by the Cross City Campaign for Urban School Reform documents, nothing changes if school conditions are not altered to better support innovation.[11] One of the least appreciated insights from the Eight-Year Study reflects this point: the recognition that schools needed assistance to experiment and to improve. Legislative mandates do not necessarily lead to change and may even worsen the situation. Commission staff could not expect busy school faculties to revise the curriculum alone. Tyler's evaluation team, the Curriculum Associates, Zachry's Adolescent Study group, Keliher's staff, and various Commission meetings and workshops brought together school and university faculty in ways that currently would be recognized as "partnerships," democratic communities committed to cooperation, for serious dialogue and engagement. Ironically, the schools called upon university researchers to free themselves from university domination, yet such was the case. And while the Eight-Year Study staff may not have understood the concept of partnership as well as those now actively working to establish and sustain professional development schools, we suspect that there are few of the many extant partnerships today that have succeeded, as did the Commissions, in elevating secondary school issues to center stage, where they garnered the active involvement of university professors and a dazzling array of social scientists who joined in common cause to improve public education.

Many of these distinguished social scientists, members of the Adolescence Study and Thayer's Subject Groups, were well aware of the plight of adolescence during the Great Depression—unemployment, unraveling social institutions, and stressful international developments. From their concern for the well-being of young people, student needs became a driving force among the Commissions. While educators now easily talk about attending to the needs of students, remarkably little clarity exists about what this phrase actually means. Our treatment of needs in chapter 5 intentionally complicates the topic even further as a way to underscore the complexity of the implicit issues. Policy makers assume student needs are lacks—inabilities—and those most discussed today are associated with securing and keeping a job, now understood as being the essential condition of productive citizenship. Minimal competency in reading, writing, and mathematics constitutes the list in addition to certain personal traits such as honesty, conscientiousness, punctuality, and the ability to get along with others. Strengthening academic performance seems to be taken most seriously by the general public which views schooling as the portal to gainful and secure employment. But parents want their children not only to learn to read and write but to have opportunities to develop a wide range of interests and abilities. These are student needs of a different sort and to which the most experimental of the Eight-Year Study schools gave particular attention.

Unlike the intense, critical exchanges among Aikin and Thayer Commission members, one seldom hears discussion of why one or another category of student needs is or is not educationally legitimate. Lacking such discourse, schooling is left without a curricular center or clear purpose other than the mandate that every young person must attend and pass an exit examination for graduation. Needs proliferate endlessly, no parental request is out of bounds, and teachers find themselves unable to adequately respond. Further, few discussions address a different sort of student needs—the importance of the teacher-pupil relationship, the quality of life lived in the school, and encounters with the academic disciplines that expand what is seen by the young as the range of real living possibilities. As Maxine Greene has maintained, "It is through education that preferences may be released, languages learned, intelligences developed, perspectives opened, possibilities disclosed."[12] A centerpiece of the Eight-Year Study was not merely creating a social philosophy by which the worth of student needs could be determined but also providing experiences that would fulfill and *create new needs*, especially those associated with valuing democracy as a unique way of life—a need to live democratically.

Our point is straightforward: while debates continue to rage over student test results, only rarely is attention brought to perhaps the most important element in obtaining an education—the quality of the relationships in schools and how teachers dramatically influence what young people are willing to learn. Giles and his colleagues well understood this link, concluding that "to be a good teacher one must be first of all be a good human being."[13] The quality of human relationships—student to student, student to teacher, teacher to teacher, teacher to administrator, and teacher to parent—was a central concern for the Eight-Year Study and ought to be a dominating issue today, particularly as the school stands almost alone as the central place where cultures meet and the young learn to accommodate more or less successfully to differences and diverse viewpoints.

IV

Even before the Committee of Ten of the National Education Association in 1893 recommended four academic tracks leading toward high school graduation, fragmentation was a vexing problem for many educators seeking to strengthen the curriculum. The issue has become more urgent with each passing decade as demands placed on schools have increased and as disciplinary knowledge has grown. Yet curricular integration is generally overlooked today as educators acquiesce to a simple organizational structure and a view of the disciplines that delineates and separates the academic subjects. Many, if not most, of the perplexing problems of our own age require for their solution interdisciplinary knowledge. Images of the lone scientist pushing the boundaries of human understanding remain compelling tales of heroic journeys, but increasingly the reality is quite different. Effective problem solving is a team affair, and sometimes the groups are very large indeed, located in centers linked across the world.

In several of the Eight-Year Study schools, core curriculum proved to be the primary means for overcoming fragmentation and focusing the secondary school program. Through a variety of approaches, including teacher-pupil planning and supported by resource units, students discovered how to effectively work with others as they planned, coordinated, and directed their own studies. Along the way, they also learned a substantial amount of traditional content and were given the opportunity to see the value of interdisciplinary knowledge. Core curriculum was closely linked to general education and, although not solely but centrally responsible, core teachers understood their role to develop democratic citizens. They recognized that citizens are made through a lifetime of experience beginning with the family, but they also knew that citizenship must be instilled and refined through practice within the school and through living democratically—exploring social sensitivity, pursuing justice, exercising rights in the quest for community. For the Commissions' staff, citizens were made, not born, and democracy was forever fragile.

The public school still remains one of the few social agencies, arguably the only institution, that pays any attention whatsoever to fostering citizenship. Unfortunately, most efforts have been reduced to generating a superficial array of mottos and slogans, a mantra about rights. This need not be so. The Eight-Year Study core teachers took advantage of the natural inquisitiveness and sociability of adolescents to help them learn to live together with their differences and to take action on their world. In our time, when questions of identity and diversity are so insistent and cultural differences are celebrated while commonalities are ignored, the work of the core teachers provides a valuable reminder that schools can become means for building a principled sense of belonging and a dynamic sense of community and cooperation. Such groups arise, of course, from serious discussions of social aims and school philosophy, conversations that are too often absent among educators today. For many of the Eight-Year Study students, community was built through similar dialogue—serious, persistent, consistent, and informed discussion of how we, as a people, wish to live together—and its strength depended, in part, upon providing venues for diverse points of view in common studies and in shared projects. Teacher-pupil planning required nothing less. This is not to suggest that all of the Aikin Commission schools were successful in this endeavor, for they were not. It is, however, to say that such dialogue was extensive then and must become so now.

V

Presently, social aims and school purposes are not often discussed by administrators or teachers, let alone by students. Generally speaking, among Americans today a very limited sense of citizenship now prevails—democracy becomes simply an expression of a consumer's right to choose and, as such, is taken for granted except when questioned or attacked. Democracy has been reduced to choice as a mere procedure, an act of voting where the majority wins. Little is said about wise choices or how decisions reverberate outward and shape our shared social and natural world. The struggle to live democratically—democracy as a way of life—became the most central concern to the schools of the Eight-Year Study. Agreements about educational aims and activities, while hard won, rested upon this experience of solving problems democratically—lived and learned rather than merely told and taught.

In our estimation the central educational and curricular challenge of our time is to determine how to rekindle and reinvigorate debate over the purposes of education and the place of schools in an increasingly diverse and contentious democracy. Fortunately, there appears to be a resurgence of interest in this important issue.[14] Yet much more must be done to raise the level of conversation so that it may compare to the discourse among the many more experimental programs of the Eight-Year Study. As John Dewey reminds us, "Democracy must be reborn with each generation, and education is its midwife."[15] When the U.S. Supreme Court ruled on the 2002 Cleveland school case, those justices supporting vouchers failed to see the necessary connection between public education, democracy, and the building of public spaces for interaction across differences of race and class. Schooling became simply a matter of choice, concluding that public funds should follow whatever form of education is desired. Everywhere we see the results of a society that largely ignores cultivating even the most ordinary obligations of citizenship. To encourage development of civic virtues among all students requires that democratic values and skills become part of every aspect of the school program—from the classroom to the lunchroom to the playground. They are practiced and turned into a way of life that is examined, criticized, and reconsidered in light of desired social goals, the life that is lived, and those interests grounded in differences of experience and background, of race, class, and gender that generally eluded educators of the progressive era.

VI

When teachers do become involved in working on the important questions in education, they are themselves enormously enriched. You cannot have significant curriculum development in any school unless this happens—unless teachers dedicate themselves completely to trying to find out what they want to do, what they're going to do it with, how they can do it, and how they're going to find out when they get through whether they accomplished what they set out to do. When you do have this happening, you get more than curriculum development: you get the development of great human beings. (A. N. Zechiel, 1964)[16]

Zechiel's conclusions to his Goddard College remarks highlight an insight from the Eight-Year Study that has only recently been rediscovered: school reform ultimately is teacher education, a form of what is now called "capacity building."[17] Better education for the young requires that the grammar of schooling, as Tyack and Cuban have described, be altered and that educators' personal and professional development be richly and generously supported.[18] Through the workshops and the various school-based activities sponsored by the Eight-Year Study, members of the Commissions learned that trust in the ability of teachers to produce thoughtful educational experiences for the young was never misplaced. This same viewpoint now underpins the work of the National Staff Development Council, which maintains that "any faculty, with no additional formal training or professional development, already [has] enough practical knowledge and ability to make continuous and significant improvements to instruction."[19] To be sure, we will be the first to admit that James Michener, Lou LaBrant, William Van Til, Chandos Reid, and Margaret Willis, our examples of the Aikin Commission's general classroom teacher, are exceptional. However, while an individual's ability is crucial for building extraordinary educational programs, of greater importance is the development of a "collective capacity," a professional community that invites, supports, and sustains exceptional performance.

The Eight-Year Study offered many opportunities for classroom teachers to become exceptional, to explore their professional and academic interests as well as the educational needs of their immediate communities. Similar possibilities are within reach today when school settings are adapted to "developing capacity among schools and teachers to be responsible for student learning and to be responsive to student and community needs and concerns," as has been described by Linda Darling-Hammond in The Right to Learn.[20] Such a commitment does not occur as an extracurricular event or as a result of occasional staff development meetings. Opportunities for dialogue, reflection, and inquiry—essential aspects of the development of a teacher—must become part of the school day and of the teacher's role as a thoughtful, reflective learner.

VII

Giles and his colleagues have reminded us that "the first requirement for growth of teachers through any means is that they work under conditions which are favorable to their growth as persons."[21] Currently, with the emphasis on testing, a growing danger exists that teachers' welfare is being ignored.[22] Outstanding teaching cannot occur nor be sustained by educators who feel unappreciated and who, at every turn, are reminded of their deficiencies as if nothing is ever good enough. At a time when schools find themselves working under hostile conditions, the Eight-Year Study reminds us that good education cannot be produced by threatening and consistently belittling teachers, and the possibility of great education is diminished by increasingly sophisticated systems of control. To be sure, such measures might raise the performance of very poor teachers, but this benefit comes at the cost of leveling the truly extraordinary teaching that occurs only when educators are able to fully and wholeheartedly invest themselves in their work.

Unlike the current situation in much of the nation, where teachers are generally excluded from policy discussions, educators at Eight-Year Study schools were treated as professionals and as knowledgeable, skilled practitioners trusted to wisely direct their work toward worthy aims. The Commissions' staff provided support by demonstrating confidence in teachers' abilities. In his summary volume for the final report, Aikin noted a condition necessary for encouraging experimentation: "Experience has taught the participating schools that no school is ready to advance until teachers have a sure sense of security in adventure."[23] In this sense, the Study was not merely an "adventure in American education" but a journey inward for each seriously involved participant. Encouraged to embark on a pedagogical life of innovation, with open and honest discourse about the aims and means of educating the young and a commitment to educational research understood broadly, these teachers worked to the very edge of their abilities, an essential condition, as Bereiter and Scardamalia note, for developing expertise.[24]

Could the Eight-Year Study be recreated today? We have heard that question posed quite often. Certainly the matched-pairs, follow-up study could be staged where the college success of graduates from some common conception of "good secondary schooling" would be compared to the outcomes of students who graduated from more traditional, separate-subject, No Child Left Behind-oriented schools. Since these programs would be selected in anticipation of a matched-pairs design (unlike the Aikin Commission), we suspect the differences between the "S group" (special curriculum, experimental group) and "C group" (control group) would be greater than before. And, if oriented more in accordance with the "Study within the Study," certainly useful empirical and qualitative data would emerge offering many possibilities for future experimentation. But to recreate the spirit of the Eight-Year Study would require establishing a number of experimental laboratory schools, perhaps similar to the Ohio State University School and the Tulsa "little schools." The intent would not be to replicate but rather to extend the boundaries of current practice in order to envision what might be possible. Being labeled an experimental school did not elicit confidence in the 1930s—Aikin even noted that most of the thirty schools were "*fearful* of such appellation"—and the term would even be less well received today.[25] Yet, as we have noted, many remarkable programs are being created around the country. The true challenge is to provide links among these schools and universities to form educational laboratories where discovery and exploration rather than demonstration and duplication become guiding principles.

Postscript

> Just after the end of the Eight-Year Study, I went as a curriculum consultant to the schools of three southern Michigan counties, full of my Eight-Year Study pep and vinegar. I tried to put across some of the things we'd done in the Study, and found they just wouldn't work. I came to this conclusion, and I think it's a significant one, that whenever an end-product is taken over, lock, stock, and barrel, by a group that hasn't gone through the mental agony of the process involved in developing it, the product's bound to fail. It's the process that makes the difference and that led dozens of dedicated teachers who took part in this kind of process to go on to make important contributions to American education. (A. N. Zechiel, 1964)[26]

Critics of the Eight-Year Study sometimes complained about the unwillingness of Aikin and his colleagues to champion one specific curriculum practice or design. Reminiscent of David Tyack's *The One Best System*, too many policy makers, then as well as now, want specific answers to specific questions, a shorthand, "best practices" fix that could be quickly and easily adapted across the tens of thousands of schools that dot the American landscape.[27] Certainly some activities are transportable and should be widely disseminated, but much about good practice is idiosyncratic and particular, a function of a specific group of teachers and students working together in a particular time and place. Those who desire sameness and predictability misunderstand the difficulty of school reform and renewal and underestimate the power of the grammar of schooling. Suspicious of the ability and motives of teachers, too many of those in power fail to grasp what the Commission's leaders came to recognize: the importance of creating in each participating secondary school a culture of inquiry, a fragile phenomenon whose painfully slow birth accentuated differences across experimental sites while fostering an underlying and recognizable faith and confidence in school experimentation. These Eight-Year Study progressives realized that the continuous process of inquiry, one of thoughtful discourse embedded in civility and grounded in a commitment to confront differences in beliefs and values while extending the range of common interests, inevitably leads to positive and fruitful educational outcomes. Truly, the Eight-Year Study was a journey with adventurous company, and the quest lives on.

Appendix A

The Thirty Schools of the Commission on the Relation of School and College

The Aikin Commission's Study within the Study identified the six most experimental schools and the six least experimental schools. While we have been able to document from written correspondence only certain schools, our designations have been compiled from interviews and correspondence with Commission staff and teachers throughout the years, from Frederick L. Redefer's dissertation, and from the complete set of original files submitted for the preparation of text for *Thirty Schools Tell Their Story*.[1]

Altoona Senior High School (Altoona, Pennsylvania) served as the city's one public secondary school with 122 teachers and a racially-integrated student enrollment, in 1932, of 3,100.[2] Students for the experimental program were drawn ultimately from a social-economic and academic cross section, and the Altoona staff organized its own control group as another comparison to the Follow-up Study's C group. The experimental group of students exceeded the Altoona control group in reading ability, cognitive development, and participation in extracurricular activities. A general education program was instituted for both college-bound and non-college-bound students and centered on a needs-based core emphasizing communication, consumership, the natural environment, and family living. Staff reported, "Every department in the Altoona High School has been affected by this new program. During the eight years that teachers and students have been working together, old courses have been revised and twenty new courses have been introduced to take care of new needs or new problems as they were recognized."[3] The school also participated in the Pennsylvania Study Inquiry Group.

The Baldwin School (Bryn Mawr, Pennsylvania), a suburban Philadelphia private girls' boarding school, was founded in 1888 and enrolled just under 400 high school students with most proceeding to post-secondary education. Staff members hoped the Carnegie unit requirement would be dropped so that they could provide more curricular flexibility, yet Redefer described the school as "quite confused in its attitudes towards the aim of the Eight-Year Study. It wanted greater freedom and yet it seemed frightened by such a prospect."[4] By the staff's own account, the curriculum changed little during the Study, and few teachers participated in summer workshops. The Baldwin School's curriculum, successfully oriented for admission to the five sister colleges, was viewed as one of the six least experimental schools.

Beaver Country Day School (Chestnut Hill/Brookline, Massachusetts) Founded in 1921, this suburban Boston private school for girls maintained an innovative progressive tradition well before its entry into the Study. Participation in the Aikin Commission permitted the school to offer to non-college-bound students experiences that had been available only in the college preparatory program, including individualized programs of study, correlated English and social studies courses, and more experiences with the arts and creative expression. The school enrolled approximately 225 students in the junior and senior high school. The experimental program established a core curriculum centered on the social studies with a cultural epoch configuration. Under Eugene Smith's direction, students were administered numerous Cooperative Test Service and Educational Records Bureau tests, and staff used extensively the cumulative record.

Bronxville High School (Bronxville, New York), a suburban New York City school, was considered one of the finest public secondary schools on the East Coast.[5] During the Eight-Year Study the high school, enrolling approximately 400 students, also served as an experimental site for the Thayer Commission's Adolescent Study and the Keliher Commission's Human Relations Film Series. By establishing three "approaches to situations"—scientific, political, and artistic—the curriculum was configured into a broad fields core program. Approximately one-third of the secondary school students chose to participate in the project and were assessed to have become more critically minded, inventive, responsible, and independent.

Cheltenham Township High School (Elkins Park; Wyncote, Pennsylvania), a public suburban Philadelphia secondary school, participated in the Eight-Year Study due primarily to being one of four featured schools in the Pennsylvania Study Inquiry Group. With an enrollment of approximately 800 students from primarily upper-middle-class families, Cheltenham teachers and staff displayed little effort to experiment with the program. One of the few schools not to present at the 1934 George School Conference, the staff's general philosophy, as they admitted, called for no radical change; however, they attempted to develop better cumulative records for parents. Students' personal journals were seen as a way for teachers to become acquainted with needs and interests, and the school served as an experimental site for the Keliher Commission's Human Relations Film Series. Cheltenham Township High School appears to be one of six least experimental schools, even though its reported participation in the Pennsylvania Study, submitted in 1940, appears much more extensive and positive.[6]

The Dalton School (New York, New York) best represents one of the more popular images of an Eight-Year Study school: a small, private, experimental (girls') school of 200 students in New York City.[7] From its inception, Dalton emphasized a laboratory approach to education; however, its most experimental work was reserved primarily for the elementary school. The secondary school, while first attempting to reconfigure the curriculum around "centers of orientation," ultimately developed an integrated curriculum for social science, English, science, and arts. The school served as a site for the Keliher Commission's Human Relations Film Series and radio programming. The teaching staff also experimented with "Grade-Faculty conferences," where the discussion of guidance topics by the teaching faculty sought to bring unity to the curricular program. The Dalton School was thought to be one of the six most experimental schools.

Denver Senior and Junior High Schools (Denver, Colorado) were considered one of the six most experimental programs in the Study. Actually, fifteen schools participated: five high schools began the project, and in 1938 ten junior high schools joined. The teaching staff ultimately conceived an adolescent needs approach—a personal, social, and social-civic problems approach—for all students, college and non-college bound, and all secondary schools developed some form of core program in English and social studies (and later, science). At East Denver High School, the largest school in the city with an enrollment of approximately 2,800 students, over one-third of the students were included in the core program. Few sites represented such an integrative approach to experimentation as depicted in the student publication, *Our Education*.[8] The Denver schools reconceived their school philosophy, evaluation, student records, core curriculum, and staff development programs and developed a comprehensive array of resource units. The Denver schools also served as a site for the Keliher Commission's Human Relations Film Series.

Des Moines Senior and Junior High Schools (Des Moines, Iowa) consisted of four racially integrated secondary schools with an average enrollment of approximately 2,000 students at each site and six junior high schools. The city was nationally recognized for its public forums and adult education programs (financed by the Carnegie Corporation). Theodore Roosevelt Senior High School was originally selected as the primary experimental site, however, "practical science programs" were developed at the three other high schools, and different fusion core programs were begun at several of the junior high schools.

Eagle Rock High School (Los Angeles, California), established in 1927, joined the Eight-Year Study in 1934. While not officially a university school, Eagle Rock is adjacent to Occidental College, a traditional teachers training college during the 1930s and a center for progressive education on the West Coast. The community, an independent, incorporated city within Los Angeles, was highly affluent, and high school enrollment doubled during the 1930s to reach, in 1940, a racially integrated population of 1,690 students. "Democracy as a way of life" was embraced by an administrative council of administrators, staff, and teachers that met bimonthly to address issues identified by an independent "agenda" committee of teachers. The experimental program included cooperative teacher planning, teacher-pupil planning, an adolescent needs core drawn from *Science in General Education,* and the integration of instruction with guidance. Students were actively involved in initiating learning plans, and by 1937 they viewed their education as a continuous series of academic projects.[9] Eagle Rock High School also served as the lead program for the "Los Angeles Plan for the Cooperating and Experimental Schools" as well as one of the four Los Angeles schools in the California Study, the Cooperating Secondary Schools' Study in California.[10] The unpublished supplement to Eagle Rock High School's final report maintained that the school "had a definite bearing on the character of secondary education throughout the city," and that the Eight-Year Study Staff members extended their services far beyond Eagle Rock as their influence was "easily discernable in the program of studies developed in Los Angeles during this period."[11]

The Fieldston School (Bronx, New York) was founded in 1928 to serve as the secondary school for the Ethical Culture Society of New York City. During the Eight-Year Study, enrollment at this private, secondary day school exceeded 500 students. The Fieldston School served as a research site and headquarters for the Commission on Secondary School Curriculum's Adolescent Study. In an effort to develop further the Fieldston Plan, the school staff adopted a social-demands approach to core curriculum and set up six pre-professional fields of interest: euthenics, economics and business, art, literature, music, and science.

Francis W. Parker School (Chicago, Illinois), founded in 1901, was a nationally known private, k–12 progressive school of 300–400 students during the 1930s and had served as a center of progressive education since its founding.[12] The staff entered the Eight-Year Study as "a total school" and did not establish smaller experimental sections. For this reason, its initial programmatic changes were somewhat modest; however, one of the more significant tasks included developing a school philosophy for both the elementary and secondary school faculties. The experimental program included a social studies curriculum with an international focus and an English program that integrated human relations. Further, as an experiment in democratic living, a faculty-elected policies committee accepted considerable administrative roles, and a teachers' council was involved significantly in hiring, promotion, and firing decisions. The Parker School was designated as one of the six most experimental programs, an original financial contributor to the Aikin Commission, and a site for the Keliher Commission's Human Relations Film Series.

Friends' Central School (Philadelphia, Pennsylvania), founded in 1845, served as the "central school" for three elementary Friends' schools. By the time of the Eight-Year Study, the k–12 school enrolled approximately 450 students.[13] The Friends' Central School joined the project in 1934 and quickly embarked on program development, according to Redefer, with "less caution. Some doubts have been expressed by faculty members as to the soundness of its purpose in participating."[14] The staff and faculty had not engaged in experimentation before the Study, but upon its entry immediately developed the Enterprise program—a cultural epoch curriculum where English and social studies were fused during double periods for the upper three grades and where the individuality of students, cooperative living communities, and the social responsibility of school life were stressed. Difficulties arose, however, and Giles, in *Exploring the Curriculum,* even cited the school as an example of unsatisfactory features of a fused core program. The school served as a site for the Keliher Commission's Human Relations Film Series and radio program.

The George School (Newtown, Pennsylvania), another private suburban Philadelphia school, was founded in 1893 by Friends and during the project served as a coeducational boarding school for approximately 400 secondary school students. The George School had developed a sequenced core program in languages, social science, and science before entering the Eight-Year Study and during the project initiated further changes in curriculum, instructional methods, guidance, and cumulative student records. The faculty members made extensive use of tests and evaluation instruments developed by Tyler's Evaluation Team; however, by their own admission the George School staff participated "without any fundamental changes in school policy or routine."[15]

Germantown Friends School (Germantown, Pennsylvania), founded in 1845, represented yet another suburban Philadelphia Friends school with over 600 elementary-secondary students. The school staff members acknowledged that their participation in the Eight-Year Study "came rather suddenly" and that the association had not been easy. "We were more easily convinced that many of the old educational devices and theories were inadequate than that certain experimental new ones were the right ones for us."[16] Little experimentation occurred other than requiring more social studies and science courses. Since the school actually reported that any changes in the curriculum were begun before its participation in the project, Redefer stated: "It is difficult to understand why [G.F.S.] entered the Study and it is difficult to understand why it was accepted."[17] Germantown Friends School must be seen as one of the six least experimental schools.

The Horace Mann School for Girls (New York, New York), founded in 1887 as an experimental school of Teachers College, was by the time of the Eight-Year Study more of an independent, private, k–12 girls' school (having separated from the boys' school in 1914). While not one of the original twenty-eight schools of the Aikin Commission (joining the program in 1933), the high school enrolled over 200 students during the mid-to-late 1930s, with approximately 95 percent proceeding onto college. The junior high school adopted a cultural epoch core ("The Story of Man Through the Ages") that led to a secondary "American/ modern civilization and culture" fusion core. The school philosophy embraced pupil-teacher planning, cooperative planning, and guidance. In 1940, the school merged with the Lincoln School, and then both were closed in 1946.

John Burroughs School (Clayton, Missouri), named after one of the more popular American nature writers of his time, was a private, six-year coeducational secondary school in the St. Louis area, founded in 1923. The Eight-Year Study offered an occasion for the staff to formulate its educational philosophy and to develop curricula fostering social sensitivity, aesthetic appreciation, creativeness, and problem solving within a more traditional separate subjects core. All fifty students in each grade participated in the experimental program that included correlating English and social studies and developing an "activity program" with daily extracurricular activities. The John Burroughs School may have taken on the impression of greater involvement in the project since its principal, Wilford Aikin, became director of the Commission on the Relation of School and College and since it was one of the four schools that contributed $200 to help begin the project.

Lincoln School of Teachers College (New York, New York), along with John Dewey's Laboratory School and the Parker School of Chicago, was perhaps one of the most famous of progressive education schools of the twentieth century. Founded in 1917 with GEB funding as Teachers College's "pioneer experimental school for newer educational methods," this k–12 private school enrolled approximately 250 secondary school pupils during the 1930s and graduated between thirty-nine and fifty-four students each year.[18] The Lincoln School established its "integrated, functional" core curriculum prior to the Study and after its entry developed "firsthand study" activities as weekend and week-long trips to local and regional communities. During 1936 and 1937, all secondary students participated in the experimental program. The Lincoln School served as a site for the Keliher Commission's Human Relations Film Series and was considered among the six most experimental schools (as well as being one of the four original contributors to the Eight-Year Study). Even with its fame, the school was near its end, merging with the Horace Mann School in 1940 and then closing within three years of the release of *Thirty Schools Tell Their Story*.

Milton Academy (Milton, Massachusetts, Boston metropolitan area), chartered in 1798 under the Massachusetts land-grant policy, represented a coeducational day school where preparation for college was its primary goal. When members of the Aikin Commission's Directing Committee were selecting schools for the project, the Carnegie Foundation staff underscored the need for more private schools. Considered one of the least experimental programs, Milton Academy requested permission upon its entry in the Eight-Year Study to continue its independent study-tutorial program. The school was one of the few that did not discuss its work at the George School Conference.

New Trier Township High School (Winnetka, Illinois) served four affluent communities in suburban Chicago and in 1940 maintained an enrollment of 2,500 students (with 85 percent college bound).[19] A small experimental program was organized with students selected for a "v group" based on school records and test results. The New Trier faculty acknowledged that these students underwent no "upsetting revolutionary methods," but teacher-pupil planning was initiated and efforts were undertaken to fuse an English-science course and to revise a cooperative English literature program and social science course. Creative and logical thinking, a scientific point of view, and the habit of suspending judgment—traits of "democratic living"—were integrated into the curriculum. The New Trier faculty and staff admitted they "quite frankly worked within the traditional subject matter headings, feeling that it is not so important what you name a class period as what you do in it."[20]

North Shore Country Day School (Winnetka, Illinois), founded in 1919, was a well-known, private, Chicago progressive school with an "enriched curriculum" implemented before entering the Eight-Year Study. The final three years of high school were organized sequentially to break down traditional patterns in specific subjects, and shop, art, and music were compulsory.[21] Grades were eliminated as incentives for students' work, and many administrative responsibilities were delegated to students. Redefer believed the school never entered into the Eight-Year Study with wholehearted enthusiasm or with complete sympathy, and the final report refers to the faculty becoming more subject-matter oriented. One student, however, described the program as focusing on "rich, creative days" rather than preparing for the future.[22] Efforts were taken to correlate the English and social studies courses, and the social studies curriculum incorporated a community outreach project. The school also served as a site for the Keliher Commission's Human Relations Film Series.

Pelham High School (Pelham Manor, New York) originally intended to develop a core curriculum for English, social science, music, and art. School staff members reported that their work differed from the regular program, "primarily in greater continuity of work, greater adaptation to individual capacity and interests, more adequate guidance, and more vital subject matter," indicating that teachers were involved in experimentation.[23] Yet no representative attended the 1933 Bennington Conference, and the school did not participate at the 1934 George School meeting. In 1936, Pelham High School, one of the original twenty-eight participating schools, withdrew with the consent and approval of the Aikin Commission after becoming more involved than it had anticipated with the Regents' Inquiry of New York State.[24]

Radnor High School (Wayne, Pennsylvania), located in an affluent suburb of Philadelphia, was a racially integrated, public school that enrolled approximately 400 college- and non-college-bound students. The experimental program included gifted as well as least-able students; literature and social studies were correlated with some effort to include mathematics and science. Experimentation at the junior high level included an integrated core for the study of the community (approaching a correlated cultural epochs approach), and at the senior high level a "cooperative course" was developed for the non-college-bound student. Radnor High School was another participant in both the Eight-Year Study and the Pennsylvania Study Inquiry Group. School Superintendent Sydney V. Rowland, who introduced an extensive assessment program and displayed much more loyalty to the testing beliefs of Learned and Wood than to those curriculum and assessment ideas introduced by Tyler and Alberty, reported that the efforts of both projects were undermined by a small vocal group of parents who believed the school was no longer preparing students for college.[25]

Shaker High School (Shaker Heights, Ohio) located in suburban Cleveland, enrolled 300 students in the tenth, eleventh, and twelfth grades; approximately 200 students participated in the experimental program. The school received national recognition during the 1927 PEA conference, held in Cleveland, and this no doubt encouraged its entry into the Eight-Year Study. Little experimentation seemed to occur until A. K. Loomis, former principal at University of Chicago High School, in 1936 became superintendent. Guided by and in conjunction with a two-year community survey program of parents, the school initiated block scheduling, developed a "life needs" core program, increased community field experiences, including an acclaimed arts program with the Cleveland Museum of Art, and eliminated "deadwood" in the curriculum.[26]

Tower Hill School (Wilmington, Delaware), founded in 1919 and guided by the educational program of the Lincoln School, was a private, coeducational secondary school that enrolled approximately 300 students during the time of the Eight-Year Study. Redefer mentioned that while the school was known for its modern educational methods well before the 1930s, staff described its program "as middle of the road and . . . assiduously avoided labeling as 'progressive.' "[27] The curriculum was based on five objectives: social cooperation, critical thinking, appreciation, mental and physical health, and skills. During the project, staff introduced block scheduling and a cultural epoch curriculum with a focus on student needs; however, emphasis seemed to be placed more upon instruction than curriculum development. The school encouraged teacher cooperation and teacher-pupil planning and used extensively the assessment instruments of Tyler's Evaluation Staff. No doubt due to the leadership of its principal, Burton P. Fowler, president of the PEA from 1930 to 1933, Tower Hill School was one of four schools that contributed $200 to help launch the Eight-Year Study.

Tulsa Senior and Junior High Schools (Tulsa, Oklahoma), considered one of the six most experimental schools, included the participation of three white high schools and, tangentially, one black high school. The core curriculum was less oriented toward college preparation and directed more toward personal and social development and the integration of social studies and social relations, notably through the efforts of Lavone Hanna. Core curriculum was organized in blocks and "little schools," and the experimental program embraced pupil-teacher planning and cooperative education.[28]

University of Chicago High School (Chicago, Illinois) was the laboratory school of the Department of Education.[29] Shortly after entering the Study, the eleventh and twelfth grades were removed from the high school and placed under the control of the university. This college component enrolled 240 students with an additional 270 students enrolled in grades 7–10. Experimentation, admittedly limited due to this administrative reorganization, focused primarily upon integrating the social sciences and refining the guidance program and assessment instruments. Redefer maintained that the staff altered its curriculum "only by reorganizing content within traditional academic departments." Even the faculty admitted that it "hesitated to join" the project.[30] Redefer concluded, "There seems to be little recognition of the spirit and purpose of the Eight-Year Study."[31]

University High School (Oakland, California), founded in 1914, served as the training school for the University of California. The three-year public high school enrolling a racially integrated population of 1,750 students, joined the project in 1934, in part due to its ongoing involvement with the UC Institute of Child Welfare's Oakland Adolescent Study. The school served as a research site for the Commission on Human Relations Film program, and its integrated core program followed more of an adolescent-needs approach with an emphasis on personal-social relations, social living, and democracy. The core was described as "teaching 'down to earth' subjects with practical daily value."[32] The school closed under great protest in 1946, and in 1966 the building became the location for the formation of the Black Panther Party.

The University School of Ohio State University (Columbus, Ohio) served as an experimental center for the state of Ohio's teachers with funding provided by the Ohio General Assembly.[33] Upon opening in 1932, the high school faculty and students permitted its organizational framework to emerge. "In line with the policy of setting up no organization in advance of need,"[34] its guidelines, regulations, and mission were drafted at the end of its first year. Approximately 400 elementary, middle, and high school students from throughout the city were enrolled. Although the majority of pupils came from the middle- and upper-middle classes, a socioeconomic, racial, and intellectual cross section was maintained, including 10 to 20 percent African American pupils.[35] Considered one of the six most experimental schools in the project, an adolescent needs core program was organized with an innovative free-reading program and mathematics instruction/Nature of Proof method. The school served as a research site for the Commission on Human Relations film and radio programs and the Thayer Commission's Adolescent Study.

Winsor School (Boston, Massachusetts), a private, girls' day school, enrolled approximately 140 secondary school students during the Eight-Year Study. The staff divided its college-bound students into two groups—a special curriculum to include social studies and community study and a traditional curriculum in accordance with Carnegie units. As the "contemporary-civilizations"-oriented program continued, the entire ninth grade class was included in the special (main unit) curriculum, since "students, parents, and teachers were convinced that the community study combined with the American history (a combination adopted after two earlier experiments) met so unusually well the needs of the students that no one should miss it."[36] The staff recognized that the correlated core curriculum added markedly to the intellectual maturity and self-direction of the students, yet the program was viewed as one of the six least experimental schools.

Wisconsin High School (Madison, Wisconsin), with an enrollment of approximately 300 students at the secondary level, served as the practice teaching center for the University of Wisconsin's School of Education. Viewed as one of the least experimental schools in the Aikin Commission, the staff's "experimental failure," by its own admission, arose more from institutional and professional restraints. Most of the teachers who initiated the experimental program left the school, and five different individuals served as principal during the time of the Eight-Year Study. The school, however, showed little participation, even at the beginning of the project. Wisconsin High School and Pelham High School (which later withdrew) were the only programs to send no delegates to the 1933 Bennington Conference.[37] Staff sought to integrate the secondary school curriculum around four "areas of living": community living, health, vocations, and leisure; however, some teachers, who also held faculty rank in the College of Education within the traditional subject matter fields, "could hardly be expected to lend their enthusiastic support."[38] The experimental program lost direction, and in 1939 the project was abandoned by a faculty vote.

Appendix B

Testing Bureaus and Projects Related to the Aikin Commission

The College Entrance Examination Board (CEEB)

The College Board, founded in 1900 and closely connected to the curricular recommendations of the 1893 Committee of Ten, prepared entrance exams in various traditional subject areas. Due to the very focused high school curriculum from which the examinations were drawn, the CEEB's essay-like answers were more objective than the interpretive responses we have come to assume from essay questions today. The Board exams, then as now, assumed a uniform curriculum, one not always well received by schoolteachers and administrators. One headmaster exclaimed, "I'll be damned if any Board down in New York City, with a college professor at its head, is going to tell me and my faculty what or how to teach!"[1] Quickly, however, school heads recognized that these subject-area, content-specific essay exams were the easiest way for their students to gain admission to elite East Coast colleges. The Board began experimenting in 1916 with a new type of psychological test, the "New Plan," by which a series of examinations was designed to assess intellectual traits rather than subject matter knowledge. Developed by Carl Brigham, the New Plan evolved into the Scholastic Aptitude Test, first administered in 1926, which grew in popularity through the late 1920s and early 1930s with nearly 9,000 candidates taking the exam in 1931. The College Board's New Plan was mentioned regularly in early Aikin Commission discussions about college admissions as an example of innovative and promising work in the area of standardized test construction.[2]

The Cooperative Test Service of the American Council on Education (ACE)

The ACE's Cooperative Test Service (CTS), formed in 1930, became "a factory for the continuous manufacture, year after year, of the particular kind of scientific measuring instrument known as the standardized objective achievement test."[3] This research bureau, directed by Ben Wood and housed at Columbia University, provided high school and college tests for the Pennsylvania Study and by 1932 had organized a Carnegie Foundation-sponsored College Sophomore Testing Program with 140 participating postsecondary institutions throughout the United States. Similar in intent to the College Board's New Plan, leaders of the CTS saw themselves as liberating high school students from the grip of the Carnegie unit. Wood believed that by administering standard intelligence tests with achievement tests, school faculties could assist individual students in becoming more aware of their interests and capabilities as part of the process of helping them plan their futures.

Educational Records Bureau (ERB)

The Educational Records Bureau, founded in 1927, was another agency seeking to determine an appropriate role for standardized testing in public education. During the early days of the testing era, the Bureau served as a forum to discuss issues concerning the use of intelligence, aptitude, and achievement tests. Bureau conferences addressed "the danger of a dogmatic faith in the dependability and significance of test results far beyond what is warranted" and warned that "any testing program inevitably becomes itself the goal of instruction and hence dominates, standardizes, stifles, and devitalizes the whole of the teaching process subject to it."[4] Founded by Eugene Smith and overseen by Herbert Hawkes and Wood, the ERB sold and popularized standardized tests as a service to member schools. Perhaps its greatest legacy, however, was the development of the Cumulative Record Card, an administrative solution for recording student progress and a means "to enable teachers to visualize both the continuity and the complexity and variability of the growing pupil."[5] Although the ERB questioned whether or not "confidential information [should] be recorded and made accessible to all teachers," this card offered a way of recording important student information that could be used by teachers and then passed on to others for use in student guidance.[6] Similarities exist between the PEA, ideologically invested yet willing to debate the uses of progressive education, and the ERB, strongly committed to testing yet serving as a forum for debate and criticism.

A surprising outcome of our research was the discovery of the parallel work of the Bureau's Committee on School and College Relations. While the ERB promoted the use of cumulative records, the Committee's three reports presented detailed information of specific colleges' and universities' adherence to the Carnegie unit and other college admission practices. The Fourth Report of the Committee on School and College Relations, released in 1943, tabulated the responses of 386 questionnaires (originally sent to 750 postsecondary institutions); previous reports served as a method of collecting data on admissions practices. The Committee requested reactions to a series of recommendations, one being that the "use of the so-called 'Carnegie Units' as a measure of secondary school work be given up." Unlike the implementative study and school experimentation of the PEA's Commission on the Relation of School and College, the ERB's Committee on School and College Relations ascertained postsecondary education's allegiance to the Carnegie unit and attempted to form a coalition that, once recognizing its own strength, could initiate change in its own settings.[7] When the Carnegie Foundation leaders decided to reject Aikin Commission grant requests, they recognized that their interests would be better served by the ERB Committee on School and College Relations.

The Pennsylvania Study of the Relation of Secondary and Higher Education

The Pennsylvania Study, described as a "landmark in the passing of the system of units and credits," was conducted between 1925 and 1938 to examine the academic careers of 45,000 students from high school into college.[8] In addition, certain students from the four designated Inquiry Group schools (Altoona, Radnor, Cheltenham Township, and Reading high schools) were followed into their after-college careers, extending the study through 1940. This project, similar to the Eight-Year Study, was initiated to examine continuity in education—the relation between school and college—and conceived of learning as "a continuous process for which the traditional horizontal divisions of our 'educational ladder' are little better than a series of arbitrary obstructions, disturbing crises, and irrelevant distractions."[9] High school achievement tests were administered to over 55,000 high school and college students, approximately 70 percent of all senior secondary students in the state of Pennsylvania, with some students tested every two years for a six-year period. In 1928 alone, tests were given to 27,000 high school seniors. The study sought to shift educators' allegiance from Carnegie units ("the package method of academic advancement") to student "demonstrated achievement" and, from the perspective of Ben Wood, "exposed the fallacies of credits, degrees, and other time-serving 'units,' . . . and denounced the professional incompetence implied by the universal preoccupation with such fraudulent counters with their underlying curriculum folklore, classroom rituals, irrelevant admission ceremonies, and hypocritical twaddle about systematically evaded standards."[10] Perhaps representing the naiveté of the time, standardized testing was associated with democracy, fairness, and opportunity, since all students could now be considered for admission to college on the grounds of intelligence rather than the accessibility to college preparatory programs.

William Learned had devised a new type of test consisting of multiple choice, true-false, and matching items. This "innovative" format represented a major breakthrough in standardization, since instruments could now be scored quickly and objectively. IBM collaborated with the Cooperative Test Service and developed means for scoring the Pennsylvania Study's exam sheets electronically. Thousands of tests could be administered, and reliable and valid data accumulated for students throughout their academic careers. In Pennsylvania, Learned was able to introduce an extensive student sampling procedure and, drawing from the Educational Records Bureau's efforts to develop a cumulative record form, he and Wood began planning a statewide system that would result in a cumulative record of all students' "knowledge attainment." They believed that six years of cumulative records would provide adequate information for admissions to Pennsylvania colleges and ultimately would have greater predictive value than any single college entrance exam. Further, Learned imagined each student's cumulative record becoming part of a registry of student ability, a national database that college admissions officers throughout the United States could tap. In 1941, at the completion of the project, Wood wrote to Learned, underscoring the profound impact of the Pennsylvania Study: "Many significant developments were attributed to the study, including establishing CTS, launching the ERB, popularizing the Cumulative Record (first used by the Pennsylvania Study), underwriting the development of the Electric Test Scoring machine and the adaptation of the Hollerith tabulating machines, and establishing the National College Sophomore Testing program, the Teacher Examination Service, and the Graduate Record Examinations."[11]

Appendix C

Excerpt from a Comprehensive Student Record

This girl is on the whole industrious and responsible. She reaches in some of her work the point where she does not need to be told what to do, but goes beyond the requirements of the teacher in her desire to get as much as she can from the opportunity and to make any contributions she can to her classes. However, she is at times a little temperamental and some work that she likes less than other kinds may not be so completely done. She is judged by all her teachers to have a good deal of creativeness and originality. The least favorable judgment given by anybody is that she is promising in this quality, and the highest judgments which are given by any of her teachers—and there is a certain significance in which ones give those judgments—is that her whole attitude toward everything she does is creative, that she puts into all activities something original. Her influence in the group is distinctly constructive, and she has a good deal of influence. I am not using the word 'leadership,' you understand. She has a very strong constructive influence. Her opinions are respected and therefore the class is the better for having that pupil in the group. The one place where that is not strictly true is in the part of the school day given to physical education. . . . She has a highly inquiring mind on the whole. Practically every teacher judges her to be one who responds with deep interest to any intellectual stimulus. She varies a good deal, however, in open-mindedness. She has certain areas of fixation where, because of her past experience or prejudice developed from family or otherwise, she thinks with a certain emotional set that does not always make it easy to change her mind. . . . This pupil has considerable ability to analyze, but she does not always meet every situation from the analytical standpoint. . . . She is definitely concerned for the good of her group; that is, she thinks beyond her own selfish interest to a degree that means that her social contribution is a thoughtful one. She is very responsive emotionally. . . . She is not physically vigorous, which has to be taken into account in what she is allowed to do or urged to do, but she has a high degree of self-reliance, of assurance in various situations, and she shows good emotional control despite the fact that she is strongly emotional. This pupil has had serious family unhappiness within a short time and has gone through distinct and powerful emotional upsets. She has controlled herself remarkably but undoubtedly has suffered somewhat perhaps from overcontrol. . . . She is definitely purposeful. She knows what she wants and why she wants it and is always moving toward something far enough ahead to be a worthwhile long-time purpose. Her work habits are on the whole quite highly effective, though they differ somewhat in different fields. They are never less than reasonably adequate for a girl of her age.[1]

Glossary

The Aikin Commission. After Aikin's small discussion groups at the 1929 St. Louis and 1930 Washington PEA Annual Conferences bemoaned the curricular control the colleges exerted on the secondary schools, the Commission on the Relation of School and College was formed in April 1930.

The Cummington Meeting. Planning for the project began in earnest in May 1931 at a three-day retreat in Cummington, Massachusetts, and continued during four subsequent meetings during 1931 and 1932 in New York City at the offices of the Carnegie Foundation.

The Plan of Cooperation. By January 1932, the Subcommittee on Principles had prepared a thirteen-page memorandum describing the project. In May 1932, the Directing Committee released the Plan of Cooperation to schools and colleges in the first detailed explanation of the yet-to-be-named Eight-Year Study. At this point the project was to include no more than twenty high schools and would follow approximately 1,000 students each year (between 1936 and 1941) into college.

The Bennington Conference. The first gathering of the "Eight-Year School Experiment" participants—selected teachers, principals, and Aikin Commission staff—occurred in early July 1933 at Bennington College.

The Thayer Commission. During the Bennington Conference the need for curriculum development in the subject fields was discussed. To this end, the Commission on Secondary School Curriculum, originally formed in May 1932, received GEB funding in 1933 and concluded its work in 1940 after completing research in general education design.

The Revolt of 1934. In April 1934, the principals and heads of the participating schools rebelled against the Aikin Commission and indirectly against the Carnegie Foundation. The direction of the project would shift from externally developed tests to a broader conception of evaluation and assessment.

The George School Conference. The second annual gathering was held in June 1934 at the George School in Philadelphia. For the first time an open invitation was extended to all teachers to attend the conference as the Eight-Year Study was redirected more toward curriculum and evaluation issues.

Tyler's 1934 Challenge. In early November 1934, at the Third Educational Conference on Testing in New York City, Ralph Tyler stepped into the national spotlight and questioned the status quo of college admission procedures and testing.

The Thousand Island Park Conference. The third annual meeting of all Eight-Year Study participants was held in June 1935 at an upper New York State park near the summer home of Eugene Smith. Assessment and evaluation permeated the sessions as schools and content area groups (art, drama, English, foreign languages, guidance, mathematics, music, science, and social studies) reported on their curricular activities. A highlight of the meeting was Burton Fowler's statement of the project's developmental stages: protest, hope, and charity.[1] Aikin reported that the general feeling throughout the conference was that "it had been the most outstanding series of meetings held to date."[2] While a fourth conference was to be arranged, no other such gathering was ever staged as the Commissions turned toward organizing teacher workshops.

Evaluation Staff and Curriculum Associates. During 1935 and 1936, program development became so "difficult, complex, and engrossing that the original problem of college entrance requirements was almost lost sight of and forgotten."[3] The orientation of the Study shifted from its original purpose, the "relation between school and college," to its second, "To find, through exploration and experimentation, how the high school in the United States can serve youth more effectively." With the formation of the Evaluation Staff in 1934 and the appointment of Curriculum Associates in 1936, the Aikin Commission seemed to focus exclusively upon assisting schools' faculties to initiate local school reform rather than to commence national educational change.

The Keliher Commission. In 1935, the Commission on Human Relations was formed after Lawrence K. Frank of the General Education Board saw the usefulness of the PEA (Thayer Commission) staff in constructing and developing educational materials. The Commission completed its work in 1942.

The Briarcliff Memorandum. To assist faculty to reexamine and confirm common beliefs and purposes, in October 1935 the Briarcliff (New York) Conference was held to prepare a statement of social objectives for the participating schools.

Proposal for College Follow-up Study. On April 17, 1936, discussions turned to a specific evaluation plan that would follow matched pairs of students into college. At this point, college records of 6,000 students from participating secondary schools (i.e., approximately 1,500 students each year) were to be examined and compared to the records of all college graduates. The 1936 proposal planned to compare the college records of 600 experimental school students with records of traditional secondary school counterparts from four specified colleges. In its final form, the Follow-up Study examined the college experiences of 1,475 pairs of students, graduates from participating schools matched with graduates from traditional schools, at numerous colleges for varying durations of one to three years.

The 1936 Ohio State Workshop. The first teacher workshop was held for six weeks during the summer of 1936 in what would become an innovative approach to teacher education. The PEA workshops offered opportunities for teachers to actually "work" on problems and issues of concern to them.

Science in General Education is published. Released in 1938, *Science in General Education,* the first volume of the Thayer Commission's reports, defined the conception of adolescent needs and general education for which the Eight-Year Study was based.

The Release of *The Story of the Eight-Year Study.* In December 1941, the first volume of the Aikin Commission's report, *Adventure in American Education,* was released. Volume 1, *The Story of the Eight-Year Study,* summarized the Commission's work; four additional volumes were published during 1942 and into 1943 as the Commission completed its work. Through the life of the Eight-Year Study, the Aikin, Thayer, and Keliher Commissions released twenty-two books along with countless related workshop materials and standardized tests.

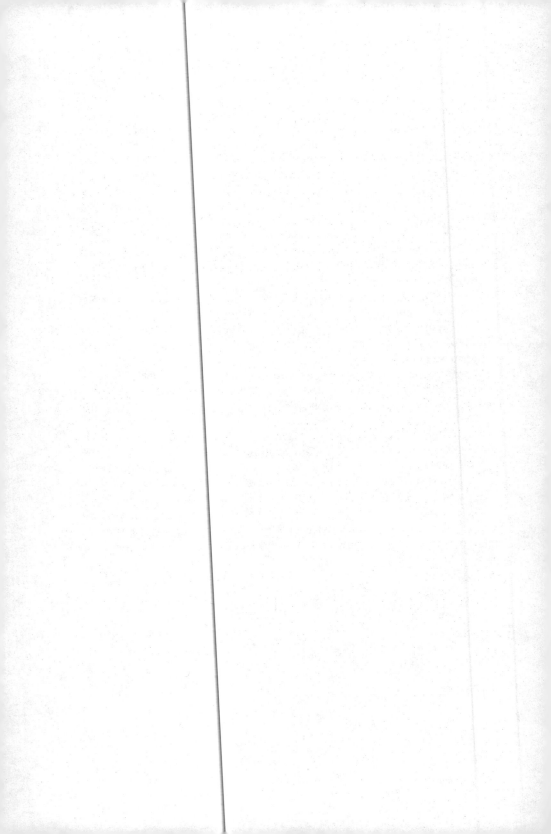

Abbreviations

ACE   American Council on Education

AVK   The Alice V. Keliher Papers, New York University Archives, Bobst Library, New York University

CCF   Carnegie Corporation Archives, Rare Book and Manuscript Library, Columbia University

CFAT   Carnegie Foundation for the Advancement of Teaching, Rare Book and Manuscript Library, Columbia University

FSA   Ethical Culture/Fieldston Schools Archives, Tate Library, The Fieldston School

GEB   General Education Board Archives, Rockefeller Archive Center, Pocantico Hills, New York

MW   Margaret Willis Professional Papers, Museum of Education, University of South Carolina

PEA   Progressive Education Association

PHC   Paul Hanna Collection, Hoover Institution Archives, Stanford University

RDL   Articles and papers prepared by R. D. Lindquist, Department of University Schools, Ohio State University Archives

TC   Special Collections, Teachers College, Columbia University

All future bibliographic references to these works will be abbreviated.

Notes

Epigraph

1. James A. Michener, correspondence to Craig Kridel, August 28, 1986. See also G. W. Dybwad and Joy V. Bliss, *James A. Michener: The Beginning Teacher and his Textbooks* (Albuquerque, NM: The Book Stops Here, 1995).

Introduction

1. Lawrence A. Cremin, *The Transformation of the Schools* (New York: Knopf, 1961): viii.

2. Richard Lipka, John Lounsbury, Gordon Vars, et al., *The Eight-Year Study Revisited* (Columbus, Ohio: National Middle School Association, 1998); David Tyack and Larry Cuban, *Tinkering Toward Utopia* (Cambridge, MA: Harvard University Press, 1995); Ellen Lagemann, *An Elusive Science: The Troubling History of Educational Research* (Chicago: University of Chicago Press, 2000); Linda Darling-Hammond, *The Right to Learn* (San Francisco: Jossey-Bass, 1997); *Education Week* staff, *Lessons of a Century: A Nation's Schools Come of Age* (Bethesda, MD: Editorial Projects in Education, 2000); Diane Ravitch, *Left Back: A Century of Failed School Reforms* (New York: Simon & Schuster, 2000): 267–268, 281–282; Alfie Kohn, *The Schools Our Children Deserve* (New York: Houghton Mifflin, 1999): 232; Patricia Graham, *Schooling America* (Oxford: Oxford University Press, 2005): 88.

3. We must note that the project was never *totally* forgotten. Fifteen years after its release, educators were summarizing the project to a European audience: James Hemming, *Teach Them to Live* (London: Longmans, Green and Co., 1957). Twenty years after its publication, Cremin stated: "Long after the other efforts of the PEA have faded into history, its work [the Eight-Year Study] may well remain as the Association's abiding contribution to the development of American education" (*The Transformation of the Schools*, 251). During the 1970s and 1980s, the Eight-Year Study was described by Daniel and Laurel Tanner as "the most important and comprehensive curriculum experiment ever carried on in the United States" [Daniel Tanner and Laurel Tanner, *Curriculum Development: Theory into Practice* (New York: Macmillan, 1975): 319]. Many other texts and reference books have featured the Eight-Year Study: William H. Schubert, *Curriculum* (New York: Macmillan, 1986); Jon Snyder, Frances Bolin, and Karen

Zumwalt, "Curriculum Implementation," in *Handbook of Research on Curriculum,*
ed. P. W. Jackson (New York: Macmillan, 1992): 402–435; Richard Gibboney,
The Stone Trumpet (Albany: State University of New York Press, 1994); William
F. Pinar, et al., *Understanding Curriculum* (New York: Peter Lang, 1995).

4. Cremin, *The Transformation of the Schools,* ix.

5. Wilford M. Aikin, *The Story of the Eight-Year Study* (New York: Harper &
Brothers, 1942): 116

6. While the final 1940s' volumes of the Eight-Year Study hyphenate "Eight
Year," not all period reports and internal documents do so. In keeping with
period documents, we have standardized all references to the Committee on
the Relation of School and College as the Commission on the Relation of
School and College. Wilford M. Aikin, "Commission on Relation of School and
College," *Educational Research Bulletin* XVII (November 1938): 211.

7. Robert Gilchrist, personal interview with author-CK, Columbus, Ohio,
July 3, 1997.

8. Alice Keliher, correspondence to Flora M. Rhind (October 25, 1937);
GEB: S 1–2, B 283, F 2960; Alice Keliher, correspondence to W. Carson Ryan
(May 16, 1938); GEB: S 1–2, B 283, F 2961.

9. *Progressive Education Advances: Report on a Program to Educate American
Youth for Present-Day Living* (New York: D. Appleton-Century Co., 1938).

10. Katharine Taylor (Chair), "Introductory Memorandum on Plans for
Experimental Work in Secondary Education" (January 16, 1932): 2; GEB: S 1–
2, B 281, F 2935.

11. "Commission on Relation of Secondary School and College," Minutes
of the Meeting of the Board of Director, PEA Minutes (February 21, 1939): 1;
American Education Fellowship Executive Committee, Vol. 4 (February 1938–
November 1940); TC: 370.62 Am 38 v.1.

12. Paul Diederich "Introduction," *Thirty Schools Tell Their Story* (New York:
Harper & Brothers, 1942): xvii–xxiii.

13. "Memorandum of Interview: FPK[epple] and Mr. Aiken [*sic*], Dean
McConn and Dean Hawkes" (August 31, 1933); CCF: III.A, B 300.10.

14. J. L. Bergstresser, "Interviews: Annual Conference of the Directing Committee and Heads of Schools" (October 12–15, 1938): 1; GEB: S 1–2, B 281, F
2933; Frederick L. Redefer, "The Eight-Year Study—Eight Years Later: A Study of
Experimentation in the Thirty Schools" (Ph.D. diss., Teachers College, Columbia
University, 1951): 193; Robert J. Havighurst, "Interviews: Meeting of the Curriculum Staff" (March 2, 1937): 29; GEB RG 12; Havighurst, 1937–1938, Box 4.

15. Dean Chamberlin, Enid Straw Chamberlin, Neal E. Draught, and
William E. Scott, *Did They Succeed in College?* (New York: Harper & Brothers,
1942): 164–175. After years of work we believe we have correctly identified the
six most experimental sites to be Dalton, Lincoln, and Parker schools among
the private programs and Denver, Ohio State, and Tulsa schools among the
public programs. The selection was ultimately made by Ralph Tyler and his
staff, and we wonder if the Dalton School would have otherwise been selected
without its close ties to Tyler and his staff, especially since from 1936 onward
Parkhurst seemed to be at the center of controversy that ultimately led to her

resignation in 1942. Also, the reputation of the Parker School seemed to demand its inclusion when, in fact, its educational practices did not change markedly as the school continued those traditional (progressive) activities established at the beginning of the twentieth century.

16. Frederick L. Redefer, "The Eight-Year Study...After Eight Years," *Progressive Education* 28:2 (November 1950): 33–36. Ironically, in that very issue of *Progressive Education*, three essays appear that illustrate the impact of the Eight-Year Study on curriculum development and school reform: Harold Alberty, "A Proposal for Reorganizing the High-School Curriculum on the Basis of a Core Program," Ibid., 57–61; Lavone A. Hanna, "Proposals for the Secondary School Curriculum," Ibid., 62–67; Kenneth D. Benne, "Eight-Year Study for the 1950's?," Ibid., 68–69.

17. Ralph W. Tyler, *Education: Curriculum Development and Evaluation* (Berkeley, CA: Regional Oral History Office, Bancroft Library, 1987): 283. A far more interesting and positive account of the Eight-Year Study "after six years" was published by Agnes Benedict, *Dare Our Secondary Schools Face the Atomic Age?* (New York: Hinds, Hayden & Eldredge, 1947).

18. Frederick Redefer had requested funding from the GEB for "A Research Project to Explore Possibilities for a Follow-Up Study" in February 1949 [GEB: S 1–2, B 281 F 2934]—in essence, to fund what became his dissertation. The GEB staff expressed concern whether he would be objective [Flora Rhind, "Inter-Office Correspondence" (March 1, 1949); GEB: S 1–2, B 281 F 2934]. No funds were forthcoming, and he begrudgingly wrote his dissertation after one of his colleagues, advising him not to tackle the ambitious topic that he had originally wanted to pursue, instead told him to "take it easy and choose a manageable topic" and to "just get his degree . . . and please a committee." In his 141-page autobiography, *The Education of an Uneducated Man,* Redefer only devotes one paragraph to its description. He does state, however, that "Graduate school was a disappointment, but it was the only road available to that necessary but meaningless Ph.D. degree" [Frederick L. Redefer, *The Education of an Uneducated Man* (unpublished autobiography, 1977): 75–76].

19. Herbert M. Kliebard, *Changing Course: American Curriculum Reform in the 20th Century* (New York: Teachers College Press, 2002): 56.

20. For example, see Ralph W. Tyler, "Studies in Progressive Education and the Direction They are Taking," Proceedings of the Fifth Annual Meeting of the Association of Colleges and Secondary School for Negroes (Tallahassee, FL; December 8–9, 1938): 83–86; Hilda Taba, "The Philosophy of the Eight-Year Study," Ibid., 87–92. Eight-Year Study workshops were attended by African American educators who served to lead the Secondary School Study. Many Eight-Year Study staff participated in this project and clearly would have been more involved if GEB funding had been available. See Craig Kridel, The Secondary School Study Project (Columbia, SC: Museum of Education, in progress).

21. We do not cite those articles and chapters that have taken such "unique" interpretations with facts. Our intent is only to encourage today's educators to reexamine the original Eight-Year Study documents and not to fall prey to other researchers' questionable explanations.

22. Cremin, *The Transformation of the Schools*; Patricia A. Graham, *Progressive Education: From Arcady to Academe* (New York: Teachers College Press, 1967); Larry Cuban, *How Teachers Taught: Constancy and Change in American Classrooms, 1890–1980* (New York: Longman, 1984); David Tyack and Elizabeth Hansot, *Managers of Virtue: Public School Leadership in America, 1820–1980* (New York: Basic Books, 1982); Herbert M. Kliebard, *The Struggle for the American Curriculum, 1893–1958*, 3rd ed. (New York: RoutledgeFalmer, 2004); Arthur Zilvermit, *Changing Schools: Progressive Education Theory and Practice, 1930–1960* (Chicago: University of Chicago Press, 1993).

23. Cremin, *The Transformation of the Schools*, x.

24. Lorraine Morgan, "Interview with Dr. Ralph Tyler" (January 16, 1993): 1; CK's copy.

25. John I. Goodlad, *Romances with Schools* (New York: McGraw-Hill, 2004): 242.

26. Ibid., 254.

27. H. H. Giles, S. P. McCutchen, and A. N. Zechiel, *Exploring the Curriculum* (New York: Harper & Brothers, 1942): 308, emphasis added.

28. Steven C. Rockefeller, *John Dewey: Religious Faith and Democratic Humanism* (New York: Columbia University Press, 1991): 561.

29. Tyack and Cuban, *Tinkering Toward Utopia*, 6.

30. Eugene Smith, "A Message from the President of the PEA," *Progressive Education* 1 (April 1924): 5.

Introduction Vignette: Wilford Merton Aikin

1. Minutes of the Meeting of the Board of Directors, PEA Minutes (February 23, 1929); American Education Fellowship Executive Committee; TC: 370.62 Am 38 v. 1.

2. Burton P. Fowler, "The New Secondary Education" *Progressive Education* 5:4 (October–November–December,1928): 299.

3. V. T. Thayer, "The Reorganization Movement and the Progressive Secondary School," *Progressive Education* 6:2 (April–May–June 1929): 127–131.

4. Wilford M. Aikin, "The Prospect in Secondary Education," *Progressive Education* 7:1 (February 1930): 28, emphasis added.

5. Thomas E. Rankin and Wilford M. Aikin, *American Literature* (New York: Harcourt, Brace and Co., 1922). Aikin no doubt was known to the PEA Executive Board, since just a few years before his John Burroughs appointment he served as the director of the Scarborough School, a private New York school and the site of various PEA committee meetings. Further, the first two PEA Executive Secretaries, Morton Snyder (1926–1927) and J. Milnor Dorey (1928–1931), came from the Scarborough School. Since Aikin had increased enrollment by 300 percent during his four years as director there, he certainly would have generated some attention.

6. Minutes of the Meeting of the Executive and Advisory Board of the Progressive Education Association, PEA Minutes (May 19–21, 1933); American Education Fellowship Executive Committee, TC: 370.62 Am 38 v. 3.

7. Attributes taken from the poem *Ode to Mr. Aikin*, written by Burroughs school staff at the occasion of Aikin's departure; PHC: Wilford M. Aikin Papers, B 1; Ralph Tyler, personal interview with author-CK, Washington, D.C., April 1987; Paul Diederich, telephone interview with author-CK, December 4, 1990; Wilfrid Hamlin, ed., "Introduction," *Teacher School Child*, (Plainfield, VT: Goddard College, 1964): 44.

8. Editorial, "The Executive Committee Holds a Special Meeting," *Progressive Education* 7:5 (June 1930): 252. Harold Rugg states that the "birth of the idea" to form the Eight-Year Study arose from a John Burroughs School survey conducted by himself, a member of the Board of Directors of the PEA, and Burton Fowler, then-president of the Association (Harold Rugg, *Foundations for American Education* [New York: World Book, 1947]: 593).

9. Wilford M. Aikin, "Report of the Committee on College Entrance and Secondary Schools," *Progressive Education* 9:4 (April 1932): 293.

10. Wilford M. Aikin, correspondence to Ralph W. Tyler (January 1946); R. W. Tyler Papers, B 1, F 3; University of Chicago Library, Department of Special Collections.

11. Rudolph D. Lindquist, correspondence to Wilford M. Aikin (April 8, 1942); PHC: Wilford M. Aikin Papers, B 1.

12. M. Heather Aikin Jackson, telephone interview with author-CK, October 30, 2003; Wilford M. Aikin, "Someone to Talk to" (n.d.); CK's collection.

13. Wilford M. Aikin, "The Eight-Year Study: If We Were to Do It Again," *Progressive Education* 31:4 (October 1953): 12. This article was written in response to Frederick Redefer's essay, "The Eight-Year Study...After Eight Years," *Progressive Education* 28:2 (November 1950): 33–36, which had appeared just two years earlier and was drawn from his dissertation research completed in 1952.

14. File clippings: *The Boston Herald*, "Progressive Students Excel in College, Survey Finds" (2/10/42); *Philadelphia Record*, "Progressive Schools Prove They're Progressive" (2/10/42); the *New York Sun*, "Rigid Curriculum Condemned: Graduates of Progressive Schools Found Superior in College Grades" (2/10/42); *Philadelphia Evening Bulletin*, "School of Future Is Taking Form: Experimental Units Here Find That Pupils Excel in Things That Matter" (2/11/42); PHC: Wilford M. Aikin Papers, B 1.

15. "The Secondary Curriculum: An American Experiment," *The Journal of Education* (September 1942): 391–392.

16. Craig Kridel, "Aikin/Aiken: Dashed Hopes and a Legacy Misspelled," *The Journal of Curriculum Theorizing* 13:1 (1997): 38–39. As we examined leading curriculum synoptic texts of the 1980s and 1990s, only half spelled Aikin's name correctly. Percentages dropped dramatically when we added all textbook references from 1970 to 2003.

17. M. Heather Aikin Jackson, telephone interview with author-CK, October 30, 2003.

18. Wilford M. Aikin, "Correspondence"; Hamlin, *Teacher School Child*, 44.

19. Aikin, *The Story of the Eight-Year Study*, 19.

Chapter 1: The Educational Context of the Eight-Year Study

1. Graham, *Progressive Education: From Arcady to Academe*; Cremin, *The Transformation of the Schools*; William J. Reese, *Power and the Promise of School Reform* (Boston: Routledge & Kegan Paul, 1986).

2. John L. Childs, "Progressive Education and the Secondary School," *Progressive Education* 16:4 (October 1939): 411.

3. Berdine Jackman Bovard, "A History of the Progressive Education Association, 1919–1939" (Ph.D. diss., UC Berkeley, 1941); Stanwood Cobb, *The New Leaven: Progressive Education and Its Effect upon the Child and Society* (New York: John Day Company, 1928); Ernest Cobb, *One Foot on the Ground: A Plea for Common Sense in Education* (G. P. Putnam's Sons, 1932).

4. Robert H. Beck, "American Progressive Education, 1875–1930" (Ph.D. diss., Yale University, 1942): 134.

5. Stanwood Cobb, "Concerning Ourselves," *Progressive Education* 6:1 (January–February–March, 1929): 72.

6. George S. Counts, "Dare Progressive Education Be Progressive?," PEA Annual Meeting, Baltimore, February 1932.

7. Harold Rugg, *Foundations for American Education* (New York: World Book Company, 1947): 560.

8. Robert J. Havighurst, "Interviews: Southern New England Regional Conference" (May 11–12, 1934): 57; GEB, RG 12, Series: Havighurst, 1934, B 4.

9. Stanwood Cobb, "Retrospect and Prospect," *Progressive Education* 4:3 (July–August–September 1927): 151.

10. "A Request for Financial Assistance" (January 25, 1933): 5; GEB: S 1–2, B 277, F 2891.

11. *Time* magazine, XXXII: 18 (October 31, 1938). Studebaker served as superintendent of the Des Moines Public Schools.

12. Cremin, *The Transformation of the Schools*, 250; Graham, *Progressive Education*, 57; Stanwood Cobb, personal interview with author-RVB, Columbus, Ohio, 1974.

13. Graham, *Progressive Education*, 57

14. Donald Cottrell, personal interview with author-CK, Worthington, Ohio, May 1978.

15. Robert J. Havighurst and Flora M. Rhind, "The Program in General Education," *General Education Board Annual Report* (New York: GEB, 1940): 7.

16. Quoted in Graham, *Progressive Education*, 21.

17. Howard M. Bell, *Youth Tell Their Story* (Washington, DC: ACE, 1938); Homer P. Rainey, et al., *How Fare American Youth?* (New York: D. Appleton-Century, 1937); *Youth and the Future: The General Report of the American Council on Education's American Youth Commission* (Washington, DC: ACE, 1942); Committee on the Cooperation Study in General Education, *Cooperation in General Education* (Washington, DC: ACE, 1947).

18. Hollis L. Caswell, correspondence to James R. Squire (January 14, 1970), RVB's copy, "Implications of the Eight-Year Study for California Secondary Schools—A Symposium," *California Journal of Secondary Education* 17:3 (March

1942); Roland C. Faunce, *Some Went to College* (Lansing, Michigan, State Board of Education, 1943).

19. Educational Records Bureau materials; FSA: RG3 A4; S5b, B 52, F 13; Eugene R. Smith, "Recent Developments in School and College Relations," *Educational Record* 16, Supplement 9 (January 1936): 86–101.

20. Educational Records Bureau, *Guidance in Public Secondary Schools* (New York: ERB, 1939); Daniel A. Prescott, *Emotion and the Educative Process* (Washington, DC: ACE, 1939); Fellowships: Educational Motion Picture Project of the ACE; GEB 1–2, B 222, F 2129.

21. George S. Counts, *Dare the School Build a New Social Order?* (New York: John Day, 1932).

22. Cremin, *The Transformation of the Schools*, x.

23. Harold Alberty, "The Report of the Committee on Philosophy of Education" (New York: PEA, September 1938). Earlier, Stanwood Cobb, in describing progressive education, recounts "It is not a plan; it is a spirit." ["The Romance of Beginnings," *Progressive Education* 6:1 (January–February–March 1929): 66]. This is also where Cobb substantiates Eliot's characterization that progressive education was "the most significant movement in American education today."

24. Harold Alberty, *A Study of the Project Method in Education* (Ph.D. diss., Ohio State University, 1927); Boyd H. Bode, *Modern Educational Theories* (New York: Macmillan, 1927); Michael Knoll, "Faking a Dissertation: Ellsworth Collings, William H. Kilpatrick, and the 'Project Curriculum,' " *Journal of Curriculum Studies* 28:2 (1996): 193–222.

25. David B. Tyack, *The One Best System* (Cambridge, MA: Harvard University Press, 1974): 196.

26. Herbert M. Kliebard, *The Struggle for the American Curriculum, 1893–1958*, 3rd ed. (New York: RoutledgeFalmer, 2004): xix; 287.

27. Harold Rugg, *American Life and the School Curriculum* (New York, Ginn and Company, 1936): 257.

28. Ralph W. Tyler, *Basic Principles of Curriculum and Instruction* (Chicago: University of Chicago Press, 1949).

29. Eugene R. Smith, "A Message from the President of the Progressive Education Association," *Progressive Education* 1:2 (1924): 99.

30. Boyd H. Bode, *Democracy as a Way of Life* (New York: Macmillan, 1937); Boyd H. Bode, *Progressive Education at the Crossroads* (New York: Newson & Company, 1938); V. T. Thayer, *The Passing of the Recitation* (Boston: D.C. Heath and Co., 1928); V. T. Thayer, "V.T. Thayer Replies," *Progressive Education* 17:8 (1940): 437–540.

31. Rainey, et al., *How Fare American Youth?*, 44.

32. Maxine Davis, *The Lost Generation* (New York: Macmillan, 1936): 327.

33. N. P. McGill and E. N. Matthews, *The Youth of New York City* (New York: Macmillan, 1940): 75.

34. Walter C. Eells, "Collegiate Success of Secondary School Graduates," *Journal of the American Association of Collegiate Registrars* XIII (April 1938): 275–284.

35. Ralph Tyler mentioned that the Rockefeller Foundation paid a ransom to Hitler to permit eight German-Austrian psychologists to immigrate to the

United States. Those project directors, supported by the Rockefeller Foundation, were given the opportunity to employ these researchers. Tyler requested Bettelheim (Ralph Tyler, *Education: Curriculum Development and Evaluation*, 76).

36. Aikin, *The Story of the Eight-Year Study*, 1.

37. Burton P. Fowler, "An Appraisal of the Eight-Year Study of the Progressive Education Association," *The Educational Record*, Supplement 14 (January 1941): 107.

38. Robert J. Havighurst and Flora M. Rhind, *1940 Annual Report* (New York: General Education Board): 19; Frederick L. Redefer, "The Eight-Year Study—Eight Years Later: A Study of Experimentation in the Thirty Schools" (Ph.D. diss., Teachers College, Columbia University, 1951): 2–3.

39. William R. Caspars, *Dewey on Democracy* (Ithaca, NY: Cornell University Press, 2000): 154.

40. John I. Goodlad, *Educational Renewal: Better Teachers, Better Schools* (San Francisco: Jossey-Bass, 1994).

Chapter 1 Vignette: V. T. Thayer

1. V. T. Thayer, *American Education Under Fire* (New York: Harper & Brothers, 1944): 148–149.

2. V. T. Thayer, *The Passing of the Recitation* (Boston: D.C. Heath, 1928).

3. Robert Gilchrist, personal interview with author-CK, Chula Vista, California, January 25, 1998; Oliver Loud, personal interview with author-CK, Seattle, Washington, January 2001; Chandos Reid, telephone interview with author-CK, Boulder, Colorado, March 30, 1992.

4. H. Standish Thayer, telephone interview with author-CK, July 15, 2001.

5. "This is Ethical Culture," The American Ethical Union pamphlet, circa 1930.

6. V. T. Thayer, *Footprints: A Partial Autobiography* (unpublished manuscript, 1971): 9.

7. Ibid., 38.

8. Ibid., 62.

9. "A Quest for Meaning," The American Ethical Union pamphlet, circa 1930.

10. Felix Adler, *Creed and Deed* (New York: G. P. Putnam's Sons, 1877).

11. Thayer, *Footprints*, 69.

12. Thayer, *The Passing of the Recitation*; Alberty and Thayer, *Supervision in the Secondary School*.

13. Thayer, *Footprints*, 70.

14. "The Fieldston Idea" (ca. 1934): 2; FSA: RG3 A4; B48, S6, F4.

15. Harold Alberty and V. T. Thayer, *Supervision in the Secondary School* (Boston: D.C. Heath and Co.,1931): 8

16. Howard B. Radest, *Toward Common Ground: The Story of the Ethical Societies in the United States* (New York: Frederick Ungar, 1969): 218.

17. V. T. Thayer, *Religion in Public Education* (New York: Viking Press, 1947); Thayer, *American Education Under Fire*.

18. Thayer, *Footprints*, 113; Frieda Moss, "Oral Interview with Dr. Vivian Thayer," December 16, 1963 and January 27, 1964; V. T. Thayer File, B I, F 4, Ethical Culture Society Archives, New York.

19. Thayer, *Religion in Public Education*; V. T. Thayer, *The Attack Upon the American Secular School* (Boston: Beacon Press, 1951); V. T. Thayer, *Public Education and Its Critics* (New York: Macmillan, 1954); V. T. Thayer, *The Challenge of the Present to Public Education* (Columbus: Ohio State University Press, 1958); *The Role of the School in American Society* (New York: Dodd, Mead, 1960).

20. Thayer, *The Role of the School in American Society*, 230.

21 M. Willis, *Three Dozen Years*; Report of the Committee on the University School, November 1, 1954; Margaret Willis Papers, b 1/f 9.

22. Exercises on Social Problems, Form A & B, ESB-SST 19A, ESB-SST 19B; CK's personal collection.

23. V. T. Thayer, "Today's Challenge to Education," November 15, 1956; V. T. Thayer File, B 2, F 5, Ethical Culture Society Archives, New York.

24. "Hudson Guild Farm Camp," GEB, S 1–2, B 281, F 2930.

Chapter 2: Tests and Records

1. Tyack and Cuban, *Tinkering Toward Utopia*, 8.

2. Brigham, as the designer of the SAT, is described by Robert Havighurst as being "rather skeptical of the objective testing movement." "Interviews: First meeting of the ACE's Committee on Review of the Testing Movement," December 12–13, 1935; GEB, RG 12; Havighurst, subseries 1935; Box 4, p. 213.

3. Max McConn, "Freeing the Secondary School for Experimentation, *Progressive Education* 10:7 (November 1933): 367.

4. Herbert E. Hawkes, "Preparatory School Pattern and College Accomplishment," *North Central Association Quarterly* 15:3 (January 1941): 253.

5. Eugene R. Smith, "Criteria for Admission to College," *Progressive Education* 5:4 (October–November–December, 1928): 346–350.

6. "Minutes of the Meeting of the PEA Committee on The Relation of School and College" (May 9–11, 1931): 18; GEB: S 1–2, B 281, F 2935.

7. Eugene R. Smith, "Judging and Recording Pupil Characteristics," *The Educational Record* 15:1 (1934): 97.

8. Nicholas Lemann, *The Big Test: The Secret History of the American Meritocracy* (New York: Farrar, Straus and Giroux, 1999): 28–29.

9. Hawkes subsequently filled Keppel's post as dean after his resignation in 1918 for WW I service. William E. Weld and Kathryn W. Sewny, *Herbert E. Hawkes: Dean of Columbia College, 1918–1943* (New York: Columbia University Press, 1958).

10. "Minutes of the Meeting of the PEA Committee on The Relation of School and College (June 20, 1931): 2; GEB, S 1–2, B 281, F 2935.

11. Ibid., 2.

12. "Proceedings of the Meeting of the PEA Committee on The Relation of School and College" (November 6, 1931): 6; GEB, S 1–2, B 281, F 2935.

13. Ibid., 7.

14. Ibid., 8.

15. Stanley R. Yarnall, correspondence to Herbert W. Smith (February 21, 1934); FSA: RG3 A4, B 46, S2.

16. Marginalia: note from David H. Stevens, July Conference Papers No. 4 (July 4, 1933 evening session); GEB, S 1–2, B 281, F 2935.

17. "Proceedings of the Meeting of the PEA Committee on The Relation of School and College" (November 6, 1931): 2.

18. "Memorandum of Interview: FPK[epple] and Dr. Learned" (August 11, 1933); CCF: III.A, B 300.10.

19. Herbert Smith, correspondence to Eugene Smith (March 28, 1934); FSA: RG3 A4; B 47, S1; F1.

20. Jesse Newlon, correspondence to Eugene Smith (April 4, 1934); FSA: RG3 A4; B 47, S4; F5.

21. Jesse Newlon, correspondence to Wilford Aikin (April 3, 1934); FSA: RG3 A4; B 47, S4; F5.

22. Minutes of the Meeting of the Committee on Evaluation of the Commission on Secondary School Curriculum (November 8–9, 1934): 2; FSA: RG3 A4; B 46, S2; F2.

23. Robert B. Leigh, correspondence to Herbert Smith (April 9, 1934); FSA: RG3 A4; B 47, S4, F5.

24. Willard Beatty, correspondence to Herbert Smith (April 9, 1934); FSA: RG3 A4; B 47, S4, F5.

25. Eugene R. Smith, correspondence to H. W. Smith (April 21, 1934); FSA: RG3 A4; B 47, S4, F5.

26. Eugene R. Smith, correspondence to H. W. Smith (April 9, 1934); FSA: RG3 A4; B 47, S4, F5.

27. Stanley R. Yarnall, correspondence to H. W. Smith (February 21, 1934); FSA: RG3 A4; B 46, S4, F5.

28. Rudolph Lindquist, correspondence to Eugene Smith (April 6, 1934); FSA: RG3 A4; B 46, S4, F5.

29. Eugene R. Smith, "The Work of the Committee on Reports and Records," *Progressive Education* 12:7 (November 1935): 443, emphasis added.

30. Eugene R. Smith, correspondence to H. W. Smith (April 9, 1934).

31. Claude M. Fuess, *The College Board* (New York: Columbia University Press, 1950).

32. Herbert W. Smith, Minutes of the Meeting at the Horace Mann School for Girls (April 26, 1934): 2; FSA: RG3 A4; B 47, S4; F5.

33. Ibid., 1.

34. Minutes of the Meeting (May 10, 1934); FSA: RG3 A4; B 47, S4; F5.

35. F. P. Keppel, correspondence to Thomas B. Appleget (October 29, 1936); CCF: III.A, B 300.10.

36. "Record of Interview: F. P. Keppel, Hawkes, Jessup, Aikin, Dean Smith, Tyler" (October 15, 1936); CCF: III.A, B 300.10.

37. William S. Learned, memorandum to F. P. Keppel (December 14, 1934); CCF: III.A, B 300.10.

38. "Blue Sheet: E. E. Day and Keppel" (March 9, 1937); CCF: III.A, B 300.10.

39. "Conversation: W. M. Aikin and Howard J. Savage" (December 17, 1941); CCF: III.A, B 300.10.

40. Memorandum for Council (June 11, 1954); CCF: III.A, B 300.10.

41. Chamberlin, Chamberlin, Drought, and Scott, *Did They Succeed in College?*, 22.

42. Herbert W. Smith, Minutes of the Meeting at the Horace Mann School for Girls (April 26, 1934): 2. At this time in the Study, these two test committees reflected their funding agencies: the Aikin Commission's Committee, with CFAT support, supported tests and measurements, while the Thayer Commission's Committee, with GEB funding, addressed testing from the perspective of curriculum design.

Chapter 2 Vignette: Eugene Randolph Smith

1. Cremin, *The Transformation of the Schools*, 197–198; Rugg, *American Life and the School Curriculum*, 257.

2. Eugene R. Smith, "Aims of Education," speech transcript (April 20, 1920): 16; CK's copy.

3. Eugene R. Smith, *Some Challenges to Teachers* (New York: Exposition Press, 1963): 21; Eugene R. Smith, *Education Moves Ahead* (Boston: The Atlantic Monthly Press, 1924): 12.

4. Harold S. Weschsler, "Eastern Standard Time: High School-college Collaboration and Admission to College, 1880–1930," in *A Faithful Mirror: Reflections on the College Board and Education in America*, ed. Michael C. Johanek (New York: College Board, 2001): 43–79.

5. Eugene R. Smith, "Modernizing Records for Guidance and Transfer," *The Educational Record* 21, Supplement 13 (January 1940): 21.

6. Stanwood Cobb, "Concerning Ourselves," *Progressive Education* 6:1 (January–February–March 1929): 67.

7. Jean Thompson Sharpless, *The Park School of Baltimore: The First Seventy-five Years* (Brooklandville, MD: The Park School of Baltimore, 1988): 16.

8. Ibid., 16.

9. Ibid., 24.

10. Smith, *Some Challenges to Teachers* (New York: Exposition Press, 1963). Smith also donated his massive and valuable clock key collection to Rollins College's museum.

11. Sharpless, *The Park School of Baltimore*, 29, emphasis added.

12. Eugene R. Smith, "Modernizing Records for Guidance and Transfer," *The Educational Record* 21, Supplement 13 (January 1940): 33.

13. *Cooperative Educational Record* (Denver: Denver Public Schools, 1935); FSA: RG3 A4; B 48, F5.

14. Smith, "Modernizing Records for Guidance and Transfer," 22.

15. Ibid., 22.

16. Ibid., 32.

17. Robert W. Butche, *Growing Up In University School: An Autobiographical Look Inside America's Most Experimental Laboratory* (Columbus, Ohio: Greenbrier House, 2005).

18. Paul Klohr, personal interview with author-CK, Columbus, Ohio; May 8, 2004.

19. Smith, "Modernizing Records for Guidance and Transfer," 33.

NB Smith prepared an autobiographical statement, "Educational Experimentation and Advances, 1894, As Observed or Taken Part In." We hope someday this document is made available to the research community.

Chapter 3: An Essential Faith: From Tests and Measurement to Appraisal and Evaluation

1. Wilford M. Aikin, "The First Years of the Eight-Year Experimental Study," *Educational Record* 16, Supplement 9 (January 1936): 71.

2. Ralph W. Tyler, *Education: Curriculum Development and Evaluation* (Berkeley, CA: Regional Oral History Office, Bancroft Library, 1987): 72.

3. Wilford M. Aikin, correspondence to Herbert Smith (April 9, 1934); FSA: RG3 A4; B 47, S4; F5.

4. Eunice F. Barnard, correspondence to Herbert W. Smith (April 26, 1934); FSA: RG3 A4; F47 S4 F3.

5. Herbert W. Smith, Minutes of the Meeting at the Horace Mann School for Girls (April 26, 1934): 2; FSA: RG3 A4; B 47, S4; F5.

6. Three schools did not participate: Cheltenham (a school from the Pennsylvania Study), Milton Academy (a school selected by the Carnegie Foundation), and Pelham Manor Day School (which would later withdraw).

7. John A. Lester, correspondence to school directors and principals (April 10, 1934); FSA: RG3 A4 B 47, S4; F2; The Second Annual Conference (program), George School June 18–23, 1934); GEB: S 1–2, B 281, F 2936.

8. Ralph W. Tyler, *Constructing Achievement Tests* (Columbus, Ohio: Bureau of Educational Research, Ohio State University, 1934).

9. Tyler, *Education: Curriculum Development and Evaluation*, 87–89.

10. Herbert E. Hawkes, "Real and Imaginary Dangers in the Testing Movement," *The Educational Record* 16:1 (January 1935); Weld and Sewny, *Herbert E. Hawkes: Dean of Columbia College, 1918–1943*, 81–82.

11. Herbert E. Hawkes, "Real and Imaginary Dangers in the Testing Movement," 58.

12. Ibid., 53.

13. Sydney V. Rowland, "The Effect of Systematic Testing on Pupil and Teacher," *The Educational Record* 16:1 (January 1935): 97.

14. Tyler, *Education: Curriculum Development and Evaluation*, 86.

15. Ralph W. Tyler, "Evaluation: A Challenge and an Opportunity to Progressive Education," *The Educational Record* 16:1 (January 1935): 121–131. Tyler's 1934 "Challenge" appeared in four publications. When he later edited this speech for the *Progressive Education* journal, the *Educational Research Bulletin*, and *Constructing Achievement Tests*, "opportunity" was deleted from the title so that evaluation proved to be the sole challenge for progressive education.

16. Robert Havighurst, "Interviews: Educational Conference and Meeting of the Educational Records Bureau, New York" (November 1–2, 1934): 127–128; GEB:, Record Group 12; Series Havighurst, Subseries 1934, B 4. While the Conference presenters objected to Tyler's position, it was noted that a very uncharacteristic crowd of first-time attendees was at the 1934 Educational Conference on Testing. "Ben Wood told RJH[avighurst] that many of the Educational Records Bureau people were not able to attend the conference and that he had been expecting a small attendance, but the influx of people from the progressive schools who were interested in the new kind of testing made the conference twice as large as he had anticipated." See Robert J. Havighurst, "Interviews, Educational Conference and Meeting of Educational Records Bureau" (November 1–2, 1934): 1; GEB: S 1–3, B 368, F 3847.

17. Tyler, "Evaluation," 124.

18. Eugene L. Baum, "History of the Commission on Relation of School and College of the Progressive Education Association: 1930–1942" (Ph.D. diss., Washington University, 1969).

19. Tyler, "Evaluation," 123–124.

20. Douglas Waples and Ralph W. Tyler, *Research Methods and Teachers' Problems* (New York: Macmillan, 1930): 20.

21. Waples and Tyler, *Research Methods and Teachers' Problems*, 20.

22. Robert J. Havighurst, "Interviews" (October 13, 1934); GEB: S 1–2, B 282, F 2946; Robert J. Havighurst, "Interviews: Eugene R. Smith" (November 19, 1937); GEB: S 1–2, B 282, F 2947.

23. Eugene Smith, Ralph W. Tyler, and the Evaluation Staff, *Appraising and Recording Student Progress* (New York: Harper & Brothers, 1942).

24. Robert J. Havighurst, "Interviews: Tyler and Buros" (October 13, 1934); GEB: S 1–2, B 282, F 2946; Robert J. Havighurst, "Interviews: R. W. Tyler" (December 16, 1934); GEB: S 1–2, B 282, F 2946.

25. Tyler was at times quite "abrupt" with staff. He decided not to employ one individual because, while quite original, the applicant appeared to lack social skills, and he pushed another from his staff because he thought this person was unable to respond to people with creativity and originality. There were also certain tensions between Tyler and Buros. See Tyler, *Education: Curriculum Development and Evaluation*, 75; Robert J. Havighurst, "Interviews" (June 14–18, 1937); GEB: S 1–2 B 282; F2947; Oscar Buros, correspondence to R. J. Havighurst (January 8, 1936); GEB: S 1–2, B 282; F 2947.

26. Four different types of assistance were offered to the participating schools: (1) recommending available evaluation instruments; (2) developing new instruments; (3) advising the testing of educational hypotheses; and (4) collecting evidence of student success.

27. Frank Freeman, *Mental Tests, Their History, Principles and Applications*, 2d ed. (Boston: Houghton Mifflin, 1939): 262–268.

28. Robert J. Havighurst, "Interviews" (December 16, 1934); GEB: S 1–2, B 282, F 2946.

29. Herbert Hawkes, et al., "Report of the Committee on Evaluation" (November 30, 1937): 3; GEB: S 1–2, B 283, F 2950.

30. Ralph W. Tyler, "Defining and Measuring Objectives of Progressive Education," *The Educational Record* 16, Supplement 9 (1936): 82.

31. Ibid., 79.

32. Ibid., 81.

33. Ruth K. Sayward, "An Evaluation Instrument," *Thirty Schools Bulletin* 1 (April 1937): 31.

34. "Evaluation in the Thirty Schools," PEA 796; FSA: RG3 A4; B 46, S2; F2.

35. Kridel, "Eight-Year Study Materials [microform]: from the Progressive Education Association's Commission on the Relation of School and College," Columbia, South Carolina: Museum of Education, University of South Carolina, 1993; two microfilm reels; 16 mm. Microfilm OCLC 400719841.

36. PEA 209 (1937); Ibid.

37. Smith, Tyler, et al., *Appraising and Recording Student Progress*, 159.

38. For example, Terman Group Test of Mental Ability, Henmon-Nelson Test of Mental Ability, Whipple's High School and College Reading Test, Iowa Silent Reading Test, Rogers Test of Mathematical Ability, Brown-Woody Civics Test, Kirby Grammar Test, Educational Records Cooperative Tests in English, Literary Acquaintance, General Mathematics, General Science (and German, French, and Latin, where appropriate for individual students); Tests 3.4, 3.5: Kridel, "Eight-Year Study Materials."

39. E. E. Day, "Interviews" (December 14, 1934); GEB: S 1–2, B 282, F 2946.

40. Hawkes, et al., "Report of the Committee on Evaluation," 5.

41. Ibid., 5.

42. Ibid., 2.

43. Waples and Tyler, *Research Methods and Teachers' Problems*, 3.

Chapter 3 Vignette: Understanding Ralph Tyler

1. David Krathwohl, "Lessons Learned from Ralph W. Tyler," in *Teachers and Mentors*, ed. Kridel, Bullough, and Shaker (New York: Garland, 1996): 39.

2. Kevin Ryan, John Johnston, and Katherine Newman, "Ralph Tyler: Education's Mr. Fix-It," *Phi Delta Kappan* 58 (March 1977): 540–543.

3. George H. Lackey and Michael Rowls, eds., *Wisdom in Education: The Views of Ralph Tyler* (Columbia, SC: Museum of Education, 1989): 15.

4. Morris Finder, *Educating America: How Ralph W. Tyler Taught America to Teach* (Westport, CT: Praeger, 2004): 12.

5. George Madaus and Daniel Stufflebeam, *Educational Evaluation: Classic Works of Ralph W. Tyler* (Boston: Kluwer Academic, 1989): 251.

6. Ralph W. Tyler, "Reflecting on the Eight-Year Study," *Journal of Thought* 21:1 (Spring 1986): 18; Robert J. Havighurst, "Interviews" (December 18, 1934); GEB: S 1–2, B 282, F 2946.

7. Ralph W. Tyler, *Education: Curriculum Development and Evaluation* (Berkeley, CA: Regional Oral History Office, Bancroft Library, 1987): 101.

8. While W. W. Charters was a close friend, Bode must have been leery of suggesting him as the director of evaluation. Charters is said to have urged

Tyler to accept the Eight-Year Study role and, according to Charters biographer Sheldon Rosenstock, was involved behind the scenes in the Study's design and evaluation (Sheldon Rosenstock, correspondence with author, December 10, 2004, February 3, 2005); Sheldon Rosenstock, "The Educational Contributions of W. W. Charters" (Ph.D. diss., Ohio State University, 1993).

9. Matthew T. Downey, *Ben D. Wood: Educational Reformer* (Princeton, NJ: Educational Testing Service, 1965). Downey maintained as well that Wood's career implemented child-centered and individualized education.

10. Tyler, *Education*, 66.

11. Madaus and Stufflebeam, *Educational Evaluation*, 4.

12. Ralph W. Tyler, "A Generalized Technique for Conducting Achievement Tests," *Constructing Achievement Tests* (Columbus: Ohio State University Press, 1934): 4–14.

13. Ralph W. Tyler, "Conducting Achievement Tests," in *Constructing Achievement Tests* (Columbus: Bureau of Educational Research, Ohio State University, 1934): 13.

14. While William Learned removed himself from the Aikin Commission activities, Wood continued. When Tyler was asked if he and Wood ever resolved their differences, he responded, "Yes, eventually. Ben was a strong-willed man. . . . But, on the whole, a person who wanted to be on the side that is winning" (Tyler, *Education*, 97).

15. Ralph W. Tyler, "The Leader of Major Educational Projects," *Educational Research Bulletin* XXXII:2 (February 11, 1953): 42.

16. W. W. Charters and Douglas Waples, *The Commonwealth Teacher-Training Study* (Chicago: University of Chicago Press, 1929).

17. Tyler, "The Leader of Major Educational Projects," 46.

18. This phrase, coined by Edgar Friedenberg, comes from an essay written by David Krathwohl, "Lessons Learned from Ralph W. Tyler," where he identified eight specific special capabilities. These same traits, according to Rosenstock, describe Charters (Sheldon Rosenstock, correspondence with author-CK, December 10, 2004, February 3, 2005).

19. Rosenstock, correspondence with author-CK, December 10, 2004.

20. I. Keith Tyler, personal interview with author-CK, Columbus, Ohio, October 1993; Tyler, "The Leader of Major Educational Projects," 42.

21. Sheldon Rosenstock, correspondence with author-CK, December 10, 2004.

22. Finder, *Educating America: How Ralph W. Tyler Taught America to Teach*.

23. Robert M. W. Travers, *How Research Has Changed American Schools* (Kalamazoo, MI: Mythos Press, 1983): 147.

24. Herbert M. Kliebard, "Reappraisal: The Tyler Rational," *School Review* 78 (February 1970): 259–272.

25. Audio tape; interviewer: I. Keith Tyler (circa 1970); audio recording; Columbus, Ohio; CK's copy.

26. Ralph W. Tyler, William Schubert, and Ann Lynn Lopez Schubert, "A Dialogue with Ralph Tyler," *Journal of Thought* 21:1 (Spring 1986): 94.

27. Robert J. Havighurst, "Interviews: Meeting of Curriculum Staff" (March 2, 1937): 29; GEB RG 12, Havighurst, 1937–1938, Box 4.

28. Giles, McCutchen, and Zechiel, *Exploring the Curriculum*, 1.

29. Attributed to Tyler: Executive Committee of the Cooperative Study in General Education, *Cooperation in General Education* (Washington, DC: ACE, 1947): 57.

30. Finder, *Educating America,* 63–80.

31. Executive Committee, *Cooperation in General Education.*

32. Robert J. Havighurst "Interviews: Ralph W. Tyler" (December 27, 1939); GEB S 1–2, B 285, F 2972.

33. Executive Committee, *Cooperation in General Education,* 181.

34. Madaus and Stufflebeam, *Educational Evaluation,* 261.

35. Martin Dworkin, *Dewey on Education* (New York: Teachers College Press, 1959): 1.

Chapter 4: Guidance, Human Relations,
and the Study of Adolescents

1. Thayer, Zachry, and Kotinsky, *Reorganizing Secondary Education,* 91.

2. Harold Rugg, *Foundations for American Education* (New York: World Book, 1947): 21.

3. Harold Taylor, personal interview with author-CK, Holderness, New Hampshire, July 1989; Stephen J. Cross, "Designs for Living: Lawrence K. Frank and the Progressive Legacy in American Social Science" (Ph.D. diss., Johns Hopkins University, 1994): xi.

4. J. R. Gillis, *Youth and History* (New York: Academic Press, 1974): 138.

5. Leta Hollingworth, *The Psychology of the Adolescent* (New York: D. Appleton-Century Co., 1928): ix.

6. Hollingworth, *The Psychology of the Adolescent,* 36.

7. N. P. McGill and E. N. Matthews, *The Youth of New York City* (New York: Macmillan, 1940): 75.

8. Flora M. Rhind, "Interviews: Dr. Zachry's Seminar on the Study of Adolescents" (May 5, 1937); GEB S 1–2, B 280, F 2925.

9. V. T. Thayer, *Footprints,* 88.

10. Thayer, *Footprints,* 89.

11. Robert J. Havighurst and Flora M. Rhind, "The Program in General Education," General Education Board Annual Report (New York: GEB, 1940): 7.

12. Thayer, Zachry, and Kotinsky, *Reorganizing Secondary Education,* v.

13. "A Description of The Study of Adolescents" (July 6, 1937): 1; GEB S 1–2, B 280, F 2926.

14. Ibid.

15. Alice Keliher, "Preface"; Langer, *Psychology and Human Living,* v.

16. Louise Rosenblatt, telephone interview with author-CK, May 2, 1998; Dennis R. Bryson, *Socializing the Young: The Role of Foundations, 1923–1941* (Westport, CT: Bergin & Garvey, 2002).

17. Bryson, *Socializing the Young,* 170–180; Dennis R. Bryson, "Lawrence K. Frank: Architect of Child Development, Prophet of Bio-technocracy" (Ph.D. diss., University of California, Irvine, 1993).

18. Jane Howard, *Margaret Mead: A Life* (New York: Simon and Schuster, 1984): 176.

19. Robert J. Havighurst, "Interviews: Dr. V. T. Thayer, LFK, and RJH" (March 20, 1935); GEB S 1–2, B 280, F 2924.

20. "Progressive Education Association: Commission on Human Relations: Appraisal" (December 1935): GEB S 1–2; B 283, F 2955.

21. "Radio Analysis, Committee on the Relation of School and College" (n.d.); GEB S 1–2, B 361, F 3727; "Appraisal: Committee on Radio and Education" (December 1940); GEB S 1–2, B 361, F 3726.

22. I. Keith Tyler and high school students, *High-School Students Talk It Over* (Columbus, Ohio: Bureau of Educational Research, 1937); 35.

23. "Preliminary Report on the Human Relations Forum" (April 15, 1938); GEB S 1–2, B 361, F 3726.

24. "Progressive Education Association: Committee on Radio and Education" (December 1940); GEB S 1–2; B 361; F 3726; "Other Program Suggestions from Human Relations Materials" (n.d.); GEB S 1–2, B 361, F 3727; Margaret Harrison, correspondence to principals (October 3, 1938); GEB S 1–2, B 361, F 3726.

25. I. Keith Tyler and high school students, *High-School Students Talk It Over*, 35.

26. The Hays Office (the Motion Picture Producers and Distributors of America) coordinated the release of film classics to the schools and the Keliher Commission establishing a film distribution network.

27. Garth S. Jowett, Ian C. Jarvie, and Kathryn Fuller, *Children and the Movies: Media Influence and the Payne Fund Controversy* (Cambridge: Cambridge University Press, 1996).

28. "Project Progress" (December 24, 1937); GEB: S 1–2, B 284, F 2965. "Appraisal, Motion Picture Project" (January 1940): 4; GEB: S 1–2, B 284, F 2962.

29. Alice Keliher, correspondence to the General Education Board (May 27, 1936): 7; GEB: S 1–2, B 283, F 2960.

30. Alice Keliher, "Commission on Human Relations Report" (January 7, 1941); GEB: S 1–2, B 283, F 2959.

31. Taylor, *Do Adolescents Need Parents?*, 70.

32. Thayer, Zachry, and Kotinsky, *Reorganizing Secondary Education*, 98.

33. L. K. Frank, "Interviews: Caroline Zachry" (April 12, 1935); GEB: S 1–2, B 280, F 2924.

34. "A Description of the Study of Adolescents" (revision of June 1938): 52–56; GEB: S 1–2, B 281, F 2927.

35. L. K. Frank, "Interviews: Caroline Zachry" (April 12, 1935); GEB: S 1–2, B 280, F 2924.

36. Flora M. Rhind, "Interviews: Dr. Zachry, Adolescent Study Seminar (October 15, 1936); GEB: S 1–2, B 280, F 2925.

37. Peter Blos, *The Adolescent Personality: A Study of Individual Behavior* (New York: Appleton-Century-Crofts, 1941); Jessie L. Rhulman, "An Approach to Revision of the Program and Procedures of Centralia High School [Ohio State

University School] through the Organization and Interpretation of School Records" (Ed.D. dis., Teachers College, New York, 1939).

38. Caroline Zachry, "Study of Adolescents to R. J. Havigurst" (March 14, 1935):7; GEB S 1–2 B 280, F 2924.

39. Zachry, *Emotion and Conduct in Adolescence*, 20.

40. L. K. Frank, "Interviews: Meeting with the Adolescent Study" (May 19, 1936); GEB: S 1–2, B 280, F 2925.

41. Benjamin Spock, *Spock on Spock: A Memoir of Growing Up with the Century* (New York: Pantheon Books, 1989): 111.

42. Nancy Zachry, personal interview with author-CK, New York City, November 4, 2004; Nancy and Stephen Zachry, personal interview with author-CK, New York City, December 2, 2004.

43. Flora M. Rhind, "Interviews: Dr. Zachry's Seminar on the Adolescent Study" (October 29, 1936); GEB: S 1–2, B 280, F2925.

44. In correspondence to the GEB, one educator claimed with racist fervor that Zachry was forcing the views of European Jews down the throat of the classroom teacher (W. B. T. correspondence [November 9, 1939]; GEB: S 1–2, B 280, F2926).

45. Robert J. Havighurst, *Developmental Tasks and Education* (Chicago: University of Chicago Press, 1948); Havighurst and Hilda Taba, *Adolescent Character and Personality* (New York: John Wiley, 1949).

46. Ruth Strang, *The Role of the Teacher in Personnel Work* (New York: Bureau of Publications Teachers College, 1935): 105.

47. *Thirty Schools Tell Their Story*, 723.

48. Ibid., 724.

49. Katherine Moran, *Curriculum Study in the Tulsa Secondary Schools* (Tulsa, OK: Tulsa Public Schools, 1940): 130.

50. A. M. Johnson, "The Contribution of the Lunchroom to the Program of Secondary Education—with Special Reference to the Ohio State University School" (M.A. thesis, Ohio State University, Columbus, 1941); OSU Archives, University School (RG 15/p/3/5).

51. Lou LaBrant, telephone interview with author-CK, March 1990; Chandos Reid, telephone interview with author-CK, Boulder, Colorado, March 30, 1992.

52. Zachry, *Emotion and Conduct in Adolescence*, 1.

53. Rosenblatt, *Literature as Exploration*, v.

54. Zachry, *Emotion and Conduct in Adolescence*, 1.

55. Thayer, Zachry, and Kotinsky, *Reorganizing Secondary Education*, 6.

56. George H. Lackey and Michael Rowls, eds., *Wisdom in Education: The Views of Ralph Tyler* (Columbia, SC: Museum of Education, 1989): 184. Stephen Corey also argued that the Eight-Year Study involved action research. See Stephen Corey, "Action Research in Education," *Journal of Educational Research* 47 (1954): 375–380.

57. Howard Good, "Wilderness Road," *Education Week* (August 11, 2004): 56.

58. Thayer, Zachry, and Kotinsky, *Reorganizing Secondary Education*, 93.

59. Lorin W. Anderson, *In Their Own Words: An Interim Report* (Columbia, SC: The Anderson Research Group, 2001).

Chapter 4 Vignette: Alice V. Keliher

1. Alice V. Keliher, "My Story" (ca. 1975): VIII; AVK: MC 139; B 16; F 8.1.

2. Lucy Prete Martin, ed., *Profiles in Childhood Education 1931–1960* (Wheaton, MD: Association for Childhood Education International, 1992).

3. Lois Meek Stolz, "Memorandum re. Lawrence K. Frank" (ca. 1968); AVK: MC 139; B 16; F15.

4. Keliher, "My Story" (ca. 1975): I.

5. Keliher, "My Story" (ca. 1975): VIII.

6. Arnold Gesell, *An Atlas of Infant Behavior: A Systematic Delineation of the Forms and Early Growth of Human Behavior Patterns . . . Illustrated with 3,200 Action Photographs* (New Haven, CT: Yale University Press, 1934).

7. Keliher, "My Story" (ca. 1975): IX.

8. Ibid.

9. Keliher, "My Story" (ca. 1975): XXVI.

10. Alice V. Keliher, "Lawrence Kelso Frank" (ca. 1975): n.p.; AVK: MC 139; B 16; F 8.3.

11. "Interviews: Alice Keliher" (March 31, 1938); GEB: S 1–2, B 283, F 2961. An offer in 1938 to establish a department of educational research in the School of Education at Yale University had not materialized.

12. Lawrence K. Frank, correspondence to Alice Keliher (May 15, 1935); AVK: MC 139; B 16; F 14. Interestingly, during the same period the American Council on Education leaders were looking for an administrator for their Educational Motion Picture Project (also funded by the GEB). While they were well aware of Keliher's extensive film background, staff members instead considered lesser-qualified, male candidates (George Zook, correspondence to David H. Stevens [July 15, 1935]; GEB: S 1–2, B 222, F 2131).

13. Correspondence: Lawrence K. Frank and Alice Keliher, May 15, 1935; May 15, 1935; July 16, 1935; July 24, 1935; July 29, 1935; July 30, 1935; July 30, 1935; August 1, 1935; August 5, 1935; AVK: MC 139; B 16; F 14.

14. Louise Rosenblatt, telephone interview with author-CK, April 24, 2002.

15. Another 183-page experimental form, *Society and Family Life*, exists for a volume on family issues written for college students, yet no final report was published, perhaps stemming from the reactions and comments received. See *Society and Family Life: Tentative Experimental Form* (New York: Commission on Human Relations, PEA); *Life and Growth: Tentative Experimental Form* (New York: Commission on Human Relations, PEA); AVK: MC 139; B 14; "Tentative Appraisal: Commission on Human Relations: Preparation of Teaching Materials" (November 1940).

16. Walter Langer-Alice Keliher correspondence (September 1937–July 1938); AVK: MC 139; B 12, F 10; Carl Van Ness, correspondence to Alice Keliher (September 5, 1940); AVK: MC 139; B 12, F 10.

17. Correspondence, Walter Langer to Alice Keliher (June 5, 1938, July 5, 1938, July 7, 1938, July 26, 1938); AVK: MC 139; B 12; F 23. Langer left Vienna with Freud and traveled to London; from there, he coordinated applications as Keliher and her brother became the sponsors for Austrian refugees, sending

documents and financial statements. Keliher's position as the vice president and associate director of the American Film Center seemed to be conceived as much to impress immigration officers as to fulfill professional responsibilities.

18. Walter Langer, correspondence to Alice Keliher (May 18, 1938): 3; AVK: MC 139; B 12; F 23.

19 The Human Relations Series of Films (New York: PEA, 1939); Motion Picture Project, 1937; GEB: S 1–2, B 284, F 2966.

20. Alice Keliher, "Human Relations Series of Films," New England Educational Film Association, p. xi (n.d.); AVK: MC 139; B 17; F 7.

21. Alice Keliher, "Human Relations Series of Films," New England Educational Film Association, p. xii (n.d.); AVK: MC 139; B 17; F 7.

22. Lea Jacobs, "Reformers and Spectators: The Film Education Movement in the Thirties," Camera Obscura 22: 29–49. Garth S. Jowett, Ian C. Jarvie, and Kathryn Fuller, Children and the Movies: Media Influence and the Payne Fund Controversy (Cambridge: Cambridge University Press, 1996); Schools Motion Picture Committee; GEB: S 1–2, 377; B 226, F 2168. Educational Motion Picture Project of the ACE; GEB 1–2, B 222, F 2128, F 2133.

23. Joris Ivens, the first production director and later technical advisor, is perhaps best known for The Spanish Earth, a 1937 documentary about the Spanish Civil War, and New Grounds, both involving Ernest Hemingway. Irving Lerner, another production director, was simultaneously filming the 1937 documentary China Strikes Back and later established Nykino/Frontier Films, a collective, left-wing documentary production group. Helen van Dongen, who would work on Robert Flaherty's The Land and Louisiana Story, served as the Human Relation Series of Film sound editor, and Joseph Losey, production supervisor for the series, was active in New York City's workers' theatre movement. Both Ivens and Losey were later named members of the Communist Party and blacklisted by the House Un-American Activities Committee. See Kees Bakker, ed., Joris Ivens and the Documentary Context (Amsterdam: Amsterdam University Press, 1999); Hans Schoots, Living Dangerously: A Biography of Joris Ivens (Amsterdam: Amsterdam University Press, 2000); Helen van Dongen, personal interview with author-CK, Brattleboro, Vermont; July 20, 2005.

24. "Summary of Secrets of Success Experiment in Character Education," 1936; GEB: S 1–2, B 284, F 2964.

25. Lea Jacobs, "Reformers and Spectators: The Film Education Movement in the Thirties," 36. While certain documents may imply that the Committee on Social Values in Motion Pictures was a component of the Commission on Human Relations, a thorough search of GEB documents shows no connection other than the sharing of technical staff for the editing of film. See "Summary of Secrets of Success Experiment in Character Education," 1936; GEB: S 1–2, B 284, F 2964.

26. "Commission on Human Relations: Motion Picture Project, Appraisal" (January 1940): 1; GEB: S 1–2, B 284, F 2962.

27. Alice V. Keliher, "Are There Basic Values in Progressive Education?," The Alice V. Keliher Papers, MC 139; B 12; F 2; Alice V. Keliher, "Current Misconceptions of Progressive Education" (ca. 1929); AVK: MC 139; B 12; F 5;

Alice V. Keliher, "Current Misunderstandings of Progressive Education; AVK: MC 139; B 12; F 75.

28. William Van Til, telephone interview with author–CK, May 11, 2005.

Chapter 5: The Conception of Needs

1. Hilda Taba, *Curriculum Development: Theory and Practice* (New York: Harcourt, Brace & World, 1962): 285.

2. With the many contemporary attacks on progressive education and life adjustment, we must note that Eight-Year Study leaders had not mandated that their schools revolve their curriculum around adolescent needs. The conception of an adolescent needs core curriculum emerged over time and even then was adopted by few of the participating school faculties. Most if not all of the Aikin Commission school programs remained centered on a content-oriented, correlated core curriculum.

3. Harold Alberty, *A Study of the Project Method in Education* (Columbus: Ohio State University Press, 1927); B. H. Bode, *Modern Educational Theories* (New York: Macmillan, 1927).

4. V. T. Thayer, *Formative Ideas in American Education* (New York: Dodd, Mead and Company, 1965): 303.

5. John Dewey, *Interest and Effort in Education* (Boston: Houghton Mifflin Company, 1913).

6. Committee on the Function of Science in General Education, *Science in General Education* (New York: D. Appleton-Century Co., 1938): v.

7. "Minutes of Meeting, Commission on Secondary School Curriculum" (May 11–12, 1935): 3; GEB: S 1–2, B 280, F 2917.

8. Giles, McCutchen, and Zechiel, *Exploring the Curriculum*, 85.

9. "Minutes of Meeting, Commission on Secondary School Curriculum" (May 11–12, 1935): 18; GEB: 1–2, B 280, F 2917.

10. Ibid., 15.

11. Ibid., 12.

12. Ibid., 18.

13. Ibid., 12–13.

14. Committee on the Study of Adolescents Seminar (January 14, 1937): n.p.; GEB: 1–2, B 280, F 2926.

15. Ibid., II, 2.

16. Ibid., II, 2.

17. Ibid., III, n.p.

18. Ibid., IV, n.p.

19. Ibid., VIII, n.p.

20. Giles, McCutchen, and Zechiel, *Exploring the Curriculum*, 5.

21. *Science in General Education*, 24.

22. Ibid., 27.

23. Ibid., 27

24. Ibid., 25.

25. Ibid.,, 25.

26. Ibid., 26.

27. V. T. Thayer, telephone interview with Robert V. Bullough, March 17, 1977; also, Robert J. Havighurst, "Interview: Boyd Bode" (October 23, 1934): 115; GEB: RG 12; Havighurst, 1934, B 4.

28. Boyd H. Bode, *Progressive Education at the Crossroads* (New York: Newson & Company, 1938): 63–66.

29. Boyd H. Bode, *Democracy as a Way of Life* (New York: Macmillan, 1937): 67.

30. Boyd H. Bode, "The Concept of Needs in Education," *Progressive Education* 15:1 (1938): 9.

31. Boyd H. Bode, "Needs and the Curriculum: Progressive Education," *Progressive Education* 17:8 (December 1940): 532–537.

32. V. T. Thayer, "V. T. Thayer Replies," *Progressive Education* 17:8 (December 1940): 538, 540.

33. Thayer, Zachry, and Kotinsky, *Reorganizing Secondary Education*, 15.

34. Ibid., 75.

35. Cremin, *The Transformation of the Schools*, 327.

36. Boyd H. Bode, *Progressive Education at the Crossroads* (New York: Newson & Company, 1938): 43–44.

37. Taba, *Curriculum Development*, 285.

38. The Committee on the Objectives of a General Education in a Free Society, *General Education in a Free Society* (Cambridge, MA: Harvard University Press, 1945).

Chapter 5 Vignette: Caroline Zachry

1. La Campanilla, New Jersey State Teachers College Student Yearbook (1930): 26.

2. Spock, *Spock on Spock: A Memoir of Growing Up with the Century*, 110. Spock acknowledged her profound influence on his work; Louise Rosenblatt, telephone interview with author-CK, May 2, 1998; Paul Diederich, telephone interview with author-CK, May 9, 1991; Nancy Zachry, telephone interview with author-CK, September 9, 2003; Stephen Zachry, personal interview with author-CK, New York City; December 2, 2004.

3. Robert Gilchrist, personal interview with author-CK, Chula Vista, California, January 25, 1998.

4. Eugene Smith, "A Message from the President of the Progressive Education Association," *Progressive Education* 1 (April 1924): 5.

5. Stephen Petrina, "Luella Cole, Sidney Pressey, and Educational Psychoanalysis, 1921–1931," *History of Education Quarterly* 44:4 (Winter 2004): 524–553; Clifford T. Mayes, "The Psychoanalytic View of Teaching and Learning: 1922–2002," *Journal of Curriculum Studies* (in press); Patrick Suppes and Hermine Warren, "Psychoanalysis and Education," in *Impact of Research on Education: Some Case Studies*, ed. P. Suppes (Washington, DC: National Academy of Education, 1978): 371–379; Rudolf Ekstein and Rocco L. Motto, *From Learning for Love to Love of Learning* (New York: Brunner/Maxel Publishers, 1969).

6. "Zachry Seminar," GEB: S 1–2; B 280, F 2925.

7. Robert J. Havighurst, "Interviews" (July 30, 1937); GEB: S 1–2, B 284, F 2967.

8. Caroline B. Zachry, *Personality Adjustments of School Children* (New York: Charles Scribner's Sons, 1929).

9. Spock, *Spock on Spock,* 110.

10. Flora M. Rhind, "Continuing Committee for Study of Adolescents" (January 10, 1940); GEB: S 1–2, B 285, F 2973; Robert J. Havighurst, "Interviews: Dr. Caroline Zachry" (May 15, 1939); GEB: S 1–2, B 280, F 2925; Robert J. Havighurst, "Interviews: Chancellor Harry Chase" (May 2, 1939): 98; GEB, RG 12, Havighurst, 1939, Box 5.

11. Margaret Mahler, *The Memoirs of Margaret S. Mahler,* edited by Paul E. Stepansky (New York: Free Press, 1988): 105.

12. "Mss. Proposal: Cultural Geography of New York," Columbia University Press (September 19, 1949); Columbia University Press Records, B 32, file: Caroline Zachry Institute of Human Development, Columbia University.

13. Robert J. Havighurst, "The Study of Adolescence in Relation to Reorganization of General Education" (March 25, 1935); Lawrence K. Frank, "Child Study Program" (September 25, 1936); GEB: S 1–2, B 369, F 3849; Dennis Bryson, "Personality and Culture and Rockefeller Philanthropy," *Research Reports from The Rockefeller Archives Center* (Fall 2005): 14–19.

14. Mary Frank Perry, personal interview with author-CK, Holderness, New Hampshire, July 30, 1989; Mary Frank Perry, telephone interview with author-CK, June 15, 2002.

15. V. T. Thayer, correspondence to Trevor Arnett (February 22, 1934): 7; GEB: S 1–2, B 279, F 2911.

16. Robert J. Havighurst, "Interviews: Telephone conversation with Dr. Caroline Zachry" (March 28, 1935); GEB: S 1–2, B 280, F 2924.

17. This is a woman who embraced change and the unexpected. While in her forties, she decided to adopt a child (during an era when a single, mature woman would not necessarily have been deemed an appropriate parent). Zachry traveled to Washington, D.C., and adopted not one but two children and, in what must be seen as one of the more unique gestures of "revision," she officially changed her daughter's name twice until finally arriving upon a suitable selection (Nancy Zachry, personal interview with author-CK, New York City, January 15, 2004).

18. "Description of the Study of Adolescents" (July 6, 1937); GEB: S 1–2, B 280, F 2926.

19. Caroline B. Zachry, "The Influence of Psychoanalysis in Education," *The Psychoanalytic Quarterly* 10 (1941): 443.

20. Active and fully participating staff members included Benedict, Erickson, Horney, Mead, Peter Blos, John Dollard, Eric Fromm, Earl Goudey, Lois Murphy, Fritz Redl, George Sheviakov, and Spock. Zachry's group was also tangentially connected to an American Council on Education research project conducted by Daniel Prescott and centered at Oakland Public Schools, with Herbert Stoltz and Harold Jones of the University of California's Institute of Child Welfare.

21. "Description of the Study of Adolescents" (July 6, 1937); GEB: S 1–2, B 280, F 2926.

22. Robert J. Havighurst, "Tentative appraisal" (November 27, 1940); GEB: S 1–2, B 279, F 2914.

23. Havighurst, "Tentative appraisal," Ibid.

24. "Description of the Study of Adolescents" (revision of June 1938): 54; GEB: S 1–2, B 281, F 2927.

25. Robert J. Havighurst, "Interviews" (July 30, 1937); GEB: S 1–2, B 284, F 2967.

26. Robert J. Havighurst, "Interviews: Regional Conference of the PEA in Detroit" (April 24–25, 1935).

27. Caroline B. Zachry, "Contributions of the Psychoanalytic to the Education of the Adolescent," *The Psychoanalytic Quarterly* 8 (1939): 102.

28. Havighurst, "Tentative appraisal" (November 27, 1940): 2; GEB: S 1–2, B279, F 2914.

Chapter 6: The Core Curriculum

1. Boyd H. Bode, "The Confusion in Present-day Education," *The Educational Frontier*, ed. W. H. Kilpatrick (New York: The Century Company, 1933): 4.

2. Diane Ravitch, *Left Back* (New York: Simon & Schuster, 2000): 262–263.

3. See Paul Shaker, "*Left Back*: Punditry or History?," *Journal of Curriculum Studies* 36:4 (2004): 495–507.

4. Patricia Graham, *Schooling America* (Oxford: Oxford University Press, 2005): 125.

5. A. E. Bestor, *Educational Wastelands* (Urbana: University of Illinois Press, 1953).

6. Wilford M. Aikin, "Division of High-school and College Relations," *Educational Research Bulletin*, Vol. XVII, No. 6 (September 21, 1938): 153.

7. William S. Learned, *Realism in American Education* (Cambridge, MA: Harvard University Press, 1932): 28.

8. William S. Learned and Ben D. Wood, *The Student and His Knowledge* (New York: Carnegie Foundation for the Advancement of Teaching, 1927); Larry Cuban, *How Teachers Taught: Constancy and Change in American Classrooms, 1890–1980* (New York: Longman, 1984).

9. W. C. Bagley, "The Textbook and Methods of Teaching," *The Textbook in American Education*, ed. G. M. Whipple (Bloomington, IL: Public School Publishing Company, 1931): 10–11.

10. L. T. Hopkins, "Differentiation of Curriculum Practices and Teaching Methods in High Schools," *The Grouping of Pupils*, Part I, ed. G. M. Whipple (Bloomington, IL: Public School Publishing Company, 1936): 173–185; L. V. Koos, Summary: National Survey of Secondary Education, United States Department of the Interior Bulletin, No. 17, Monograph No. 1 (Washington, DC: Government Printing Office, 1932).

11. Aikin, *The Story of the Eight-Year Study*, 77; Cuban, *How Teachers Taught*, 2d ed. (New York: Teachers College Press, 1993): 88.

12. A. K Loomis, E. S. Lide, and B. L. Johnson, "Program of Studies, National Survey of Secondary Education Bulletin," *United States Department of the Interior Bulletin* 17:19 (Washington, DC: United States Government Printing Office, 1932). Further, from a national survey of courses of study and curriculum materials published between 1934 and 1937 (secondary and elementary programs combined), Leary found that 88 percent were "organized by single subjects or groups of unrelated subjects," while 12 percent of the courses showed signs of "full or partial integration of learning activities" (most of these likely at the elementary level). See Bernice E. Leary, "A Survey of Courses of Study and other Curriculum Materials published since 1934," *United States Department of the Interior Bulletin* No. 31 (Washington, DC: United States Government Printing Office, 1937): 25, 62.

13. Aikin, *The Story of the Eight-Year Study*, 25.

14. R. D. Leigh. "Twenty-seven Senior High School Plans," *Progressive Education* 10:7 (November 1933): 373–380.

15. Other classifications of core programs were developed by the Curriculum Associates during the next nine years but by the time of their final report, curricular experimentation took three forms and reflected the degree of organizational flexibility at a school as much as the creativity of its teachers. Quite similar to Leigh's original description, school curricula were conceived as *broad field courses*, survey courses representing a concept of general education. The Curriculum Associates maintained that all of the school sites had implemented some form of broad field courses with many programs emphasizing a problems-based approach for instruction (Giles, et al., *Exploring the Curriculum*, 310). The second category was quite loosely defined as *core curriculum* and included different configurations—unified studies, cultural epoch, social demands, and adolescent needs. The third form, *the reorganization of subjects*, signified the many instances when an individual teacher revised a single course, since some school faculties were unwilling or unable to initiate overall program redesign.

16. Leigh, "Twenty-seven Senior High School Plans," 378.

17. S. P. McCutchen, "Social Studies," *Educational Research Bulletin* 17:8 (September 21, 1938): 231–236.

18. Aikin, *The Story of the Eight-Year Study*, 25.

19. Denver Public Schools, *Handbook for the Application of Progressive Education Principles to Secondary Education* (Denver, Colorado: Denver Public Schools, 1936): 115, 114; Giles, McCutchen, and Zechiel, *Exploring the Curriculum*, 307.

20. Robert J. Havighurst, "Interviews" (February 28–29, 1936); GEB S 1–2, B 277, F 2893.

21. J. L. Bergstresser, "Interviews: Annual Conference of the Directing Committee and Heads of Schools" (October 12–15, 1938): 5; GEB: S 1–2, B 281, F 2933.

22. Giles, McCutchen, and Zechiel, *Exploring the Curriculum*, xx.

23. Associates included Paul Diederich, formerly a Latin teacher at the Ohio State University School and since 1934 a member of the Evaluation Staff, who had special responsibility for foreign languages, English, and the arts; H. H. Giles, also of the University School, was a consultant in English and the

arts; Henry Harap, who in 1937 coordinated a curriculum laboratory at Ohio State; Walter Kaulfers of Stanford University, who visited schools during the fall of 1938 to assist foreign language teachers; S. P. McCutchen, who left the John Burroughs School in 1936 and worked full time until 1940 as a consultant in social studies; A. N. Zechiel, who had been on the faculty of the Tower Hill School and was a consultant in science and mathematics, John Lester, who worked part time from 1935 to 1941 in English, primarily with schools along the Atlantic seaboard.

24. Wilford M. Aikin, "Division of High-school and College Relations," *Educational Research Bulletin* (September 21, 1938):153.

25. Giles, McCutchen, and Zechiel, *Exploring the Curriculum,* 311.

26. Aikin, "Division of High-school and College Relations," 153.

27. Harold B. Alberty, "Development of Core Curriculums," *Educational Research Bulletin* 17:8 (September 21, 1938): 223–224.

28. Chamberlin, Chamberlin, Draught, and Scott, *Did They Succeed in College?,* 164–175.

29. Lou LaBrant, telephone interview with author-CK, March 1990.

30. Margaret Willis, *Three Dozen Years;* Report of The Committee on the University School, November 1, 1954; Margaret Willis Papers, b 1/f 9; Museum of Education, University of South Carolina; Robert W. Butche, *Image of Excellence: The Ohio State University School* (New York: Peter Lang, 2000).

31. Rudolph D. Lindquist, "The Public Secondary School as it Might Be" (May 19, 1935): 7; RDL: RG 16/e-3/3.

32. Rudolph D. Lindquist, "Memo to the Faculty" (December 29, 1934): 2. RDL: RG 16/e-3/3; Lindquist, "The Public Secondary School as it Might Be, 10.

33. Rudolph D. Lindquist, "Memo: The Organization of Educational Experiences" (May 27, 1935); RDL: RG 16/e-3/3; Lindquist, "Memo to the Faculty," 1–5, RDL: RG 16/e-3/3.

34. Giles, McCutchen, and Zechiel, *Exploring the Curriculum,* 293.

35. Rudolph D. Lindquist, "Purposes of the School Program" (December 3, 1934); RDL: RG 16/e-3/3.

36. Rudolph D. Lindquist, "Values as Reflected in Organization and Teaching Procedure" (May 15, 1934); RDL: H 52434, RG 16/e-3/3; Lindquist, "The Public Secondary School as it Might Be," 5.

37. Class of 1938, Ohio State University High School, *Were We Guinea Pigs?* (New York: Henry Holt and Company, 1938): 24.

38. Class of 1938, *Were We Guinea Pigs?,* 24–25.

39. H. H. Giles, "Travels of a Curriculum Associate among the Secondary Schools," *Educational Research Bulletin* 17:8 (September 21, 1938): 247.

40. H. H. Giles, *Teacher-pupil Planning* (New York: Harper & Brothers, 1941): 40.

41. Class of 1938, *Were We Guinea Pigs?,* 204–205; Harold Fawcett, *The Nature of Proof* (New York: Teachers College, 1938).

42 Class of 1938, *Were We Guinea Pigs?,* 211.

43 Class of 1938, *Were We Guinea Pigs?,* 209.

44. See the current website of the Alumni Association of University School, http://www.aaus.net.

45. Giles, *Teacher-pupil Planning*, 76–77.

46. *Thirty Schools Tell Their Story*, 745.

47. Denver Public Schools, *Handbook for the Application of Progressive Education Principles to Secondary Education* (Denver, Colorado: Denver Public Schools, 1936).

48. Class of 1938, *Were We Guinea Pigs?*, 80–81).

49. Oliver Loud, personal interview with author-CK, Seattle, Washington, January 2001; William Van Til,, telephone interview with author-CK, November 18, 1993; Lou LaBrant, telephone interview with author-CK, March 1990; Robert Gilchrist, telephone interview with author-CK, June 2002.

50. William Van Til, *My Way of Looking at It: An Autobiography* (Terre Haute, IN: Lake Lure Press, 1983): 114.

51. Paul Klohr, personal interview with author-CK, Columbus, Ohio; May 8, 2004.

52. Giles, McCutchen, and Zechiel, *Exploring the Curriculum*, 75.

53. Ibid., 74.

54. Henry C. Morrison, *The Practice of Teaching in the Secondary School* (Chicago: University of Chicago Press, 1926).

55. Giles, McCutchen, and Zechiel, *Exploring the Curriculum*, 72.

56. William G. Wraga, "Patterns of Interdisciplinary Curriculum Organization and Professional Knowledge of the Curriculum Field," *Journal of Curriculum and Supervision* 12 (Winter 1997): 98–117.

57. Patricia Wasley, *Stirring the Chalkdust* (New York: Teachers College Press, 1994).

Chapter 6 Vignette: Harold Alberty

1. Harold B. Alberty, *Reorganizing the High-School Curriculum* (New York: Macmillan, 1947, 1953); Harold B. Alberty and Elsie J. Alberty, *Reorganizing the High-School Curriculum*, 3rd ed. (New York: Macmillan, 1962).

2. Harold B. Alberty, *Public Education in the Sixties: Trends and Issues* (Columbus: College of Education, Ohio State University Press, 1963): 2; W. W. Charters, *Curriculum Construction* (New York: Macmillan, 1923).

3. Victor B. Lawhead, "Harold Alberty, Teacher and Guide," in *Teachers and Mentors*, ed. C. Kridel, R. V. Bullough, and P. Shaker (New York: Garland, 1996): 153.

4. Alberty and Alberty, *Reorganizing the High School Curriculum*, 234, 235.

5. Ibid., 202.

6. Harold B. Alberty, "Designing Programs to Meet the Common Needs of Youth," *Adapting the Secondary School Program to the Needs of Youth*, Part I, ed. Nelson B Henry (Chicago: University of Chicago Press, 1953): 119.

7. Herbert Kohl, *The Discipline of Hope* (New York: Simon and Schuster, 1998): 176–263.

8. See Alberty and Alberty, *Reorganizing the High-School Curriculum*, 204–223.

9. Roland C. Faunce and Nelson Bossing, *Developing the Core Curriculum* (Englewood Cliffs, NJ: Prentice Hall, 1951): 7.

10. Harold B. Alberty, *A Study of the Project Method in Education* (Columbus: Ohio State University Press, 1927).

11. William H. Kilpatrick, "The Project Method," *Teachers College Record* 19:4 (September 1918): 319–335; William H. Kilpatrick, *Foundations of Method* (New York: Macmillan, 1925).

12. Alberty, *A Study of the Project Method in Education*, 50.

13. Paul Klohr, personal interview with author-CK, Columbus, Ohio; May 8, 2004.

14. Alberty, *A Study of the Project Method in Education*, 98.

15. Harold Alberty and V. T. Thayer, *Supervision in the Secondary School* (Boston: D.C. Heath, 1931).

16. University School, *How Children Develop: A Revision of Child Development Study* (Columbus, Ohio State University Press, 1946).

17. Van Til, *My Way of Looking at It: An Autobiography*, 2d ed. (San Francisco: Caddo Gap Press, 1996): 120–129.

18. Erwin Brundage, correspondence to Paul R. Klohr (December 15, 1975); RVB's collection.

19. Ibid.

Chapter 7: The Importance of Social Philosophy

1. John Dewey, *Democracy and Education* (New York: Macmillan, 1916): 22.

2. George S. Counts, "Dare Progressive Education Be Progressive?," *Progressive Education* 9:4 (1932): 258.

3. George S. Counts, *Dare the School Build a New Social Order?* (New York: John Day Company, 1932): 40.

4. Counts, *Dare the School Build a New Social Order?*, 41.

5. Committee on Social and Economic Problems, *A Call to the Teachers of the Nation* (New York: John Day Company, 1933): 19.

6. Aikin, *The Story of the Eight-Year Study*, 9.

7. Ibid., 30.

8. E. E. Day, "Heads of Schools Conference, Columbus, Ohio" (October 22, 1936): 1; GEB: S 1–2, B 281, F 2932.

9. July Conference Papers No. 5 (July 5, 1933): 1 GEB, S 1–2, B 281; F 2935.

10. July Conference Papers No. 8 (July 7, 1933): 1 GEB, S 1–2, B 281; F 2935.

11. Aikin, *The Story of the Eight-Year Study*, 29.

12. Boyd H. Bode, "Achieving Democratic Education in Contemporary Society," *Democracy Faces the Future* (New York: PEA, 1937): 23.

13. Harold Alberty, "The Social Philosophy of the School," *Thirty Schools Bulletin* I (April 1937): 7.

14. Wilford M. Aikin, personal correspondence to H. Smith (October 8, 1935); FSA: RG3 A4; B47, S4, F3a.

15. "Second Memorandum on Central Objectives" (November 5, 1935): 2; GEB: S 1–2, B 281, F 2932; The Briarcliff Conference of Heads of Schools, Briarcliff Manor, New York (October 25–27, 1935); GEB: S 1–2, B 281, F 2936.

16. Denver Public Schools, *Handbook for the Application of Progressive Education Principles to Secondary Education* (Denver, Colorado: Denver Public Schools, 1936): 27.

17. E. E. Day, "Heads of Schools Conference, Columbus, Ohio" (October 22, 1936): 4; GEB: S 1–2, B 281, F 2932.

18. Frederick L. Redefer, *The Education of an Uneducated Man* (unpublished autobiography, 1977): 57.

19. Frederick L. Redefer, correspondence to R. Havighurst (November 3, 1937); GEB, S 1–2, B 284, F 2970; W. Carson Ryan, "A Request" (October 27, 1938); GEB, S 1–2, B 284, F 2970.

20. Harold Alberty, "The Social Philosophy of the School," *Thirty Schools Bulletin* I (April 1937): 7–10.

21. Aikin, *The Story of the Eight-Year Study*, 30.

22. H. H. Giles, "Travels of a Curriculum Associate among the Secondary Schools," *Educational Research Bulletin* 17:8 (1938): 238.

23. Committee on Philosophy of Education, *Progressive Education: Its Philosophy and Challenge* (New York: PEA, 1940).

24. John Dewey, "The Social-Economic Situation and Education," *Essays, How We Think, Contributions to the Educational Frontier* (1933): 48; *The Later Works of John Dewey, 1925–1953*, vol. 8 (Carbondale: Southern Illinois University Press, 1985).

25. Katherine Moran, *Curriculum Study in the Tulsa Secondary Schools* (Tulsa, OK: Tulsa Public Schools, 1940): 19.

26. Ibid., 37.

27. Ibid., 37.

28. Ibid., 19.

29. Ibid., 9.

30. *Thirty Schools Tell Their Story*, 659

31. Ibid., 156.

32. Ibid., 156.

33. Margaret Willis, "Democracy in the Formulation of School Policies," *Educational Method* XIX:4 (January 1940): 216.

34. *Thirty Schools Tell Their Story*, 400–401.

35. Margaret Willis, "Democracy in the Formulation of School Policies," 216.

36. Ibid., 216.

37. Radnor High School, *Report to the Commission on the Relation of School and College* (Wayne, PA: Radnor High School, 1940): 17.

38. J. L. Bergstresser, "Interviews: Annual Conference of the Directing Committee and Heads of Schools" (October 12–15, 1938): 3; GEB, S 1–2, B 281, F 2933.

39. Benjamin R. Barber, *A Passion for Democracy* (Princeton, NJ: Princeton University Press, 1998): 220.

40. Ibid., 225.

41. Corliss Lamont, *Dialogue on John Dewey* (New York: Horizon Press, 1959): 58.

42. Boyd H. Bode, "Dr. Childs and Education for Democracy," *The Social Frontier* 5:39 (November 1938): 38–40.

Chapter 7 Vignette: Boyd H. Bode

1. E. E. Bayles and B. L. Hood, *Growth of American Educational Thought and Practice* (New York: Harper & Row, 1966): 246.

2. "Progressives Progress," *Time* magazine, XXXII: 18 (October 31, 1938): 35; R. V. Bullough Jr., *Democracy in Education: Boyd H. Bode* (Bayside, NY: General Hall).

3. Boyd H. Bode, correspondence to Max Otto (June 4, 1913); Max Otto Papers, State Historical Society of Wisconsin.

4. H. Gordon Hullfish, correspondence to Hendrik Bode (February 29, 1956); H. Gordon Hullfish Papers, Thompson Memorial Library, Ohio State University.

5. Boyd H. Bode, correspondence to Max Otto (March 3, 1937); Max Otto Papers, State Historical Society of Wisconsin.

6. Dewey wrote: "Bode seems to me from the standpoint of philosophic originality one of the two or three strongest of his generation in this country" quoted in a letter from Arthur Daniels to President James [January 22, 1909]; Bode Appointment File, RS 2/5/15; University of Illinois Archives.

7. John Dewey, *Democracy and Education* (New York: Macmillan, 1916): 386.

8. Boyd H. Bode, *Fundamentals of Education* (New York: Macmillan, 1921): 62.

9. Boyd H. Bode, correspondence to Max Otto (March 11, 1937); Max Otto Papers, State Historical Society of Wisconsin.

10. Boyd H. Bode, *Modern Educational Theories* (New York: Macmillan, 1927); Bode, *Fundamentals of Education* (New York: Macmillan, 1921); Bode *Modern Educational Theories*; Boyd H. Bode, *Conflicting Psychologies of Learning* (Boston: D.C. Heath, 1929); Harold Rugg, *American Life and the School Curriculum* (Boston: Ginn and Co., 1936): 461.

11. William B. Brown, "A Great Man Spoke," *Educational Scene* III (November, 1937): 35.

12. Boyd H. Bode, *Democracy as a Way of Life* (New York: Macmillan, 1937): 114.

13. Boyd H. Bode, "Dr. Childs and Education for Democracy," *The Social Frontier* 5:39 (November 1938): 39.

14. Bode, *Democracy as a Way of Life*, 75.

15. Ibid., 62.

16. Ibid., 95.

Chapter 8: Staff Development Teacher Workshops as Personal and Professional Growth

1. C. J. Lucas, *Teacher Education in America* (New York: St. Martin's Press, 1991).

2. M. S. Garet, A. C. Porter, L. Desimone, B. F. Birman, and K. S. Yoon, "What Makes Professional Development Effective? Results from a National

Sample of Teachers," *American Educational Research Journal* 38:4 (Winter 2001): 915–945.

3. Giles, McCutchen, and Zechiel, *Exploring the Curriculum*, 231.

4. Ibid., 217.

5. Aikin, *The Story of the Eight-Year Study*, 16.

6. Giles, McCutchen, and Zechiel, *Exploring the Curriculum*, 230.

7. B. W. Frazier, "Development of State Programs for the Certification of Teachers," *United States Department of the Interior Bulletin* No. 12 (Washington, DC: United States Government Printing Office, 1938).

8. Frazier, "Development of State Programs for the Certification of Teachers," 62, 70.

9. See G. C. Kyte, "Conclusions Derived from Experimental Studies on the Value of Supervision," *Educational Method* 10:7 (April 1931).

10. O. G. Brim, "Changing and Conflicting Conceptions in Supervision," *Educational Method* 10:3 (December 1930): 133.

11. Larry Cuban, *How Teachers Taught: Constancy and Change in American Classrooms, 1890–1980* (New York: Longman, 1984).

12. D. B. Brady, "An Analysis of the Objectives and Functions of Supervision," *Educational Method* 13:3 (December 1933): 140.

13. Burton P. Fowler, "Supervision in the Progressive Secondary School," *Addresses and Proceedings of the National Education Association* (Washington, DC: The National Education Association, 1932): 686.

14. William H. Burton, *Supervision and the Improvement of Instruction* (New York: D. Appleton and Co., 1924).

15. Denver Public Schools, *Handbook for the Application of Progressive Education Principles to Secondary Education* (Denver, Colorado: Denver Public Schools, 1936): 44.

16. Giles, McCutchen, and Zechiel, *Exploring the Curriculum*, 210.

17. *Thirty Schools Tell Their Story*, 724.

18. Denver Public Schools, *Handbook for the Application of Progressive Education Principles to Secondary Education*, 44.

19. J. M. Gwynn, *Curriculum Principles and Social Trends*, rev. ed. (New York: Macmillan, 1950): 368.

20. Giles, McCutchen, and Zechiel, *Exploring the Curriculum*, 210.

21. Lawrence K. Frank, "Interviews: Mr. Willard W. Beatty" (March 9, 1933): 2; GEB: S 1–2, B 279, F 2911.

22. Kenneth L. Heaton, W. G. Camp, and Paul B. Diederich, *Professional Education for Experienced Teachers: The Program of the Summer Workshop* (Chicago: University of Chicago Press, 1940): 2–3.

23. Louis Raths, "The Workshop," *Educational Research Bulletin* 20:5 (May 14, 1941): 118, 117.

24. Giles, McCutchen, and Zechiel, *Exploring the Curriculum*, 260–261, 263.

25. Alan Griffin, "Workshops in Secondary Education," *Educational Research Bulletin* 20:5 (May 14, 1941): 122.

26. H. E. Hawkes, E. C. Foster, and B. P. Fowler, "Report of the Committee on Evaluation" (November 30, 1937): 4; GEB: S 1–2, B 283, F 2950.

27. Heaton, Camp, and Diederich, *Professional Education for Experienced Teachers*, 5.

28. H. E. Hawkes, E. C. Foster, and B. P. Fowler, "Report of the Committee on Evaluation."

29. Heaton, Camp, and Diederich, *Professional Education for Experienced Teachers*, 7.

30. W. C. Ryan and Ralph W. Tyler, *Summer Workshops in Secondary Education: An Experiment in the In-service Training of Teachers and Other Educational Workers* (New York: Progressive Education Association, 1939): 22.

31. Denver Public Schools, "Report to the Commission on the Relation of School and College on the Participation of the Denver Public Schools in the Eight-year Study of the PEA, 1933–1941" (Denver, Colorado: Denver Public Schools): 145.

32. Heaton, Camp, and Diederich, *Professional Education for Experienced Teachers*, 8.

33. "PEA Service Program Report" (March 26, 1941): 2; GEB: S 1–2, B 284, F 2971.

34. Giles, McCutchen, and Zechiel, *Exploring the Curriculum*, 231.

35. Rocky Mountain Workshop, "Arts Activities: Why Not Cut Loose" (1938): n.p.; The Ohio State University Archives, Alberty Faculty Papers, RG 40/41 A.

36. Ibid., n.p.

37. Ibid., n.p.

38. Wilford M. Aikin, "Division of High-school and College Relations," *Educational Research Bulletin* 17:8 (September 21, 1938): 152–155.

39. Paul R. Klohr, correspondence to R. V. Bullough Jr., January 11, 2002.

40. K. L. Heaton, "A Report of Progress to the Executive and Advisory Committees on the Development of Summer Workshops for 1939" (February 20, 1939): 4; GEB S–1, B 285; F 2975.

41. Hollis L. Caswell, correspondence to R. J. Havighurst (September 26, 1939); GEB: S 1–2, B 285, F 2972.

42. Katherine Moran, *Curriculum Study in the Tulsa Secondary Schools* (Tulsa, OK: Tulsa Public Schools, 1940): 133.

43. Ryan and Tyler, *Summer Workshops in Secondary Education*, 37.

44. W. Carson Ryan, "Notes on Visits to the Summer Workshops" (1939): 8; GEB: S 1–2, B 285, F 2976.

45. C. E. Prall and C. L. Cushman, *Teacher Education in Service* (Washington, DC: ACE, 1944): 210.

46. Giles, McCutchen, and Zechiel, *Exploring the Curriculum*, 211–212.

47. M. S. Garet, A. C. Porter, L. Desimone, B. F. Birman, and K. S. Yoon, "What Makes Professional Development Effective? Results from a National Sample of Teachers," *American Educational Research Journal* 38:4 (2001): 933.

48. Kevin Ryan interview with Ralph Tyler (May 7, 1976), original transcript for use in "Ralph Tyler: Education's Mr. Fix-It," Phi Delta *Kappan* 58 (March 1977): 540–543 RVB's private collection.

Chapter 8 Vignette: Margaret Willis

1. Ninth-grade core course transcript (October 4, 1934); MW: b1/f6.
2. Margaret Willis, personal correspondence to M. Stickney (April 5, 1931); MW, b5/f12; Museum of Education, University of South Carolina.
3. Margaret Willis, memorandum to Harold Alberty (n.d.); MW: b1/f1.
4. Willis, memorandum to Harold Alberty (n.d.), Ibid.
5. Margaret Willis, "Teaching Abroad" manuscript, for publication in the *Wellesley College Alumnae Magazine* (January 24, 1953); MW: b5/f 3.
6. Margaret Willis, correspondence to W. Aikin (September 3, 1940); MW: b2/f2.
7. Giles, McCutchen, and Zechiel, *Exploring the Curriculum*, 307.
8. M. Willis lecture (November 28, 1959); MW: b5/f9.
9. Paul Klohr, personal interview with author-CK, Columbus, Ohio, January 8, 2000.
10. Class of 1938, Ohio State University Laboratory School, *Were We Guinea Pigs?* (New York: Henry Holt, 1938): 295.
11. Ibid., 1.
12. Ibid., 298–299.
13. Margaret Willis, correspondence to R. Lindquist (April 5, 1936); MW: b5/f2.
14. Margaret Willis, *The Guinea Pigs After 20 Years* (Columbus: Ohio State University Press, 1968): 11.
15. Class of 1938, personal interviews with author-CK, Class of 1938 class reunion, Columbus, Ohio; May 20, 21, 1988.
16. Willis, *The Guinea Pigs After 20 Years*, ix.
17. Margaret Willis, letter to R. Lindquist (April 5, 1936); MW: b5/f2.
18. Willis, *Three Dozen Years*, 77.
19. Ibid., 72.
20. Robert W. Butche, personal interview with author-CK, Columbus, Ohio, July 3, 1997.
21. Margaret Willis, "To many" manuscript (n.d.): 1; MW: b 5/f 9.
22. Giles, McCutchen, and Zechiel, *Exploring the Curriculum*, 308.

Chapter 9: Reexamining Secondary Education

1. A. N. Zechiel, "Comments," *Teacher School Child*, ed. Wilfrid Hamlin (Plainfield, VT: Goddard College, 1964): 57.
2. John Dewey, "Why Have Progressive Schools?," *Current History* (July 1933): 448.
3. Harold Alberty, "Comments," *Teacher School Child*, ed. Wilfrid Hamlin (Plainfield, VT: Goddard College, 1964): 51.
4. Herbert M. Kliebard, *Changing Course: American Curriculum Reform in the 20th Century* (New York: Teachers College Press, 2002): 136–137.

5. The *New York Times* references: S. Dillon, "Houston's School Violence Data under a Cloud" (November 7, 2003): A1, 16; D. J. Schemo, "Texas Lifts Its Probation on Schools in Houston" (August 5, 2004): A12; D. J. Schemo and F. Fessenden, "Gains in Houston Schools: How Real Are They?" (December 3, 2003): A1, 27; M. Winerip, "A 'Zero Dropout' Miracle: Alas! A Texas Tall Tale" (August 13, 2003): A19.

6. Patricia Graham, *Schooling America* (Oxford: Oxford University Press, 2005): 125.

7. John Dewey, *School and Society* (Chicago: University of Chicago Press, 1900): 19.

8. Ronald J. Newell, *Passion for Learning: How Project-based Learning Meets the Needs of 21st Century Students* (Lanham, MD: Rowman and Littlefield, 2003).

9. Russell W. Rumberger and Gregory J. Palardy, "Test Scores, Dropout Rates, and Transfer Rates as Alternative Indicators of High School Performance," *AERJ* 42:1 (Spring 2005): 3–42.

10. Rick Stiggins, "Assessment for Learning," in *On Common Ground*, ed. Richard DuFour, Robert Eaker, and Rebecca DuFour (Bloomington, IN: Solution Tree, 2005): 65–83.

11. Cross City Campaign for Urban School Reform, *A Delicate Balance: District Policies and Classroom Practice* (Chicago: Cross City Campaign for Urban School Reform, 2005)

12. Maxine Greene, *The Dialectic of Freedom* (New York: Teachers College Press, 1988): 12.

13. Giles, McCutchen, and Zechiel, *Exploring the Curriculum*, 231.

14 John I. Goodlad, C. Mantle-Bromley, and S. T. Goodlad, *Education for Everyone: Agenda for Education in a Democracy* (San Francisco: Jossey-Bass, 2004).

15. John Dewey, *Democracy and Education* (New York: Macmillan, 1916): 22.

16. Zechiel, "Comments," 57.

17. R. V. Bullough Jr. and K. Baughman, *First Year Teacher–Eight Years Later* (New York: Teachers College Press, 1997).

18. Tyack and Cuban, *Tinkering Toward Utopia*.

19. Mike Schmoker, "No Turning Back," *On Common Ground*, ed. R. DuFour, R. Eaker, and R. DuFour, 148.

20. Linda Darling-Hammond, *The Right to Learn* (San Francisco: Jossey-Bass, 1997): 6.

21. Giles, McCutchen, and Zechiel, *Exploring the Curriculum*, 231.

22. DuFour, Eaker, and DuFour, *On Common Ground*.

23. Aikin, *The Story of the Eight-Year Study*, 130.

24. C. Bereiter and M. Scardamalia, *Surpassing Ourselves: An Inquiry into the Nature and Implications of Expertise* (Chicago: Open Court Press, 1993).

25. Aikin, *The Story of the Eight-Year Study*, 19, emphasis added.

26. Zechiel, "Comments," 57.

27. David B. Tyack, *The One Best System* (Cambridge, MA: Harvard University Press, 1974).

Appendix A

1. Personal interviews: Paul Diederich, Robert Gilchrist, Lou LaBrant, I. Keith Tyler, and Ralph Tyler; Frederick L. Redefer, "The Eight-Year Study— Eight Years Later: A Study of Experimentation in the Thirty Schools" (Ph.D. diss., Teachers College, Columbia University, 1951); Craig Kridel (arrayer), "Eight-Year Study Materials (microform): from the Progressive Education Association's Commission on the Relation of School and College" (Columbia, SC: Museum of Education, University of South Carolina, 1993), 2 microfilm reels, 16 mm (Microfilm OCLC 40071984I).

2. *Handbook of the Altoona High School* (Altoona, PA: Altoona High School, 1932): 9.

3. *Thirty Schools Tell Their Story,* 16–17.

4. Redefer, "The Eight-Year Study—Eight Years Later," 65.

5. See Claudia Keenan, *Portrait of a Lighthouse School* (Bronxville, NY: The Bronxville School History Committee, 1997).

6. I. R. Kraybill, correspondence to W. S. Learned (April 26, 1940); CFAT: V-I.B B 26 F; Pennsylvania Study of Higher and Secondary Education, 1935.

7. See Susan F. Semel, *The Dalton School* (New York: Peter Lang, 1992).

8. *Our Education: A Report written by the Students of Core Classes of East High School* (Denver, Colorado: East High School,1939).

9. Eagle Rock High School Totem (June 1937): n.p.

10. Robert J. Havighurst, "Interviews" (1935): 118–162; GEB, RG 12, Havighurst, 1935, Box 4.

11. Helen Babson, "Eagle Rock High School Eight-Year Study Statement, Part II: Curriculum Developments in Los Angeles City Schools" (February 7, 1941): 30–31. "Implications of the Eight-Year Study for California Secondary Schools—A Symposium," *California Journal of Secondary Education* 17:3 (March 1942).

12. See Marie Kirchner Stone, *The Progressive Legacy* (New York: Peter Lang, 2001). M. Kirchner Stone (Ed.) *Between Home and Community* (Chicago: F. W. Parker School, 1976).

13. See Joseph E. Haines, *A History of Friends' Central School* (Overbrook, PA: Friends' Central School, 1938); Clayton L. Farraday, *Friends' Central School 1845–1984* (Philadelphia: Friends' Central School, 1984); Bradford R. Smith, *Curriculum Integration in the Eight-year Study of the Progressive Education Association, 1932–1940: Three Schools Tell Their Story* (Ph.D. diss., Pennsylvania State University, 1996).

14. Redefer, "The Eight-Year Study—Eight Years Later," 99.

15. *Thirty Schools Tell Their Story,* 348.

16. Ibid., 379.

17. Redefer, "The Eight-Year Study—Eight Years Later," 99–100.

18. See Lester Dix, *A Charter for Progressive Education* (New York: Teachers College, 1939).

19. See T. A. Dohrer (ed.), *1901–2001, The New Trier Century* (Wilmette, IL: New Trier High School, 2000).

20. *Thirty Schools Tell Their Story*, 521.

21. See Nancy Geyer Christopher, *The North Shore Country Day School* (Winnetka, IL: The North Shore Country Day School, 1993).

22. Charles F. Haas, "One Boy's Education: A Remembrance of NSCDS, 1919–1931," *The North Shore Country Day School Bulletin* (Fall 1990): 6.

23. "Brief Statement of the Experimental Study in the Pelham High School" (ca. January 1935): 2; RG3 A4; S5b, B 48; S7 F1.

24. Kathleen Kennedy Manzo, "Legacy of the Eight-Year Study," *Lessons of a Century* by staff of Education Week (Bethesda, MD: Editorial Projects in Education, 2000): 159.

25. Sydney V. Rowland, correspondence to William S. Learned (April 23, 1940); CFAT: V-I.B B 26 F; Pennsylvania Study of Higher and Secondary Education, 1935.

26. H. H. Giles, correspondence to Nicholas Mosley (December 22, 1938): 1; GEB S 1–2, B 281 F 2933. Shaker Heights History: Clipping File: "School Year Plan Embroils Shaker," Cleveland Plain Dealer (February 22, 1938); "Step up in Shaker Curriculum Set, Cleveland Plain Dealer (December 11, 1939); School Archives, Shaker Height City School District.

27. Redefer, "The Eight-Year Study—Eight Years Later," 114.

28. See Katherine Moran, *Curriculum Study in the Tulsa Secondary Schools* (Tulsa: Tulsa Public Schools, 1940).

29. See Ida B. DePencier, *The History of the Laboratory Schools* (Chicago: Quadrangle Books, 1967).

30. *Thirty Schools Tell Their Story*, 662.

31. Redefer, "The Eight-Year Study—Eight Years Later," 190.

32. "University High Wins U.S. Praise" (October 16, 1940); University High School File, Administration Building, Oakland United School District.

33. See Class of 1938, Ohio State University High School, *Were We Guinea Pigs?* (New York: Henry Holt and Company, 1938); Robert W. Butche, *Image of Excellence* (New York: Peter Lang, 2000).

34. Margaret Willis, "Democracy in the Formulation of School Policies," *Educational Method* XIX:4 (January 1940): 218.

35. Willis, *Three Dozen Years*, 8–9.

36. *Thirty Schools Tell Their Story*, 759.

37. "Conference of Participating Schools in the Eight-Year Study Experiment, Bennington College" (July 2–7, 1933); GEB 1:2, B 281: F 2935.

38. *Thirty Schools Tell Their Story*, 780.

Appendix B

1. Claude M. Fuess, *The College Board* (New York: Columbia University Press, 1950): 57.

2. Ibid., 105.

3. Max McConn, "Educational Guidance is Now Possible," *The Educational Record* 14:4 (1933): 480.

4. Max McConn, "Putting the Tests to Work," *The Educational Record* 19, Supplement 11 (January 1938): 68, Max McConn, "Measurement in Educational Experimentation," *The Educational Record* 15:1 (1934): 116.

5. Ben Wood, correspondence to William S. Learned (September 1941): 4; CFAT: V-I.B B 26 F; Pennsylvania Study of Higher and Secondary Education, 1935.

6. McConn, "Putting the Tests to Work," 68.

7. Third Report of the Committee on School and College Relations of the Educational Records Bureau, October 1935; Fourth Report of the Committee on School and College Relations of the Educational Records Bureau, February 1943 (New York: Educational Records Bureau).

8. William S. Learned and Ben D. Wood, *The Student and His Knowledge* (New York: The Carnegie Foundation for the Advancement of Teaching, 1938): xii–xiii. Originally, this eight-year study was conceived to examine (1) the seven-year progress of a group of sixth-grade children through high school; (2) the five-year progress of 40,000 high school seniors through college; and (3) the one-year progress of 5,000 college seniors (Agenda for Trustees and Executive Committee [December 14, 1927]: 12; CFAT: V-I.B B 26 F; Pennsylvania Study of Higher and Secondary Education, 1926–1934).

9. Ben Wood, correspondence to William S. Learned (September 1941): 1; CFAT: V-I.B B 26 F; Pennsylvania Study of Higher and Secondary Education, 1935.

10. Learned and Wood, *The Student and His Knowledge*, xiii; Ben Wood, correspondence to William S. Learned (September 1941): 2–3; CFAT: V-I.B B 26 F; Pennsylvania Study of Higher and Secondary Education, 1935.

11. Ben Wood, correspondence to William S. Learned, ibid.

Appendix C

1. Eugene R. Smith, "Modernizing Records for Guidance and Transfer," *The Educational Record* 21, Supplement 13 (January 1940): 26–27.

Glossary

1. Burton P. Fowler, Tuesday Evening Session, *Report of the Third Annual Conference of the Eight-Year Study* (New York: PEA): 5–8.

2. "Conclusion," *Report of the Third Annual Conference of the Eight-Year Study* (New York: PEA): 72.

3. Chamberlin, Chamberlin, Drought, and Scott, *Did They Succeed in College?*, xviii.

Annotated Bibliography

(Aikin) Commission on the Relation of School and College Final Reports

Adventure in American Education, Volumes 1–5

Volume 1. Wilford M. Aikin, *The Story of the Eight-Year Study.* New York: Harper & Brothers, 1942.

Volume 2. H. H. Giles, S. P. McCutchen, and A. N. Zechiel. *Exploring the Curriculum: The Work of the Thirty Schools from the Viewpoint of Curriculum Consultants.* New York: Harper & Brothers, 1942.

Volume 3. Eugene R. Smith, Ralph W. Tyler, and the Evaluation Staff. *Appraising and Recording Student Progress: Evaluation, Records, and Reports in the Thirty Schools.* New York: Harper & Brothers, 1942.

Volume 4. Dean Chamberlin, Enid Straw Chamberlin, Neal E. Draught, and William E. Scott. *Did They Succeed in College? The Follow-up Study of the Graduates of the Thirty Schools.* New York: Harper & Brothers, 1942.

Volume 5. *Thirty Schools Tell Their Story: Each School Writes of Its Participation in the Eight-Year Study.* New York: Harper & Brothers, 1942.

(Thayer) Commission on Secondary School Curriculum Final Reports

V. T. Thayer, Caroline B. Zachry, and Ruth Kotinsky. *Reorganizing Secondary Education.* New York: D. Appleton-Century Company, 1939.

Committee on the Function of Science in General Education. *Science in General Education.* New York: D. Appleton-Century Co., 1938.

Committee on the Function of Mathematics in General Education. *Mathematics in General Education.* New York: D. Appleton-Century Co., 1940.

Committee on the Function of the Social Studies in General Education. *The Social Studies in General Education.* New York: D. Appleton-Century Co., 1940.

Committee on the Function of Art in General Education. *The Visual Arts in General Education.* New York: D. Appleton-Century Co., 1940.

Committee on the Function of English in General Education. *Language in General Education.* New York: D. Appleton-Century Co., 1940.

Elbert Lenrow with the Creative Writing Committee of the Commission on the Secondary School Curriculum. *Reader's Guide to Prose Fiction: An Introductory Essay, with Bibliographies of 1,500 Novels Selected, Topically Classified, and Annotated for Use in Meeting the Needs of Individuals in General Education.* New York: D. Appleton-Century Co., 1940. This guide served as a teacher's sourcebook and an annotated bibliography to help select works of (primarily) contemporary fiction. Lenrow arranged the bibliography in terms of adolescent interests and problems and organized the publications in broad categories to include the individual's need for entertainment and escape, the individual's personal environment, and the individual's social environment.

Lawrence H. Conrad. *Teaching Creative Writing.* New York: D. Appleton-Century Company, 1940. Conrad's publication examined student's writing in the context of the needs and aptitudes of the adolescent.

The Study of Adolescents Committee Final Reports

Lois H. Meek. *The Personal-Social Development of Boys and Girls with Implications for Secondary Education.* Camden, NJ: PEA, 1940. Attending to the personal and social dimensions of adolescence, Meek interpreted "needs" as a way to achieve emotional support through social relations. Drawing upon materials from the Zachry Committee, Keliher Commission, PEA Committee on Workshops, and the (ACE-sponsored) Adolescent Study of the University of California, Meek and others constructed a working conception of personal-social development for secondary schools.

Caroline B. Zachry, in collaboration with Margaret Lighty. *Emotion and Conduct in Adolescence.* New York: D. Appleton-Century Co., 1940. While written for school staff, Zachry examined adolescent tasks for life adjustment and focused on dimensions of social development in relation to the self.

Peter Blos. *The Adolescent Personality: A Study of Individual Behavior.* New York: Appleton-Century-Crofts, 1941. This work included four detailed case studies, and with psychological and psychiatric interpretations, Blos developed a theory of adolescent development.

After writing at a rather abstract level, he concluded the volume in a practical manner by exploring how teachers could respond to adolescent behavior.

Unreleased: Elizabeth Hellersberg, *Adolescence: A Period of Transition.*

Unreleased: Wilma Lloyd, *Observation and Objectivity.*

Unreleased: Gladys Oaks, *Fictionized Case Histories* (oriented for parents).

Unreleased: Caroline Zachry and Regina Weiss, *Case Book.*

Unreleased: *The Voice of Experience* (various studies of expressive movement).

Unreleased: *Collected Papers* (with a sociological and an anthropological approach).

(Keliher) Commission on Human Relations Final Reports

Alice V. Keliher. *Life and Growth.* New York: D. Appleton-Century Co., 1938. Keliher wrote in the second person and oriented this book for high school students. She presented human relations as a way to understand oneself as well as others, thus creating an interesting balance between the personal and social dimensions of adolescence. Specific chapters were aligned to the Thayer Commission's *Science in General Education,* and the entire volume was linked to other Commission on Human Relations volumes (five of six being released within the next twelve months). *Life and Growth,* the most popular book among the Commission's final reports, focused on normality—adolescents' concern and fear of being different versus being abnormal—and was used as a textbook for courses in social relationships, sex education, and physical education.

Louise M. Rosenblatt. *Literature as Exploration.* New York: D. Appleton-Century Co., 1938. Rosenblatt addressed the social implications of the act of appreciation and interpretation and was prepared both as a guide for teachers of literature and for instructional methods courses. Rosenblatt saw *Literature as Exploration* as the genesis of her "reader-response theory" and "transactional theory," perspectives that have guided generations of language arts teachers.

W. Robert Wunsch and Edna Albers, Eds. *Thicker Than Water.* New York: D. Appleton-Century Co., 1939. This publication served as a companion to *Literature as Exploration* and consisted of a sourcebook of stories selected to illuminate problems of family and family member relationships.

Bernhard J. Stern, Ed. *The Family, Past and Present.* New York: D. Appleton-Century Co., 1938. Stern prepared another sourcebook reflecting material accumulated at the 1934 Hanover Seminar. Oriented for postsecondary education, this volume examined the evolving trends and conceptions of family life and was to be accompanied by an edited collection for secondary schools, *Society and Family Life*, a compilation never released.

Katharine Whiteside Taylor. *Do Adolescents Need Parents?* New York: D. Appleton-Century Co., 1938. Taylor's work reflected Lawrence Frank's interest in parent education and was written specifically for parents whose children were going through adolescence. The title is, of course, a rhetorical question, since the volume attempts to reconsider ways in which adolescents need their parents and, as noted by Keliher, ways in which parents need their children.

Walter C. Langer *Psychology and Human Living*. D. Appleton-Century Co., 1943. Langer addressed the conception of needs from a more theoretical, developmental perspective and presented a Freudian primer of social and physical needs, personality, and adolescent development for teachers and parents.

Unreleased: Lorine Pruette and Leo Huberman. *The Family in Our Times; Society and Family Life*.

Unreleased: Earl S. Goudey, manual on sex education.

Index